A DIFFERENT TOUCH

A Study of Vows in Religious Life

by

JUDITH A. MERKLE, S.N.D.deN.

A Liturgical Press Book

THE LITURGICAL PRESS
Collegeville, Minnesota

Cover design by Fred Petters

1   2   3   4   5   6   7   8

Library of Congress Cataloging-in-Publication Data

Merkle, Judith A.
    A different touch : a study of vows in religious life / by Judith
A. Merkle.
        p.   cm.
    Includes bibliographical references.
    ISBN 0-8146-2465-0
    1. Vows.   2. Monastic and religious life.   I. Title.
BX2435.M443   1998
248.8'94—dc21   97–49888
                                                              CIP

To the Sisters of the Ohio Province
of the Sisters of Notre Dame de Namur
with love and gratitude

Contents

Preface   vii

PART I. CULTURAL QUESTIONS

Chapter One: Life-Style Issues   3

Chapter Two: Progress: Which Way Is Ahead?   13

Chapter Three: Beyond Progress: Ecological Wisdom   28

Chapter Four: Toward a New Vision   38

PART II. THEOLOGICAL FOUNDATIONS

Chapter Five: Freeing Freedom   53

Chapter Six: Getting Direction   63

Chapter Seven: The Reach of Salvation   74

PART III. FOUNDATIONS OF THE VOWS

Chapter Eight: A Different Touch   85

Chapter Nine: Touched by God   95

Chapter Ten: A Framework for Loving   103

PART IV. HISTORY

Chapter Eleven: Hearts for a New Age   113

Chapter Twelve: New Forms of Energy   125

Chapter Thirteen: Toward a New Synthesis   136

Chapter Fourteen: New Times for Community   146

PART V. THE VOWS

Chapter Fifteen: Poverty: The Transformation of Desires   163

Chapter Sixteen: Poverty: Beyond Isolation   173

Chapter Seventeen: New Times for Poverty   186

Chapter Eighteen: Obedience: An Affair of the Heart   197

Chapter Nineteen: Obedience: A Path of Becoming   205

Chapter Twenty: New Times for Obedience   221

Chapter Twenty-One: Celibacy: From Ambiguity
                              to Integrity   234

Chapter Twenty-Two: Faces of Sexual Integration   248

Chapter Twenty-Three: From Cost to Consolation   266

Chapter Twenty-Four: New Times for Celibacy   277

Index   287

Preface

We live in a situation of paradox today. After thirty years of renewal of religious life, its future and meaning stand in question. This book seeks to articulate this paradox and also express the foundations of religious life in face of current theological and socio-cultural questions. It is written with a belief in the future of religious life. It holds the conviction that changes in secular and democratic culture demand its rearticulation.

These chapters invite reflection on religious life as a "different touch" in the Christian life. Religious life is based on a distinctive religious experience, is a countercultural stance in society and embraces a unique style of loving in the Church. This book explores the theological foundations of religious life. It engages in cultural critique as well as envisions new roles for religious in the next millennium. Religious life is a distinctive adult life-style in the Church, as well as a "way" on the common road of conversion traveled by the entire People of God.

This book is not written to say everything about religious life. However, through cultural criticism, social sciences, history, and theology, it reflects on the vowed life. It hopes to further the conversation on the meaning of the vows in secular and democratic culture. Religious life is a framework of Christian living outlined by the vows. Yet, the vows involve processes of conversion undertaken by all adults in the Church. We examine the vows developmentally as well as in their social ramifications. The context of religious life is considered through an evolutionary and ecological perspective.

Part I examines the current situation of religious life today as one of paradox. It attempts to name this paradox, as well as link problems in religious life with broader patterns of fragmentation and transition in the society. It asserts that religious face four critical discernments or choices today: 1) the discernment between cultural religion and gospel living, 2) the choice of hope over nostalgia, 3) the decision to overcome moral hazards to rediscover community, 4) the adoption of a realistic vision of evolution to the future. This last issue deals with the challenge of ecological wisdom.

Parts II and III reflect on the theological foundations of religious life. Part II briefly treats the theological themes upon which religious life is based: revelation, faith, freedom, salvation, sin and grace, life in the Church community. Part III examines religious life as a framework within the Christian life and a distinct "way" of adult conversion. Religious life is seen in light of four types of moral calls of Christian living as well as in relationship to the gospel counsels. Through the model of framework, we reflect upon the core elements of religious life, and those which change historically, in different cultural circumstances and in the life of a religious.

Part IV looks at religious life in the nineteenth century, asking how issues raised in that century still affect us today. The twin development of the new congregations with simple vows and the secular institutes is noted. We examine the coordinates for our own future which can be gleaned from this first large-scale attempt to bridge the charism of religious life with secular and democratic culture. We point to the new circumstances in which core elements of vowed living must be expressed.

Part V examines the individual vows. The vows are means for the transformation of person, the creation of community, ministry or the "defeat of death," and as ecclesial energy. Through the lens of the work of the developmental psychologist Erikson we suggest that the vows engage the life challenges of the adult years, but also reframe and restructure unfinished issues from earlier periods of life. We suggest that each vow must face "new times" for its expression today. The personal, social, and political-mystical ramifications of the vows are outlined.

There are many people to thank in the preparation of this book. It has been written over a period of time and is the fruit of discussions, not only within the Ohio province of the Sisters of Notre Dame de Namur but also with sisters across the congregation in Japan, Africa, Europe, Latin America, and the United States. I have also had the privilege of talking with sisters and male religious from various congregations in the United States, Canada, Europe, and Australia and have been enriched and encouraged by their experience and responses.

I wish to thank especially Lucia Borzaga, librarian at the Office for Religious and Secular Institutes in Rome, for her assistance during the two periods of time I did research there, and to the Sisters of Notre Dame at Paciotti in Rome for their warm hospitality. I wish also to thank the sisters at the Loretto Christian Life Center in Niagara Falls, Canada, for sharing their home with me during the final writing of this book.

I am grateful to the editors of The Liturgical Press for their help in publishing this text and for their interest in the continuing renewal of religious life. Finally, I wish to thank the sisters of my own province and my family and friends for their love and support.

PART I
CULTURAL QUESTIONS

Chapter One

Life-Style Issues

It is difficult to consider the future of religious life without a sense of paradox. Religious have moved forward in crucial ways since renewal. Living at the turn of a millennium, they are enlightened by postwar insights from the sciences. They enjoy a renewed spirituality, able to bring their own experience to an understanding of faith. Vatican II personalism relates spiritual and human growth. Religious are free to be human. Their ministries are chosen and suited to their talents.

Yet the institutions and congregations of religious are often in serious financial trouble. Significant numbers of corporate ministries have collapsed, or lack their intended congregational thrust. There are few new members. Still, these external issues would be tolerable if congregations were not facing more insidious internal pressures today.

Fed by what appears to be an insurmountable pluralism, a new type of conflict troubles religious communities. Many struggle with this conflict today. Too often, effort at corporate action or dialogue is fraught with an atmosphere of antagonism.

If we reflect on what we set out to do thirty years ago, in many ways we have accomplished it. Still, we find ourselves in a situation which Arnold Toynbee aptly describes as a "sense of having all we need and still feeling alienated."[1] Toynbee was referring to the alienation of the proletariat during the nineteenth century. As

1. Joseph Tetlow, "The Human Person and Sexuality," *The Way Supplement* 71 (1991) 44.

the muscle behind the Industrial Revolution, the proletariat still failed to receive the benefits of the better life which it promised. Is this an analogy for the situation of religious today?

Many would answer yes, but from different perspectives. Some religious feel let down by the promise of Vatican II. The cooling of the spirit of renewal in the Church stands in sharp contrast to the hopes raised by the council.[2] Others find their lives perched precariously on fragments of institutions and beliefs that once supported them. They have not lost their faith; they still believe. However, they find fewer echoes of those beliefs around them.[3] One religious put it this way, "I did not leave my congregation, it left me."

Another group are drained by the gender battles in the Church. Energies are continuously wasted, opportunities for ministry missed, and unnecessary alienation grows in a Church they love. All the while needs mount, especially those of the poor. When will it end, and how will it get resolved, they ponder.

Quietly, in the privacy of their own thoughts, religious ask, is this what we struggled for? This is the same critical question as the workers above ask, however, at a different time and place. It is a common human question of those who struggle for progress, or seek to change in the face of new times. To what have we progressed? Whom has this "progress" served?

These concerns of religious are deeper than the progressive-conservative dialogues of the past. Then religious argued over the direction of renewal. Some still put energy in that regard. Yet today, religious experience a different kind of struggle. Torn between not wanting to think critically about religious life for fear it will feed a return to pre-Vatican II practices, and a desire to ask hard questions necessary for further renewal, religious venture to ask new questions.

2. Edward Schillebeeckx, *Church: The Human Story of God* (New York: Crossroad, 1990) xiii.

3. For a discussion of moral fragmentation in the wider society, see Larry L. Rasmussen, *Moral Fragments and Moral Community* (Minneapolis: Fortress Press, 1993).

The questions are different than those which marked renewal years. They reflect a new hope and a willingness to examine our situation of paradox. The questions center in the following areas. At a point where the reforms of Vatican II have been "achieved," such as freedom in ministry, respect for personal differences and need, collegial movements in authority, freedom of initiative, why are not things better in religious life? Why is it we have done the "right things," yet our problems are significant? Why has renewal moved to a point where the future of our existence is in question?

A recent study by Ukeritis and Nygren speaks to our situation succinctly. The issue of anomie haunts religious. There is loss of conviction about the vows, lack of clarity about the role of religious, negative reactions towards authority, lack of corporate mission and ministry, and disillusionment with leadership. All pose significant threats to the future of religious life.[4] For those who have lived these last thirty years of renewal, the study names experiences which they desire to move beyond.

Looking closer at the paradox

We do not want to take on the "doomsaying" of the millennialism that pervades our culture. The world is not coming to an end, nor is the world of religious life. Signs of life and hope in religious congregations witness much is right in them. Nevertheless, if a paradox is a situation which contains seemingly contradictory elements, naming the paradox helps us learn its challenge. We will point out three aspects of this paradox, knowing others will come to the mind of the reader.

The paradox of diversity

Religious struggled after Vatican II to bring the personalism of the council into an overly institutionalized way of life. Congregational identity was so strong in religious orders, that individual-

---

4. David Nygren and Miriam Ukeritis, "Future of Religious Orders in the United States," *Origins* 22:15 (1992).

ity was too often lost.[5] Under a crippling institutionalization, personal gifts of members and aspects of founding charisms often remained untapped for mission.

After the council, congregational identity formed from years of communal living held groups together as they experienced the changes of renewal. Differences in ministry, community, and living arrangements could be safely created as "experiments" because the norm or center, left over from the past, still held. New needs and situations were treated as "exceptions." There remained sufficient sameness in congregations, to which the "different" could be subordinated. What legitimated the "different" was that it filled a new need or personal calling not met ordinarily.

Our first paradox arises out of this context. After years of following this pattern, religious discover a reverse situation is true today. Identity appears to be contingent upon the chance that the "different" or individual choice will create a bond of sameness. Religious who desire to live in a local community cannot count on there being one which can support them ministerially and personally. Those who have invested in a ministerial project cannot assume someone from the congregation will continue the work in the name of the community. Things once considered necessities, community and ministry, are displaced by contingencies, the hope for an adventitious play of individual choices. Today religious question the nature of their center or identity as communities.

The paradox of communication

Our second paradox springs from our new communication patterns. Congregations have fostered increased communication among members as indispensable to renewal. Yet, increased communication often reveals that words do not mean the same

5. This was true not only for individuals but for congregations as a whole. One hundred years of canonical efforts to protect religious life resulted in a homogenization. See Eutimio Sastre Santos, C.M.F., *El ordenamiento de los institutos de votos simples según las Normas de la Santa Sede (1854–1958)* (Roma-Madrid: Urbaniana University Press, 1993).

among them. Once we assumed that Church, community, vowed life, and mission had a common meaning in a community. Today, instead of being signs of unity, these words mirror the differences among members. We desire to talk about deeper issues of our lives with each other, yet we sense a widening gap of experience and belief inform meanings for each of us. Has not this always been the case?

Differences in theology, spirituality, and most human realities have always existed in religious orders. Our paradoxical situation comes from roots deeper than these traditional differences. Formerly, we argued over issues of church, celibacy, sacramental life, and community, but we assumed each topic had an imagined center. "Givens" regarding these issues formed a reality outside the members that "held" the truth of the issue, and which allowed a certain play about ideas. We often experienced this as a unity in diversity.

As we argued about what idea was going to hold sway, or we tried to deepen our understanding of an issue, we assumed there was a "truth," if not absolute, at least an adequate one, toward which we were moving. Such "givens" fended off anxiety, and established a sense of order and meaning. Differences regarding church or sacramental life would not destroy the group because the differences had a fundamental place beyond the reach of the play of the conversation. Today this is not the case. Herein lies the roots of our paradox.

Postmodern condition

Religious share in the postmodern condition in the culture, and this "new situation" contributes to our situation of paradox. Formerly, our world was controlled by a metaphor which attested to the order and unity of the world. People, animals, nature, and the cosmos each had a place in the order of things. Even scientific discoveries were believed to point to a world which existed within and beyond the world of the appearances. Key definitions of reality which affected our lives as religious were grounded in this metaphor. There was a link between reality as we saw it and a sense of truth which was mediated through the Church.

Today our culture lacks a broad interpretative metaphor which explains the order and meaning of the world. Instead, the uncertainty of any knowledge is more widely held. The meaning of any idea is constantly in flux and no one meaning or interpretation has any authority over another.

People more readily doubt one can know the truth today. It is more widely held that only through the interplay of competing ideas, which vie with one another for acceptance, that the "truth" can be known. Criticism of any and all ideas hold sway, since the ability to know anything is seriously held in doubt. The closest one can come to knowledge is to see what idea prevails in the interplay of ideas. This is a brief description of what authors term "postmodernism."[6]

Postmodernism is our cultural framework in first world society. All knowledge has meaning only within paradigms, and loses validity when one steps outside the paradigm. For example, Jungian thought, Marxism, eco-feminism, and Catholic doctrine are seen simply as paradigms or systems of thought. In the postmodern system, conclusions reached in one paradigm are meaningless in another. Since people do not believe they can know reality beyond limited models or paradigms, talking across paradigms is difficult, or thought impossible or fruitless.[7] Ideas different than one's own easily get dismissed.

Postmodernism influences religious life since religious no longer live apart from society. We sense this cultural shift among us, as we joke "everything is up for grabs." When a sense of "givens" is not present, consciously or unconsciously, discussion meant to create unity becomes a reminder of the unity that is not there.

---

6. See Gary Eberle, *The Geography of Nowhere: Finding One's Self in the Postmodern World* (Kansas City: Sheed and Ward, 1994).

7. Understanding the phenomenon of postmodernism sheds light on contemporary interest in the ecological movement. Beyond its concern for the future of the planet, the ecological movement is also searching for a new cosmology or explanation of how humans, the world, and the cosmos are related. This overarching metaphor is missing in our culture, contributing to a deep sense of drift.

Add together the cultural atmosphere of postmodernism; differences in life experience and spirituality; generational, ethnic, and cultural distinctions, and one observes an enormous pluralism in religious life today. Along with pluralism can come a paralyzing relativism. If all is good, can any good give us identity and meaning? We are left with a paradox. Difference is no longer the exception, difference is celebrated. Yet it is getting harder and harder to know how one belongs.

The new journey

Respect for difference and open-mindedness led to massive change in religious life as "journey" became a major metaphor of religious life. Religious tended to give less attention to the foundations of religious life; foundations could be taken for granted. Rather, the quest was to move forward. Religious tried not to close down any direction of thought, or to homogenize differences. Toleration was a high value. Issues once thought unchangeable became contingent and arbitrary.

We learned that many elements of our way of living were fallible and ultimately revisable. We recognized even the sinfulness and unnaturalness in some aspects of past structures. We found, in spite of our unassailable beliefs about people and living, what was otherwise could also be proven. We realized that there were many possible solutions to the problem of human living, and that ours took only one place among them.

At times traditional ministries were set aside to meet new needs. New groups of people became a focus of our ministry, as we tried to learn fresh ways to reach out to people not previously served. We took up with eagerness the burdens of church and society, entering into people's hurts, discovering new joys and profound relationships. Struggling to make a difference in a world in transition, we found that living in paradox was not all bad.

The paradox of openness

We also experience, in the midst of these changes, moments of self reflection when we ask, where is this journey leading? A friend recounts, "I find myself spending time talking to others in my ministry, being compassionate and understanding. Yet if a member of my community would ask for similar time, I would feel nervous and constrained. I wonder why." Or a middle-aged brother remarks, "There is a promising man in my New Testament course. I believe he could have a vocation. However, I am hesitant to invite him because I wonder if we will be around. To what am I inviting him?"

Many, happy with the fact we are no longer plugged into a ministry or "slot," also wonder how we can assess today our impact as a congregation. We ask the meaning of our vows. We observe greater lay participation in the Church, and wonder about the place of religious congregations in this new situation. Our "journey" has led us into a third paradox. We are open to many people and situations. In our openness and willingness to revise our ways of thinking, however, we have created a world in which we live with a gnawing fear that we, with our life-style, no longer have any place or relevance.

How do we create a unity without returning to the limitations of the past? How do we keep communicating yet reach deeper than the differences among us? How do we stay on the journey without despairing of our relevance and our future?

Ideally, it would be wonderful to write this book about the next steps in renewal. Regrettably, no one person is that kind of prophet. As we stand at these crossroads of renewal, however, it is important to remember that a situation of paradox is not new in the Christian experience. St. Paul says it succinctly: "We are afflicted in every way possible, but we are not crushed; full of doubts, we never despair. We are persecuted but never abandoned; we are struck down, but never destroyed" (2 Cor 4:8–10).

It is not in spite of the paradox of suffering that a follower of Jesus ministers. Rather, it is through wrestling with the paradox that one is a sign and instrument of the divine life. We hear this clearly in the Scriptures. "For God, who said, 'Let light shine out of darkness,' has shone in our hearts, that we in turn might make known the glory of God shining on the face of Christ" (2 Cor 4:6). The experience of paradox calls forth eschatological faith, a faith that holds that God's last word about the meaning and direction of our lives has not yet been spoken. God's pledge of an ongoing and deeper communication, "at the right time," is the promise of the Spirit, a covenant made not just for generations past, but for us and for the future.[8]

Religious are called to a faith in this time of transition that goes beyond mere belief in their survival. Rather, the quality of faith required of them is needed in the entire Church on the cusp of a new millennium. Religious life was called by Vatican II to be a "sign and a reminder of the future life to which the pilgrim church is constantly moving . . ."[9] This refers not just to a life in the hereafter, but to the life of the Spirit guiding us in this age. Religious are called to believe that their own journey is part of the coming of the kingdom, not just for themselves but for the Church and world as well.

Renewal involves such an active hope in our own time. For if we are not living in these times, how can we do our part to witness to the life of God in our history, a life which transcends and penetrates the deepest paradoxes of our day? The times at the turn of the millennium are not the times of the '60s and the '70s. Ours is an age of fragments of meaning. Religious are called to help gather these fragments so as to feed a hungry world. In this process, they will continue to discover their meaning and relevance.

While no one person is a prophet or can predict the future, in the faith tradition we all share in the prophetic experience of discipleship. As disciples we are invited to facilitate the prophetic in each other and as communities to discover the next steps in renewal. This requires an eschatological faith which is twofold. We are called to be critical of all that lives by illusion in our lives and does not hold up to the light of God. Secondly, we are summoned to constructive efforts to build the future in response to the needs of the Church and society.

---

8. Thomas McKenna, "Memories of the Future," *Review for Religious* 51 (March–April, 1992) 249–59.

9. *Lumen Gentium*, no. 44.

Critical thinking about our situation and concrete efforts will help us discover that a paradox is only an apparent contradiction. Deep within it lies the light of truth to lead us forward. While we all do not have the same role in this process, each religious has some part in the common effort to build the future. As a first step, let us critically reflect on the the way we think about our situation as religious, and ask whether it can provide us with sufficient direction for the future.

Chapter Two

Progress: Which Way Is Ahead?

While in formation, I was given a Vatican II holy card which had no picture, simply a large arrow stretching across the entire card. It read, "Problems are solved by moving ahead." Often I thought of that card in situations of confusion. I never lacked the desire to move ahead, but my question often was, which way is ahead? The discussion of progress inevitably invites this consideration. Progress, yes, but to what? How do you measure it?

Progress implies "movement toward" something. The word progress suggests a vision of a goal and the presence of criteria for movement. In this chapter and the following we will consider some of the challenges this simple formula presents to religious today.

Our idea of progress

My hunch is that religious think about progress in renewal much the same way people of their culture think about progress in their lives. Simply stated, we ask, are things better than they were?

A recent publication investigates the paradigm Americans use to measure progress, and questions it. Americans once defined progress with a religious outlook, but today Americans (and others in first world societies) use mainly a secular yardstick.[1]

---

1. Christopher Lasch, *The True and Only Heaven: Progress and Its Critics* (New York: Norton, 1991). While Lasch comments on progress in American society, his concerns touch first world societies and their impact on the culture of second and third world nations.

An attitude toward progress is usually unconscious. It involves a view of the "inevitable" in life. The substance of "progress" answers the question, "How will our past and present limitations be fulfilled in the future?" An individual's or group's vision of progress reveals the assumptions used to arrive at an answer.

First world culture and a religious view of life differ in their approach to progress. A religious outlook sees the judgment and love of God as inevitable. A secular view holds that progress itself is inevitable.

Why do "moderns" think this way? The modern view of progress came out of a seventeenth-century conviction that human beings could master nature. Since the human person has desires that are insatiable, the drive of human wants requires us to indefinitely expand our range of material and human choices. We will continue to create in order to fulfill these wants, so went the theory, and history will move forward. The result is that today's luxuries are tomorrow's necessities.

Progress itself was believed inevitable because of the cause-effect relationship between increasing wants and the human drive to meet them. "Progress" in this way was seen as the driving force of all history. The common assumption grew to be that the life of the next generation will be or should be better than our own.

Religious and progress

We should not be surprised to find traces of the cultural view of progress in the yardsticks religious use to measure the success of renewal. It is difficult to determine to what extent this cultural view of progress entered into the vision of renewal in religious orders in the '60s and '70s; however, we certainly see fingerprints of its presence. The size of formation houses built in the '60s testify to an operative belief that religious life would be expanding in new proportions.

"Progress" was certainly given as an explanation for change. When liturgy changed, loved buildings torn down, community practices dropped, "progress" was at work. The direction of the changes in religious life often did "satisfy wants." Renewal legitimized even having preferences for some religious. The lived experience of religious in many cases reinforced the cultural theory. In many ways things got easier rather than harder.

Religious could adopt the cultural view of progress almost uncritically. It was true to their experience. The restrictions and rigidity of pre-Vatican life were removed. While it is true that new responsibility also brought struggle and suffering, it seems fair to say that for many religious life got substantially better.

A view of salvation

The cultural view of progress is not just a theory about how life changes, it contains a theory of salvation. It answers questions such as where are we going, what saves us, what can we hope for, where should we place our trust? Here again a religious and a societal view of life differ in their response to these questions.

Faith holds that our past and present finitude will be completed in the future by a God who saves us. This overarching story or narrative gives meaning to our lives as Christians, meaning which spans all aspects of our experience: health, relationships, work, money, and social change. It helps us to grow yet to live with the inevitable limits that enter our lives. The faith community explains all the dimensions of life as a participation in the death and resurrection of Jesus Christ. The paschal mystery is inevitable in this faith vision of things.

In a secular view of salvation, human progress is inevitable. What makes this attitude secular is not its optimism, which attracts us, or the partial truth it bears, which corresponds to our experience. Its secularity rests in the explanation that our finitude will be completed in the future by human perfectibility and self creation alone.

Do both views of salvation work equally well? Critics hold that the secular view lacks a way to examine the complete experience of human living. The cultural vision of progress works as long as people progress. This view of "salvation," however, has no room for the human experiences of failure, tragedy, and calamity which are also part of life.

Limitations are not treated in this view of reality. On the contrary, natural limits on human power and freedom are denied. With this evasion of life's limits in secular salvation comes the spiritual emptiness that such an evasion produces. If one is one's own source of strength and reason to be, there is no one to turn to when the limit experiences of life occur.

The cultural view of progress generates its own vision of success. Success is defined by upward mobility in a profession which has its own rules and standards of excellence, not by personal integrity or community regard following some standard of human living.[2] The absence of an ideal of human living further feeds spiritual emptiness in our culture today.

This view of success weakens community ties. Success in modern society is linked to upward mobility which moves one farther and farther away from the sanctions or the supports of community. Modern "progress" feeds an environment where people feel more and more isolated from one another. Religious can sense this change in atmosphere in their own religious communities.

Exactly what "salvation" do we pursue as religious? Is our vision of the future one of a prosperous corporation, held in esteem, filled with competent members who operate according to the success measurements of their profession? While competency and well-managed communities are important values, are they our ultimate ones?

If a cultural view of progress alone is our yardstick of success as religious, it is understandable that we feel a sense of hopelessness and anomie as we age, have fewer people enter, and experience the diminishment of institutions and ministries. We are facing serious limitations in religious congregations, limitations which the cultural view of progress cannot integrate.

Choices before us

Some find an atmosphere of spiritual euthanasia in religious congregations. Members believe religious life is dying and someone should mercifully pull the plug. To what extent does the cultural view of progress influence this mentality? By what criteria do we measure the life or death of religious life?

2. Robert Bellah, *Habits of the Heart: Individualism and Commitment in American Life* (Berkeley: University of California Press, 1985) 170–77.

The cultural view of progress must not be our measure of success. But how do we think counterculturally about our lives and future? What are the signs that our thinking is on a better track? In facing these questions we truly ask, which way *is* ahead?

I suggest we have four choices which can dramatically affect our future as religious congregations in the next several years. We must choose a) between gospel living and cultural religion; b) hope over nostalgia; c) to overcome moral hazards in order to rediscover community; d) to adopt a realistic vision of evolution to the future. In the following pages we will explore these choices.

Gustavo Gutierrez tells us in *A Theology of Liberation* that the struggle against what oppresses us actually creates a new person. As religious congregations turn away from an uncritical adoption of cultural standards to choose their future, they will create more intentionally and effectively the life for which they hope.

Choosing our faith

Modern life places a great deal of emphasis on the individual and self creation. Focus on the individual has been a breath of fresh air in religious life. It has taken years for religious to internalize the healthy link between self-actualization and holiness.[3]

Theologian Johannes Metz claims, however, that the secular view of salvation, not the gospel, can subtly set the tone for what self-actualization really means in modern society. Secular salvation can replace religion in forming our ideal of "progress" as individuals and communities. When this is the case, religion ceases to be what it should be and becomes "bourgeois."

In the nineteenth century the bourgeois were the middle class. They were considered the recipients of the benefits of the Enlightenment and definers of the boundaries of reality. "Bourgeois" religion is the distortion of religious practice that accompanied this social change.

---

3. Judith A. Merkle, *Committed by Choice* (Collegeville: The Liturgical Press, 1992). Comments on the value of autonomy and religious life in our age.

"Bourgeois" became a mentality that everything is simply for the use of those in mainstream society. People, nature, religion, and society are simply there for personal fulfillment. None of these relationships requires anything from individuals in return. When religion becomes bourgeois, religious practice patterns itself according to these distorted relationships. Another name for this phenomenon is cultural religion.

A cultural religion no longer calls to growth because people create it and, characteristically, do not create a religious practice which can challenge. Religion becomes only a tool of self-actualization, a self-actualization whose standards are set in purely secular terms.[4] A cultural religion no longer transforms; rather, mainstream society makes religion fit into what it considers reasonable.

Current research on people's expectations when they come to church uncovers this mentality.[5] A growing number of adults hope for some small group experience allowing them to feel like they belong, but in a style where the belonging has few commitments or responsibilities. Desire for belonging without commitment is a cultural trend. In religious life our current concerns around membership reflect this tendency. Do we find ourselves expecting a sense of belonging without wanting to define boundaries of membership?

Healthy religion, in contrast, affirms and questions us. It fosters a critical consciousness of culture, society, and church, along with a healthy self criticism. It checks the tendency to nest in our own perspectives and to find imperfection only outside ourselves. Cultural religion constructs its own church and its own community which only affirms and never questions. Healthy religion calls members to be challenged by a broader reality which mirrors the Mystery of God at the heart of true religion.[6]

When church and community become only a tool of self creation, they cease to be accountable to any reality outside them-

---

4. Johannes Metz, *The Emergent Church* (New York: Crossroad, 1986) 1–16.

5. Barbara Hargrove, *The Emerging New Class: Implications for Church and Society* (New York: Pilgrim Press, 1986)

6. Bellah, *Habits of the Heart*, 219–49.

selves. In turn, they become places of vague belonging. In religious life a "bourgeois" approach to church and community leads to fragmentation and alienation which cannot carry a congregation into a common future. Metz reminds us that we need to be careful we are renewing according to the gospel and not according to the "bourgeois" religion of our culture. How, though, do we know the difference?

Resentment of the world's imperfection

Cultural religion relates only to what confirms its outlook on life. It avoids people and reality which do not mirror its beliefs; in other words it lacks community. In turn, cultural religion gives us little help in facing limits. It searches for a future without the paschal mystery and creates a world which does not need God for meaning.

When we find ourselves being diverted with these mentalities, we know we are following a cultural religion. One day some friends reflected on the difference between healthy religion and cultural religion as they were speaking of eucharistic symbols. One said, "At times Jesus is more like broccoli than pizza." Cultural religion offers a Jesus "lite" who does not save as the Jesus Christ of the gospel.

Theologians and social critics today link unbelief in a decaying North American church with a secular view of life which promises us health, wealth, and happiness. Who needs a church which makes demands when our culture urges us to look at only one side of life, the sweet without the bitter? When human life is understood and liberated on its own terms, there is no need of God. We can save ourselves.

However, human experience reveals that it is precisely the awareness of our limits, our finitude, that reveals our dependence on God and poses the question of faith. Do I allow myself to be open to a Mystery which I cannot manipulate or control?[7] Do I

7. John O'Donnell, S. J., "Faith" in *The New Dictionary of Theology,* eds. Joseph A. Komonchak, Mary Collins, Dermot A. Lane (Wilmington: Michael Glazier, 1987) 375.

believe in the Goodness at the heart of life, despite disappointment and struggle?

Only an affirmative answer to these questions satisfies the longing of the human heart. A yes to Mystery allows our lives to become whole in spite of the fragmenting experiences which come into every life.

When the prevailing philosophy of life has no room for finitude, no one can survive very long in a world in which awareness of human limitations becomes inescapable. The weakness of society's view of life and progress is that it tries to answer what is essentially a religious question. It offers only secular tools to respond to a question that touches the absolute, trying to prove scientifically what is not scientific.

A focus on mere personal development is also not enough to overcome the major challenge to belief today, resentment of the world's imperfection. Another vision is needed to explain why we should be expected to love life when it is full of pain and suffering as well as love. Society's view of salvation in this light is not really that satisfying.

Religious life is built on the faith vision that integrity comes from trust in God in the face of the inherent contradictions of the human spirit and societal life. It is this faith that grounds its capacity to stand with those who may be "losers" in the cultural view of things. True religious faith feeds an active hope and creative love according to the needs of the times.

Religious seek to recover this faith today as well as its impact on community and ministerial life. Choosing the gospel, or healthy religion, over cultural religion involves the embrace of the cross. Accepting this challenge is key to the future.

Hope or nostalgia?

As religious search for identity, they struggle before the same vicissitudes that religion itself faces in postmodern society; indifference, continuing dechristianization, fanaticism, consumerism, stress, and individualism.[8] One sign of an identity grounded in

8. Jan Kerkhop, "The Synod Lineamenta: European Religious Respond," *Religious Life Review* 32 (Sept.–Oct. 1993) 287.

faith is the presence of hope in spite of limits. Hope overcomes the paralysis brought on by a false view of progress. It spawns the imagination to plan realistically and effectively and fosters a ministerial accountability in spite of limits.

Society's view of progress does more than give us false information; it causes us harm. It weakens our imagination to make intelligent provision for the future by distorting our attitudes to the past and our hopes for the future. Following it we relate to the past with nostalgia and the future with ambiguity and pessimism.

A societal view of progress weakens our imagination to make intelligent provision for the future. Nostalgia, its ideological twin, undermines our ability to make intelligent use of the past. While our attitudes toward the past and the future are linked, let us first consider how religious relate to their past.

During renewal years religious researched their original charism and spirit. Numerous celebrations of the institutional contribution of religious orders in the last century occurred as groups celebrated anniversaries of their ministerial commitments. Recently groups have invested in better archives to preserve the history of their contributions to an immigrant church in the United States and respective countries. We have celebrated and remembered as part of renewal.

Deep communal values are commemorated and expressed during celebrations. These events are gifts to a community and important occasions of its life together. Memory is wonderful. However, instead of being renewed and enlivened in remembering the past, some religious have become de-energized and depressed. Another attitude found its way into our communities, nostalgia.

Nostalgia creates a relationship between the past and the present characterized by the contrast between simplicity and sophistication.[9] The past is viewed as the "simple life" and the present as complex and sophisticated. Remembering the good old days casts the past into a childlike vision of simplicity and security. In the past, things never changed, or so it seems when viewed from the

---

9. Lasch, *The True and Only Heaven*, 82–83; 537–8.

rapid change of today's society. Subtly, the idealism and faith of the past are linked to an unreal state of innocence, an innocence which real life in modern society no longer supports. Depression stems from the frustration such a vision suggests.

Nostalgia attends to values, but not adequately. The deception of nostalgic thinking is the subtle suggestion that these values cannot survive exposure to modern experience. Through the lens of nostalgia the past is lost. Its values are locked in a time to which we no longer have access. There is no path from the past to the present.[10] Nostalgic thinking poses the false alternative to return to the past, which we cannot do, or to languish in the fragmentation of the present. Trapped by nostalgia, our energies are paralyzed for the future.

Nostalgia is a phenomenon of contemporary life. The more the modern age insists on its own wisdom, experience, and maturity as something set apart from the moorings of the past, the more appealing simple unsophisticated times appear in retrospect. Nostalgia offers to religious a subtle deceit.

Memory takes a different approach. It is an active type of remembrance that seeks to grasp the past's formative influence on the present. Memory asks the meaning of the past for today. Values are freed from the past to be expressed in contemporary times.

Memory locates the past in a broader system of meaning and value which retains its validity in the present and future. The act of remembering links a religious community to the gospel and its founding identity. Memory finds that this charism is so rich, it is not yet exhausted. Linking our past to our present, in order to connect our future, memory presents us with values worth pursuing.

Memory calls us beyond ourselves; in this is it countercultural. The modern mind sees its wants as the main criteria for action.

10. As religious around the world reviewed the Synodal Lineamenta on Religious Life they were concerned that the modern world was perceived as a dangerous place in which religious life was to grow. This seems to be a caution against slipping into a posture of nostalgia. See Austin Flannery, ed. *Towards the 1994 Synod: The Views of Religious* (Dublin: Dominican Publications, 1994).

Memory, on the other hand, moves us beyond these wants to our deeper desires. It challenges us to the call of the gospel which gives behavior meaning beyond that of the moment or even the will of the group. To remember is to be open to a program of moral and spiritual change, for today and for tomorrow.

As religious seek new routes for the future of their communities, memory rather than nostalgia is a better compass. Nostalgia links us to a lost innocence and a lost hope. As a ritual of stagnation, it allows us to wallow in the past without drawing meaning for the present. Members feel the chains of nostalgia as their present reality is denied, and ideals are relegated to the past. Nostalgia triggers the downward spiral of desolation rather than a forward thrust to renewal. While nostalgia symbolizes a community's fear to face the future, memory leads to gratitude, wisdom, and a hope which gives vision for tomorrow.

A friend drove past a large institution built by my own community in the nineteenth century, marvelled at the courage it took to undertake such as endeavor, and wondered what we will leave the next generation. We respect the exceptional contribution to the Church made by nineteenth-century religious, yet we know our times and theirs are different. However, we face the same challenge they did, to collectively choose love over egotism in the circumstances of our day. Religious of today face this challenge in a new context. Let us continue to examine our new situation in a third choice before us.

Moral hazards

A striking difference between religious life in the nineteenth century and today is the unity which existed between work and life. Religious life was lived in a total institutional context. All the needs of the religious—relational, ministerial, financial, spiritual—were often met by the same institution. This is not the case in modern living. Today we live in segmented spheres: family, work, politics, and religion operate often without reference to one another. For religious, home and the workplace are frequently separate.

A practical consequence of this way of living is that we have less knowledge of each other. We operate with what Charles

Wilbur, the economist, calls imperfect information. Today in many congregations, years of not working together in the same institutions create gaps in knowledge and understanding among members. On the one hand, we have more personal freedom and a broader scope of relationships. On the other, lack of knowledge often feeds a low trust level.

When a low trust level enters into our dealing with each other, we have what Wilbur calls a moral hazard.[11] This he identifies as a situation where people are mutually affected by the behavior of each other, but where a low trust level causes them to engage in self-defeating behaviors. Wilbur's description, while directed toward industry, reflects a situation found in religious congregations today.

A scenario of moral hazard is the vicious circle of distrust which can occur between an employer and employee. The employer fears the employee isn't doing her job. The employee fears the employer will require too much work or will fire her if given the chance. In response, the employee begins to withdraw and shirk her job. To remedy the situation the employer supervises more to stop the expected laziness.

If the employee could self-supervise, work would be more efficient and the company would profit. Instead, what results is a situation where each, the employer and employee, pursues his or her self interest: the employer, the need to exert appropriate control; the employee, the need to maintain self-esteem and autonomy. The result is that as individuals, both are worse off and the group is worse off than if they had been able to work together.

Since the employee and employer are locked into an interdependent relationship, they affect one another. Both have a common interest in their situation and both attempt to choose the best possible course of action from their point of view. However, the result is not what anyone desires. This is the nature of a moral hazard, according to Wilbur.

---

11. Charles K. Wilbur, "Incentives and the Organization of Work: Moral Hazards and Trust," in *One Hundred Years of Catholic Social Thought*, ed. by John A. Coleman, S.J. (New York: Orbis Books, 1991) 212–33.

Why is it so difficult to cooperate in such a situation?[12] Because exit is cheap and voice is expensive. To exit is to withdraw, to drop out of a conversation which would be needed to create a solution. Solutions require the capacity to move beyond untested perceptions based on distrust. Solutions require new behaviors which serve both the individual's interests and the group's interest. The ability to exit is facilitated by the availability of choice and alternatives.

Voice, in contrast, involves the communication of one's concern to another, the openness to test one's perceptions and the willingness to work out a solution. Why is voice so difficult? The cost to an individual to do this often exceeds the benefits which the individual receives. Hence, the individual exits.

A situation of moral hazard places those involved in a Catch 22. One's individual actions can make his or her own situation better. However, the solution to the situational problem requires group effort and consensus. It cannot be solved by any one person. The action which makes an individual's situation better may, in the long run, erode group life.

An individual may be willing to forego a preferred behavior and choose one that is more consistent with group goals. However, if one does this *alone*, no matter how hard an individual tries, he or she can produce no greater benefit to the group than the original behavior which is ultimately more self interested. A moral hazard exists because the alternative line of action requires some level of trust and this cannot be accomplished by one individual. The "hazard" is intensified when the group offers no incentive to the individual to risk.

The problem of "free riders" also adds to the situation of moral hazard. Free riders are those who cannot be excluded from the benefits of a collective action, even if they do not cooperate with it. They receive the benefits of the group, even without accountability to its decisions. They have little incentive to join a group agreement which requires movement beyond self interest, yet have power to block a common solution.

12. *Ibid.* 215.

Even though this is an example from the business community, there are parallels in religious life today. Problems in congregations require group decisions. We are in a situation in which we need group decisions more than ever, yet our life-style is such that to take up the challenge of voice instead of exit is getting more and more "expensive" emotionally, spiritually, and personally.

A group decision is difficult because trust level is low, fed by imperfect knowledge. Moving beyond self interest often delivers fewer benefits than exiting in a situation which depends upon mutuality. Weak methods of accountability and unclear expectations of membership make free riding harder to overcome.[13] Religious life cannot prosper in such a situation.

Dealing with the situation of moral hazard is critical. Researchers point to the fragmentation which a climate of moral hazard can create. They indicate there is "affiliative decline" among religious, or that kind of commitment that has more to do with a sense of belonging than a sense of mission.

Mistrust, inability to work together at common problems, and lack of accountability contribute to a climate of "moral hazard" which erodes a sense of belonging. The researchers believe congregations will decline if members have no stronger reason to remain than mere bonding.[14]

The third choice before religious today involves a call to be countercultural by naming and facing our situations of moral hazard. We live in a culture which seldom offers an overarching sense of meaning beyond that of personal interest. Religious are groups who have and live by a meaning deeper than accommodation of self interest. Their rootedness in a meaning beyond themselves motivates them to face the moral hazards of group life today.

Religious are challenged to be accountable because they are groups whose meaning touches on universal needs of the world

---

13. Experience in religious life teaches that any life-style can be an occasion for free riding. The question is, how is accountability practiced?

14. Nygren and Ukeritis, "Future of Religious Orders"; and Thomas Stahel, "Whither Religious Life?" *America* (Sept. 26, 1992) 180.

around them. Their witness lies in their choice to be people who can inquire, grasp, and formulate the relationships of their lives so as to respond to questions which are deep enough to explain why one should take up voice instead of exit in our world today.

In the next chapter we will look at the fourth choice before religious today: the development of a realistic view of evolution to the future.

Chapter Three

Beyond Progress: Ecological Wisdom

Religious life is grounded in belief in the ongoing revelation of God. Revelation, in this sense, is not just information about God. It involves knowing about God who is loving and operating in our lives and history.

The future of religious life is measured not only by institutional vitality, financial stability, and increase in members. Religious life is a relationship with God. This relationship involves a dialogue with God at a particular time in history. To speak of this dialogue plunges us into the realm of mystery. We need more than theories of progress and cultural criticism to address it. We must turn to the language of revelation.

Some consider revelation as a mystical experience which comes privately to an individual. Revelation is a more pervasive Christian experience. The faith community holds that God reveals through Scripture and Tradition. Yet God also reveals through personal and communal history and in movements in society. All communication from God requires our response. It is awesome to think that the expression of God's own self-understanding needs a human partner for its full meaning to be understood in history.[1]

There are elements in our lives today that make it difficult to comprehend and respond to God's revealing action. Changing

---

1. See Mary E. Hines, *The Transformation of Dogma* (New York: Paulist Press, 1989) chapters 1 and 2.

understandings of truth, freedom, and suffering influence our interpretation of God. Today people question if there is anything in which they can find certitude. Is life run by chance, or is there a plan? Our response to these questions governs our understanding of God's direction also.

Today we listen to God's revelation through the signs and symbols of an evolutionary world, not a static one.[2] The science of hermeneutics studies how symbols, questions, and thought systems influence interpretation of reality. The term "paradigm shift" refers to changes in fundamental ways of interpreting reality. Becoming familiar with evolutionary thinking can help with discernment of God's action in our lives as religious.

This raises the fourth choice before us, to develop a realistic view of evolution to the future. This involves attention to new patterns of evolutionary thinking and selection of those which are helpful. Exploration of these categories of thought can help us to better discern our future.

Ecological wisdom

"Progress" is one of many explanations of how people and nature change. The search to explain the direction of human events, or history, goes hand in hand with the quest to understand the origin of the diversity found in nature.

Since the scientific discoveries at the beginning of the eighteenth century, there has been interest in patterns of change in nature. Awareness that the earth has changed triggers questions about how human beings and institutions change. Does humankind and nature progress in a random manner, or by chance? Is there an end or purpose, a *telos*, to it all? Answers to these questions reach deep into the human psyche. They outline the relationship of our past to our future, and the significance of our present.

---

2. See John F. Haught, *Science and Religion: From Conflict to Conversation* (New York: Paulist Press, 1995) for a treatment of the relationship of an idea of God to the universe of evolutionary biology, relativity, and quantum physics and to the latest findings in astronomy.

Charles Darwin, and the social theorists who followed him, said only the fittest survive the turmoil of change.[3] Through natural selection, the weak are weeded out. Those capable of adaptation live on.

Social theorists used this biological observation to explain changes in society also. It explained poverty in the nineteenth century, why some prospered and others did not. Poor people were not as "fit" as those who succeeded. Obviously, this theory was erroneous. Yet, the survival of the fittest is deep in our culture. Its "wisdom" is used also in religious circles to explain change and difference.

People turn to the study of nature or ecology to get bearings in a transition. A disordered understanding of nature is a poor compass to the future, so better theories are sought. For instance, critics charge that the cultural view of "progress" is inadequate because of its faulty view of nature. It considers nature only as an instrument in technological progress, rather than a life force with which to live in harmony.[4]

How we think about nature affects how we think about life itself. Some claim we need a new cosmology, or understanding of the human in relationship to the universe as a whole, in order to know the way ahead as a human community.[5] What possibilities does evolutionary thinking hold for religious as we think about our future?

Evolution and religious

An evolutionary outlook holds that there is a fundamental unity in all that exists. All living and nonliving things form an interdependent life system. The unity of matter creates a possibility of uni-

3. Richard Hofstadter, *Social Darwinism in American Thought* (Boston: Beacon Press, 1955).

4. Vincent J. Donovan, *The Church in the Midst of Creation* (New York: Orbis Books, 1989) 120–3. Paula Gonzalez, S. C. "An Eco-Prophetic Parish?" in *Embracing Earth: Catholic Approaches to Ecology*, eds. Albert J. LaChance and John E. Carroll (New York: Orbis Books, 1994) 214–24.

5. Thomas Berry, C.P., with Thomas Clarke, S.J., *Befriending the Earth: A Theology of Reconciliation Between Humans and the Earth,* eds. Stephen Dunn, C.P., and Anne Lonergan (Mystic, Conn: Twenty-Third Publications, 1991).

versal analogy which links all levels of life. Information at one plane of reality can shed light on another. For example, chemical reactions have a "half-life." Those interested in mid-life crisis draw on this analogy. Since there are similarities between natural life and human life, these can be read and interpreted by the human mind.

Nature does not provide a blueprint for human meaning and direction. Nature gives the appearance of both randomness and purpose. Its meaning is left to interpretation. Some modern biologists judge that evolution lacks purpose and is not headed in any particular direction. If the evolutionary process has any goodness at all, it is that of chance.[6] Other scientists find that physical data has a mysterious order and points to the unity of the universe.[7]

Theology, evolution, and religious life

Theologians use evolutionary thinking to interpret Christian revelation. Teilhard de Chardin is one theologian who combines the perspectives of faith and science. Chardin sees the cosmos as a process which mirrors the inner life of God. Despite its pain, failure, and apparent absurdities, all life is developmental and moving in a process of cosmogenesis. Chardin sees the universe as a cosmos or whole developing in a precise direction. It goes from the Alpha point to the Omega point, under the ever present care of God the creator and preserver.[8]

Religious, too, calculate their future using broad theories of the meaning of history and the universe. They produce their own theories of growth, decline, and evolution.[9] Some even resort to a

6. Jacques Monod, *Chance and Necessity: An Essay on the Natural Philosophy of Modern Biology* (London: Fontana/Collins, 1974).

7. Fritof Capra, *The Tao of Physics* (New York: Bantam Books, 1984); Haught, *Science and Religion.*

8. Teilhard de Chardin, *The Phenomenon of Man,* trans. Bernard Wall (London: Wm. Collins and Company, 1959). See also Denis Carroll, "Creation," in *The New Dictionary of Theology,* 246–58.

9. See for instance: Raymond Hostie, S.J., *Vie et mort des ordes religieux* (Paris: Desclee de Brouwer, 1972); Lawrence Cada S.M., et al., *Shaping the Coming Age of Religious Life* (New York: Seabury Press, 1979). Most recently, Patricia Wittberg, *The Rise and Decline of Religious Orders: A Social Movement Perspective* (Albany, N.Y.: SUNY Press, 1995).

version of Darwinism to calculate the future of their congregations. Orders with ancient traditions will survive, some claim. Newer groups with flexible rules and inclusive boundaries are fit for the future, others assert.

Is the growth and decline of religious orders open to scientific rationality? Some religious study patterns to get a sense of direction. Others, more intuitive, draw from images in the mystical tradition to name the present. They see these times as the "dark night of the soul."

Certainly these approaches have something to offer today. The more rational ones offer the truth that God reveals through normal human processes.[10] The mystical approaches resist that scientific rationality alone is capable of predicting the future.

Empirical scientists today understand the universe with much humility. They now admit that only very small areas of life can be predicted through cause-effect relationships which once were held as windows on nature itself. Direction for the future is more likely to reside in some combination of the above approaches. Religious need facts and faith to envision the future. But can new science help in this process?

New science and religious

For several centuries people saw the universe as predictable. They measured order in nature in linear terms. In high school science many participated in this linear measurement of the universe. They measured changes in natural processes by marking straight lines on a graph. Natural processes were phenomena that could be traced along a sequence of causally related steps. Any final outcome could be predicted if one knew the starting conditions.[11]

Science affects thinking about life. The world was once conceived as a mechanism where the uncertain or spontaneous occurrence is at a minimum, and necessity and predictability were at the maximum. The Church and culture before the council mirrored this scientific worldview.

10. Philip S. Keane, *Christian Ethics and the Imagination* (New York: Paulist Press, 1984).

11. Haught, *Science and Religion,* 144.

Predictability makes engineering and technology possible. However, scientists know that it accounts only for the simplest happenings in nature. In the twentieth century, science has shifted. Today scientists see nature as composed largely of intricate, self-organizing patterns.

Most of these patterns are better characterized by complexity rather than predictability. Cells, organisms, brains, and ecosystems are elaborate, adaptive, and self-organizing. The theory of relativity and quantum theory in physics lead scientists to use terms seldom heard in scientific circles: freedom, contingency, and finality. Ideas once rejected as explanations of the universe are central now.

Today the cosmos and human life are realities in the making, not finished processes. An expanding and evolutionary universe challenges the vision of a rigid and mechanistic world. Not only are cells complex, but so are economic systems and religious congregations. Religious can interpret the future from older worldviews. However, if they do so, they may be shortsighted.

For instance, just as there is no "inevitable" process in history, there is likely no inevitable progress or demise of religious life.[12] How then do we use good scientific research to view the future, yet realize it does not have the entire story? Evolution sees both chance and finality operate in the universe. Understanding this can shed light on our future.

Thinking evolutionarily

An evolutionary perspective is based on the assumption that energy on the human level is analogous to energies and breakdown of energy in more primitive forms of matter.[13] Evolution is not a mechanical process. It is the result of the tension of two opposing yet complementary principles in the world. The first is *entropy*, the tendency of all energy toward dissipation into increasingly

12. Lasch claims this leads to hopelessness. See *The True and Only Heaven,* 527ff.

13. Juan Luis Segundo, *Evolution and Guilt,* trans. John Drury (New York: Orbis Books, 1974) 25; *De la sociedad a la teología* (Carlos Lohle: Buenos Aires, 1970) 155–73. Chardin, *The Phenomenon of Man.*

simple forms. The second is *negentropy,* the countermoving movement against the force of entropy.

Entropy is a principle of conservation of energy. It holds that every natural transformation involves the same sum total of energy. No energy is lost but no new energy is created in nature. Instead, evolution occurs through the displacement of energy. Energy is concentrated, drawn away from one function and put into another.[14]

The energy used to drive a car does not disappear, it remains intact somewhere. But where is it? Can it be harvested again to drive another car? The answer is no. The negative component to entropy is that all energy is conserved, but it is also degraded. The energy used to run a car is transformed into a simpler energy, difficult to concentrate and put into use again. It is converted into heat, the most simple of all energy.

If entropy has the power to create greater pools of unusable energy, how does evolution happen at all? Evolution moves toward ever more complex and potent concentrations of energy. To do this it has to work counter to entropy. True evolution moves contrary to entropy. The work of concentrating energy and running counter to the thrust of entropy belongs to the second force, negentropy.

Negentropy acts against entropy. Evolution occurs whenever more concentrated and powerful syntheses of energy are formed by running counter to the statistically greater tendency toward ever simpler syntheses of degraded energy.

We can image throwing a rock into a pond and forming a ripple effect. In the center, where the rock hits, is the highest concentration of energy. At the edges of the ripples is the repetition of the simplest kind of energy, the molecules of the undisturbed pond.

While at first glance the entropy of the undisturbed pond seems to act against the concentration of energy of the design created by hurling the rock. Yet, without the entropic state of the pond, the creation of the effect could not occur. The new effect is

14. Segundo, *Evolution and Guilt,* 22.

a result of the relationship between negentropy and entropy or that between minority and majority phenomena.

Evolutionary thinking draws an analogy between natural occurrences and other levels of life. These patterns in nature can provide insight into human affairs, like renewal, and the costs of change.

Minority and majority phenomena

Negentropy moves evolution toward a higher synthesis. This synthesis is a richer and more concentrated combination of energy. But precisely because this synthesis is a more concentrated form of energy, there is less of it in the universe.

There is less living matter in nature than physico-chemical bodies which are simple and inorganic. Life which has a nervous system is sustained by life which is more simple. Life which can think is even a smaller minority. Conscious life is sustained by the energies of all the other planes, yet is capable of concentrating and liberating energies that are dormant in them.

Evolution indicates that every new synthesis costs energy. The easiest and most plentiful synthesis will be the one that is easiest to come by, the one that is less rich and effective.

Jumping by analogy to the human plane, this bears out in experience. When congregations or individuals stand on the cusp of change, they feel a strong pull to slip back into familiar, repetitive behaviors. When this tendency is overcome it is remarkable, and we name it a movement of the Spirit.

While the forces of entropy and negentropy are opposing and complementary, they are not equal. Quantitatively, entropy is greater. More matter is found in simple arrangements than in the richer synthesis of higher forms of life. Qualitatively, negentropy prevails. As matter is arranged in increasingly complex forms, consciousness, or the "within" of things is a dominant and visible force. This evolutionary insight can carry meaning for religious.

Chance or purpose

In evolutionary thinking there are two kinds of energy: "energy of the within" and "energy from the without." What is commonly understood as energy, "energy from without," is subject to entropy. The "energy of the within" is not. Because of this, "energy of the within" is the thrust of the evolutionary process.

There are debates as to how the energy of negentropy functions. Does change occur by chance and randomly or does it follow some purposeful process? Those who take chance as the explanation of evolution reason in this way.

The first living molecule appeared by chance in evolution. In the infinite number of possible transformations of energy and against the odds of a living molecule ever appearing, one just did one day. However, for evolution to continue, the process reoccurred, by chance. Whatever the odds were in that first molecule appearing, the odds were the same for the next and the next.

Others feel this was not the case. The first living molecule was replicated and more copies of the *same* appeared. To attribute that to chance would be like attributing a winner of fifty successive bingo games to the good fortune of luck. Most, on the contrary, would look for a fixed game. These thinkers find a principle of order in the universe.

Neither outlook can be conclusively proven by science alone. Yet, in evolution, the most complex processes do occur at the end rather than at the beginning of a process. In the human species, for example, *homo sapiens* evolves from more simple forms. Our experience is that in order to read the beginning, we start at the end and trace backward.

Many find a purposefulness and a sense of chance mixed in their reading of the evolutionary process. Nature masters opposing forces through a combination of chance and adaptation or purposefulness without ever nullifying either.[15] Before human beings, nature itself overcame entropy. Nature did a good job overcoming entropy even before human beings got involved in the process.

Believers identify the spirit of God as the dynamic principle of the universe. St. Paul intuits the unity between levels of the cre-

---

15. Juan Luis Segundo, *An Evolutionary Approach to Jesus of Nazareth* (New York: Orbis Books, 1988) 51.

ated universe as he observes "creation itself groaning in labor pains" (Rom 8:22). Faith recognizes that human energy shares in an Energy source far more primitive and foundational to the universe than itself. The unity of the created order of the world is a key area of theological reflection today.

Toward the future

We have said that the fourth challenge before religious today is to develop a realistic view of evolution to the future. An evolutionary perspective can provide a balance in thinking about the future. Just as natural evolution involves a blending of expansive and constricting forces, so does evolution as religious congregations. Change for the better is not an automatic process. Nature contradicts the promised "inevitable progress" of the culture. Change in nature occurs over the long term with many twists and turns.

Evolutionary thinking supports that new combinations of "energy" in religious life are not a sign of its ultimate demise, but of its life. However, costs need to be evaluated and wise energy calculations made. Evolutionary thinking incorporates setbacks as well as forward movement into a view of the future. It gives stability, as well as change, a role in common life.

An evolutionary mindset helps religious see the change in their lives in a larger picture. God's revelation and ways are cast in light of processes which precede religious and will continue long after they are gone. It calls each to responsibility by showing how each element plays a part in the total evolution of the whole.

The new science also raises questions for religious. How can we insure that our future proceeds from a healthy balance between chance and purposefulness, between risks and planning? How can faith impact the future and help us identify God's grace in the midst of a culture focused on a scientific explanation of the world?

Chapter Four

Toward a New Vision

"Truth" is difficult to find in modern society. Cynics hold there is no truth to be found. Life is absurd, and human existence and the universe do not make sense.

The faith community believes that truth can be sought and truth can be found (John 1:14). Humans desire and need truth. They yearn for what is real, beyond their illusions. The human community continues to hope that reality is responsive and will unfold its meaning in the passing of time.

Truth is elusive. Truth is savored more as a goal of a desire within than as a possession held firmly in hand once and for all. Truth is larger than we are, hence it calls us forth. Encounter with truth is often more a case of being grasped by it than of our actually grasping it.[1] Yet, without truth there is no reason to search. In the faith community, Truth is another name for God.

Religious, too, search for truth in our times. However, a vision of the whole is needed to interpret truth. Today there are gaps in this vision. People are unsure of the yardstick of measurement. Concepts which once held human vision together are no longer convincing. There is no satisfactory evolutionary theory at this time which adequately links the interconnections of the universe at the scientific level, and categories of thought which unify the various levels of reality into a whole. We only have fragments of this vision.

---

1. John F. Haught, *What is God? How to Think about the Divine* (New York: Paulist Press, 1986) 92–114.

Previously, culture had an all-inclusive view of the universe and the place of humans in it. This conveyed a sense of "truth." Religious relied on it, even if it overstated the type of certitude it could convey. Today a weakened sense of truth in modern culture creates an atmosphere of relativism. One truth seems as good as another. A sense that life has no ground or basis makes thought about the future difficult.

Evolutionary thought contributes to the human search for truth by its belief in the unity of creation and analogous relationships found in it.[2] Yet, there is no consensus whether we read this order because it is in nature itself or because it exists in the order of the knowing mind. The origin of this order is an insoluble question, yet because of it, connections between our lives and other life processes can be made.

Humans find, in their search for truth, that their own minds and freedom reflect the purposefulness found in evolution. Truth is sought within as well as without. People not only have the desire for truth, but the means for its search.

Today, religious search for many faces of truth. One is for a fresh purposefulness in their congregations. Religious also question whether their resources for this quest are sufficient. They feel at times the cultural pressure to just stop looking. Yet, evolutionary insights into mind and freedom indicate some assets and responsibilities religious have on this journey.

The mind

In the evolutionary process as a whole, we find a constructive evolutionary dynamism in the face of entropy. This force is capable of complementing the tendency toward disintegration and breakdown in the universe. Evolutionary thinkers call this phenomenon *mind*.[3]

2. Juan Luis Segundo, *Faith and Ideologies*, trans. John Drury (New York: Orbis Books, 1984) 30.

3. Segundo, *Evolution and Guilt*, 130, n. 85; here Segundo follows the thought of Gregory Bateson. See Gregory Bateson, *Steps to an Ecology of Mind* (New York: Ballantine, 1972) and *Mind and Nature: A Necessary Unity* (New York: Bantam, 1979). It seems that wisdom as Sophia carries the same meaning. See Elizabeth Johnson, *She Who Is* (New York: Crossroad, 1992).

"Mind" refers to the tendency in evolution to involve a project, to contain a momentum toward the realization of change in face of contravailing forces.[4]

The "Mind" found in evolution is linked to the human mind through redundancy. The force of entropy produces redundancy or structural repetitions at all levels of nature as each plane of reality is involved in the evolutionary process. It is these redundancies or constancies which science studies.

Redundancy forms a similarity in structure at all levels which can be perceived and codified by our minds. My nose and an elephant's nose serve a similar function, even though the relationship between them is not exact.[5] Our lives as religious and those of early monastics have some similarities. However, they cannot be equated precisely.

Through analogy, the human mind shares the same patterned structure that exists in the universe as a whole. The mind possesses the capabilities to understand the basic structure of realities at different stages of evolutionary development because the human mind follows the same patterns in its own structures.

Mind and God

Some laws operative in evolution apply to the operation of the mind itself. One of these laws has been formulated by Chardin: "In this world, nothing could ever burst forth as final across the different thresholds successively traversed by evolution (however critical they be) which has not already existed in an obscure and primordial way."[6]

The human mind finds order in the world because there is order at the beginning. The "Mind," present since the beginning, makes possible the human comprehension and direction of the world. The human mind and this "Mind" are not only linked. We

---

4. Frances Stefano, "The Evolutionary Categories of Juan Luis Segundo's Theology of Grace," *Horizons* 19 (1992) 7–30. In the following I will draw heavily on her work on Segundo, published posthumously.

5. Segundo, *Faith and Ideologies*, 30–8ff, 101.

6. Chardin, *The Phenomenon of Man,* 71.

find that the human mind manifests the same purposefulness of evolution. Through the human mind, "Mind" finds a new way to create order.

Believers take insights from evolutionary theory to another level of meaning. The faith community holds that God coincides with the Mind in evolution. God creates order and meaning from the beginning and gives each human being a purpose. Each religious has a purpose, as well as each religious congregation in the Church.

Analogies between belief and evolutionary thinking are not total. The faith community does not see God just as a force or principle. God is a person who calls human beings as persons to relationship through freedom. God's person entered the order of creation in Jesus Christ. Because of this, the forces of the evolutionary process are not absolute. Everything in it, both past and future, has been reconciled in Christ (Rev 22:13).

God, present in the evolutionary process, does not create order in a manner which makes the ordering of human minds unnecessary. On the contrary, it is through human minds that order is created. The human mind is capable of consciously shouldering the battle against entropy in new and creative ways. We, as individuals and congregations, share in a struggle with all creation as it groans for its future (Rom 8:19-25).

Theology ponders these relationships as it recognizes that God is not the universe; God is transcendent. Nothing in the universe is God, nor do we ever catch up with God in our knowledge of the universe. Yet, every created reality participates in the reality of God. All is to evoke a sense of the sacred. Creation itself is a sacrament.

Our knowledge of the universe never captures God, yet God is present to it. God is the horizon of all knowing, whether we are thinking of God or not; if we are thinking of reality, God is there. New knowledge never threatens God, since God is a dimension of all human knowledge.[7] Using our minds to understand the world, its future, and our part in it, is a door to union with God.

7. Berry, *Befriending the Earth*, 32–3.

God does communicate in this endeavor. Mind continues to create order in this world by communicating through signs in history. The universal analogy in nature is one of these signs.[8] On our part, we are called to read order and purposefulness in the world and to recreate it. We are called to cooperate with God.

The world community is not to be destroyed by new forces, nor to drift before the challenges of our times. It is called to shape meaning and order in human life now. Religious communities, too, as constellations of energy and stimulators of others, have a special role in this process.

Getting direction

Each religious community has a "mind" at its beginning. This "mind," or charism, summons it to do more than reminisce. It challenges it to contact the living purposeful reality of its charism as it orders life today. This "mind" calls religious to live in the present in a manner that has a future.

Thinking of the future with evolutionary concepts calls religious to the discipline of "nonfulfillment." Nonfulfillment is a spirit of acceptance that we will not control the future simply through our calculations.

If we mistake the future for something less, as in saying "we have no future," evolution shows the future will stand steadily before us. If we demand the future before its time, it will resist us. There is no future in evolution that is not grounded in cycles of birth, death, and new life, each having its moment in a movement of change.[9] The real future is whatever in the now is grounded in truth and beckons us to strive beyond the present.

When religious set out on a purposeful path they often raise an important theological question: how do we hope for a future in the face of evil and destruction? Evolutionary thinking cannot re-

---

8. Moral theologians point to a moral order in reality which places on us a sense of obligation. This order also can be known. See Vincent MacNamara, "Christian Moral Life," in *The New Dictionary of Theology,* 676–88.

9. Margaret Farley, *Personal Commitments* (New York: Harper and Row, 1986) 511.

place Christian faith. Yet it can be a fertile ground to re-express Christian belief as we face this question.

The ground of our hope

The faith community hopes for a future in the face of evil and destruction because of the existence of God. God grounds life as a center of goodness. The presence of God in our lives is grace.

Grace is the free and gratuitous communication of God's life to each human being and to every level of creation. Grace creates a new birth and new creation in time. In evolutionary terms, grace is the power that starts all earthly dynamisms toward their full utilization and meaning for human life. It moves men and women beyond their egotism, making them capable of bonding with others. Grace, in Christian thinking, is invitation to faith in Jesus Christ.[10]

Grace is an aspect of negentropy. As one theologian puts it, grace is "that which enables us to journey forward as human beings—without interruption but through the effort of an essential gift—from the natural human condition to the creative liberty of sons and daughters of God (Rom 8:21)."[11]

Grace is the most profound dimension of human life and history. Yet, grace is often indistinguishable from everyday experience. As negentropy is qualitatively more present in the evolutionary process than entropy, grace is more definitive of human life and history than sin. Since entropy is quantitatively more present than negentropy, grace is obscured because of the apparent prevalence of sin.

Experientially, it appears that sin prevails in human life. For this reason, grace is only grasped through faith. It is faith which grounds hope in more than optimism.

Evolutionary thinking links grace and creation. Classical theology reminds us that all creation is created good. However, evolu-

10. James W. Fowler, *Faith Development and Pastoral Care* (Philadelphia: Fortress Press, 1987) 24.

11. Juan Luis Segundo, *Grace and the Human Condition,* trans. John Drury (New York: Orbis Books, 1973) 70.

tionary thinking stresses that creation is not a finished product. Goodness is not something God gives only in advance. God also wants to create goodness each moment through the freedom of human beings and in companionship with them.

Evolutionary thinking translates this for religious as each generation of religious has a task. They are to create with God the good that does not yet exist. In this way they cooperate with God. This charges us to examine another means we have for purposefulness, our freedom.

Is freedom for something?

If God is already our ultimate source of life in grace, what is the purpose of freedom? Are we given human freedom *for something*? Is it really that important that we use it? Does freedom have relevance for our future, our small time in the evolutionary process of religious life, of the Church and our societies? Questions like these are raised by an evolutionary perspective.

Theologically, if too much emphasis is placed on creation which has been made good by God from the beginning, a type of passivity can emerge. Human freedom can seem to be in competition with God. Goodness is finished and static.

Such thinking can devalue the use of freedom as well as responsibility. Holiness and passivity get too closely aligned. Drifting as persons and congregations finds the theological support, "God will provide."

However, an evolutionary perspective gives a different emphasis. If, at the end of time, God will also pronounce creation good in a new way, then making the world capable of being pronounced good is a goal of human freedom. Human freedom participates in the freedom of God in a project of love. The document *Gaudium et Spes* echoes this evolutionary perspective.

> The Word of God, through whom all things were made, Himself made flesh and dwelling on earth (John 1:3, 14) entered the world's history as complete human being [*Perfectus Homo*], shouldering and recapitulating it in Himself (Eph 1:10). It is He who reveals to us that God is Love (1 John 4:8), at the same time

teaching us that the fundamental law of human perfection, and hence of the world's transformation, is the new commandment of love" (GS: 38).

Love is the trajectory of grace in the evolutionary process. Love flows from the gratuitous initiative of God towards the world and a free response of the world to God. Religious life finds its basis as one center of response in this process of evolution.

This grounds religious life in a tradition in Catholic theology which has understood grace in terms of *mutuality*. Grace is a response to God's initiative in faith, a response that originates in a real sense in the action of human agents, and does not proceed in an extrinsic way from the action of God alone.[12] In the relationship of grace, human beings are not God's puppets. Nor is God a consultant invited to concur with "saving" plans made independently of God's intent. Grace involves a relationship of cooperation.

The '70s and '80s and today

In the '70s and '80s the evolutionary categories of Chardin were helpful to religious in considering their future. Yet, Chardin's thinking has been criticized for overstating continuous evolutionary progress. Chardin's vision was attractive because it provided a context for religious to interpret the forward progress experienced in the early days of renewal. Today, in face of the many crises facing our world, perspective has changed.

Visions of progress which suggest any mechanical type of development are losing ground in the modern imagination. People have too many experiences of the opposite. Ecology offers more nuanced paradigms of human meaning today through its ability to incorporate patterns of life, death, and regeneration. Ecological science stresses a profound *equilibrium* which holds everything in the universe together in relationship. In this way, ecology provides a new way to conceive the whole and a new lens for the faith community to envision its life with God.

12. See Quentin Quesnell, "Grace," in *The New Dictionary of Theology*, 437–50.

New models of the interconnections of reality aid religious in considering their lives as a whole. A model of relationship based on equilibrium is one where living, interacting, and dynamic change hold together in a life system of mutuality and purpose. Maintaining equilibrium, however, involves the continuity necessary to bring about significant and qualitative change. Religious ponder how they, too, can live in a way that holds change, continuity, and purpose in equilibrium. Continuity is a particular problem in this balance.

The issue of continuity

New science asks how to measure continuity in change. Recognition of continuity is simple in a system where future developments are predicted from knowing initial causes. Continuity was easy to measure in religious life in the past. Thoughts of institutions closing or lack of replacements in ministry were not big problems. Chapters moved pins in habits or decided a prayer could be dropped from daily practice. Continuity in institutions was easily discerned.

Continuity is a human desire. Many hope to pass values on to the next generation. Since there are few in the next generation in religious life, the linear, cause and effect way of thinking, suggests continuity is over. The logical conclusion to the question of continuity in linear thinking is that religious life is dead.

Yet, evolutionary thinking understands change and continuity, utilizing the two important elements of randomness and time. If we think of movement toward change as a process in which we have to choose between negentropy and entropy, we have not caught on to evolutionary thinking. The path of evolution is more like a circle or spiral than a straight line. Into this circle of forward movement, both entropy and negentropy are combined. Continuity is envisioned differently through this lens.

A circle rather than a straight line

Forward movement does not come from a simple choice of negentropy over entropy. The path of evolution is circular. This occurs because entropy in nature is more pervasive. Entropy is the natural version of Murphy's Law—things naturally move toward muddle and messiness. Ordinarily we think the best way to place order, negentropy, into messiness, is through planning and application of energy and will. Nature creates order differently.

Since the supply of energy in nature remains constant, the richest and most complex syntheses of energy attempted by nature—those which involve the more decisive and transformative phenomena—are those which pay the highest price in energy. They are few in number and are the most fragile.

The largest numbers, however, predominate at every level of reality. They demand a "cheap" energy or a less intense expenditure of it. Their synthesis is simple, involving accumulations of similar elements and mechanisms of a repetitive and routine sort.[13]

These patterns prevail at the human level. "Laws" of human behavior which maintain life and institutions act like entropy. Repetition and common usage make change difficult.

While entropy seems negative, it serves a positive function. The givenness and the sheer multiplicity of the ordinary and routine conserves energy. Because "the ordinary" is numerically superior at each level of reality, it provides possibilities for the experience of chance, since chance increases with numbers. Entropy creates the possibility for randomness to occur.

Ask a young professional looking for a date whether he or she would like to work in a small town or a large city. Many find their "chances" are better with a larger selection of people gathered in one place. Randomness is enhanced. In nature, a large collection of sameness is an entropic force which sets the conditions by which change can occur.

Entropy has a mixed relationship to change. When presented with creative action, entropy blocks newness. The "weight" of entropy can block creativity, turning it into ordinariness. To the eyes of history, the innovation fails. While creative efforts appear to lose, negentropy can still occur.

Negentropy will happen when it is flexible enough in the face of the laws and requirements of entropic determinism to inte-

13. Segundo, *Faith and Ideologies*, 191.

grate these negative aspects of the process into the more efficacious synthesis. For this reason, negentropy takes more energy.
Time is also needed to recognize its presence. The continuity of
purposefulness in evolution is recognized only through incorporation of the randomness created by entropy and time. For
human beings, negentropic action involves the cross, a love which
endures as ultimately victorious.

A circuit of change

In evolutionary change, a circuit is a better image of how
change occurs than a linear cause-effect relationship. A circuit of
change is observed in the operation of electricity:

> If contact is made at A, then the magnet is activated.
> If the magnet is activated, then contact at A is broken.
> If contact at A is broken, then the magnet is inactivated.
> If the magnet is inactivated, then contact is made.[14]

The above represents the successive sequence of a circuit. At
first glance it seems that if contact is made, then contact is broken—not a normal cause-effect relationship. One can only escape this apparent contradiction, or paradox, with time. It is only
the successive and consecutive activations and deactivations of
energy which bring about change.

In a circuit of change, entropy, with its disorder, disintegration,
and death actually prepares the moment of appropriateness in
which the new can occur. Entropy contributes to the randomness
required for change.

Evolutionary thinking can provide a new framework for religious to interpret change. A linear model of change provides a
mental paradigm which puts them in a quandary. It can appear
to religious that either all past change is good, or they must go
back to a former way of living. On a line there is no place to go
except forward or backward. Yet this type of mental framework
can close the door to important reflection. A more nuanced sense
of change is needed.

14. *Ibid.,* 71

Religious can reflect critically on their lives without going back to a former way of living. They can adopt a realism which imitates the "mind" at the heart of evolutionary change.[15] They can resist forces of entropy and maintain the flexibility to engage in a circuit of change. They can thoughtfully review past decisions and correct them with innovations, not regression. They can do this because the "mind" in each religious congregation continues its search to express the heart of religious commitment in new times. They must have the will, however, to search for this mind. Their purposefulness has the resources of mind which is coupled with human freedom. Yet, new steps on the road of purposefulness may cause religious to rethink their use of freedom.

15. Merkle, *Committed by Choice,* 50.

PART II
THEOLOGICAL FOUNDATIONS

Chapter Five

Freeing Freedom

Ordinarily, freedom is our capacity to bring about change. Freedom is the power to plan and invent, to harness the powers of the universe or market and create a better life. There is truth in this cultural vision. Freedom, however, is viewed differently in an evolutionary perspective.

Culture has a linear view of freedom. A free person progresses in a successive straight line of forward movement in life, usually one of upward mobility. Yet, many lives do not follow this model. What about the poor? Society claims the poor do not use their freedom. Laziness or bad character obstructs progress.

What about the sick? Sickness is a blemish on freedom. The cultural ideal is one of control in the face of sickness and death. Autonomy is stretched to the point where self-inflicted death is an option before the inevitability of suffering and death. A sick person is not culture's image of a free human being. Sickness is a detour on the forward path of freedom.

Religious allow this cultural view of freedom to influence their vision of renewal. Thirty years ago we did not predict the situation of today. We assumed people would enter. We anticipated a "better" type of candidate, more professionally trained, usually a leader. We thought we would have more impact on civic systems. We saw ourselves as shaping the Church. We did not think we would struggle as we are. Religious are failures in this linear model of change.

However, evolutionary thought sees the path of freedom differently. It factors in negative and apparent contradictory forces in its vision of forward movement. It goes beyond recognition of contravailing forces. It gives them a place in a circuit of change. To move from a vision of freedom as sheer purposiveness to one vis-a-vis obstacles is an important consideration for religious.

Freeing freedom

Freedom follows a similar pattern of efficacious change found in nature. The creation of something new in the evolutionary process results not from purposeful action alone. It stems from the capacity of this or that atom, molecule, or organism to learn a wisdom of *flexibility* in the face of two evolutionary forces: the tendency toward the conservation of energy on the one hand, and the tendency toward the expenditure of energy on the other.

Change occurs this way in evolution because the energy supplies of evolution are limited. Evolution cannot count on new supplies of energy to be created. Since its supply of energy is constant, the critical question facing the process of change is *how to make use of the energy it has.*

Flexibility is the chief characteristic of evolutionary change. It is the capacity to store energy when it can, and to use stored energy when it must to bring about the most critical changes needed for adaptation and growth.

A better understanding of human freedom can be drawn from this evolutionary model. Freedom is not just the capacity to expend energy to bring about change. Freedom involves the capacity to bring about change in face of obstacles. First, this means freedom acts in the face of those things ignored by the culture: setbacks, tragedy, and injustice. Second, freedom needs flexibility to not only act but to be effective before obstacles. It must store energy and expend energy only for the changes needed for growth and adaptation. In the language of the spiritual tradition, freedom must act with discernment.

Nature and change

Evolutionary thinking holds that energy patterns found on one level of the scale can be found analogously on another level. Thus human relationships are governed to some extent by the same energy supply and redistribution that is found on all levels of existence.

Structural repetitions of energy-saving patterns occur at all levels of evolution. The genetic structure is such a framework in human life. Genetic inheritance saves energy. There are many aspects of life that are not decided; they are received genetically. This frees energy for use in other decisions and activities.

Humans also imitate nature by creating structures to save energy in their relationships. One generation passes on laws to another. No generation regulates its life starting from scratch. Through the gift of a basic process of living codified by law, each generation saves energy. The new generation is then free to meet new problems and crises. This pattern also exists in the history of religious life.

In face of the multiple calls for adaptation to new environments, natural evolution moves forward through its capacity to maintain enough continuity to survive. Through repetition, it avoids expenditure of costly energy for change. Through flexibility, it expends energy for problems that are variable and unforeseeable. Key to evolutionary wisdom is an equilibrium between continuity and flexibility to change.

The ecology of change

Theologically, human freedom is the capacity to express one's self as a center of meaning through decision and action in the world. However, the object of human freedom is not just any change.[1] Change initiated without energy calculation will be overcome by the inevitable movement toward disintegration and breakdown in life (Luke 14:28-30). Evolutionary wisdom calls religious to a wiser use of freedom.

Human freedom always faces the limitations and resistances from opposition of human wills or the inherent contradictions of life. There is no such thing as freedom without restrictions. Yet even relationships which are characterized by limits can be incorporated into the fabric of freedom's action. Chardin's con-

---

1. Merkle, *Committed by Choice*, 32ff.

cepts of tangential and radial relationships point to the role relationships play in a cycle of change.

Radial and tangential relationships

Chardin claims that all energy operates in two general directions. *Radial* energy tends to draw an element forward into structures of greater complexity; *tangential* energy unites elements of the same order and the same complexity. By using these insights, we can characterize relationships from the perspective of the energy it takes to maintain them.

In the early stages of the earth it was radial energy that led to the production of larger and more "centered molecules." This occurred until the first "critical" point of evolution was reached and there was the sudden appearance of life. Yet, tangential energy provided the material organization for this change to occur.

Tangential relationships are characterized by social convention, function, and the impersonal manner which society dictates. These relationships are based on "automatic" responses necessary in every society and situation. No one has the energy to decide every movement. If we go to the store to buy bread, there is a social convention which dictates how to pay the cashier and how to receive change. No one has the energy to "work out" each of these exchanges each time they occur. There are many relationships in religious community of a tangential nature.

Radial relationships are those in which people encounter each other in interpersonal communion. Tangential relationships link persons to one another according to their likeness with others, their class, beliefs, and common interests. In radial relationships people embrace each other as unique individuals and centers of meaning.

Radial relationships involve going beyond automatic and prescribed relationships with others. They incorporate individual freedom and recognition of personal identity. Since radial relationships require enormous amounts of energy, they are a minority phenomenon.

People do not have a hundred best friends. One revolution in a lifetime is usually plenty, even for an avid political activist. No one has the energy! Without the stability of tangential relationships, radial ones would be impossible. While tangential and radial relationships involve different energy levels, relational patterns also have another dimension.

Mass and minority

Most people create relationships in light of the types of relationships available to them. In the evolutionary structure, a larger numerical quantity in any level follows the tendency toward the easiest synthesis. When people follow this pattern, their relationships by analogy have similar patterns. They relate in a manner which involves the least amount of radial encounter with others. Theorists describe this as "mass" behavior. Those who engage in mass behavior form the majority in any group. Religious community counts on "mass" behavior.

The majority of the "mass" is necessary for the health and function of the society. If this majority dominates numerically, a smaller number of elements can attain growth, or a higher or more complicated synthesis. This latter group is always a minority.

Minorities are those who have the richest and more complex syntheses of energy. In nature and human relationships, they also pay the highest price in energy expenditure. They are the most fragile and the smallest in number.

Groups need both minority and majority elements. When society is in such turmoil that the majority cannot be stabilized, the total health of the society is in jeopardy.[2] People also need mass and minority experiences. In religious life both elements serve the health of individuals and the group.

Change occurs when majority and minorities, and mass and minority experiences are held in equilibrium. Sufficient majority experience provides stability for minority experience to occur. Yet, minority experience should foster higher forms of life for the group.[3] The delicate balance between minorities and majorities involves energy calculation.

---

2. Segundo, *Faith and Ideologies*, 285–9.
3. Segundo, *Evolution and Guilt*, 24.

Time spent in mass behavior requiring tangential energy has to be balanced with radial energy needed for minority behavior. If radial energy is called upon extensively, overextension occurs. If mass behavior takes over, there can be great stores of energy, yet an inability to confront new challenges, exercise critical judgment, and solve problems creatively. People find themselves in a rut. They are like those who maintain a yacht to sail in a bathtub. Religious attuned to evolution realize that flexibility is crucial for life and mission.

Flexibility and religious

In energy terms, flexibility involves using energy-saving structures to solve the problems they do well. This conserves energy to meet new problems these structures do not meet. Maintenance of energy-saving structures in religious life requires discernment. We do not keep all practices useful in the past as hereditary structures today. Renewal tried to eliminate practices which no longer saved energy in a modern context.

Yet a new problem occurs today as religious feel a lack of stored energy. Flexibility does not mean liberating minority living to the point where the system of religious life is overwhelmed with differences. The course of evolution has made a more intelligent use of flexibility.[4] Religious also need to take a wiser path.

Evolution mixes its costly radial energy with its habitual, tangential energy to bring about change. To move toward the future, we need to ask not just whether to change or not, but how to use energy to make changes that make a difference.

Differences for what?

In evolution, minority experience has little meaning outside the total matrix of majority life. Majority life is always influenced by minority occurrences. We find the same mix in healthy human relationships. Healthy stability is not the result of juxtaposing already "finished" individuals. Rather, newness and difference need

---

4. For a discussion of this concept as applied to global culture today, see Segundo, *Faith and Ideologies*, 310ff.

to be fostered by the group and allowed to enter into each life and the group as a whole. A good communal situation is a system of human relationships characterized by this balance. Such stable systems are needed by every individual.[5]

Just like nature does not choose between negentropy and entropy, humans do not choose between a private life and a social life. No one can be an individual without the group, nor can the group flourish without the free decision of individuals.[6]

The process of interaction between individual freedom and the "freedom" of a stable social life is like a circuit. The goal is to establish factors on a social and communal level so that personal and communal growth can mutually "set off" or stimulate one another.

Freedom faces many challenges in this process. On the one hand, humans need structures of family, community, church, and society. Participation in their construction is integral to human development. On the other hand, these structures naturally bring a limitation to freedom; they "repress," in a way, some possibilities in life.[7]

Sometimes these limitations are excessive. They serve no positive function in the total fabric of human association. No longer supportive structures, they must be changed. When energy is expended to make these changes, not just any change is occurring. Freedom creates a difference which makes a difference.

We recognize that a difference has been made when factors on a social and communal level better facilitate the circuit by which personal and communal growth mutually "set off" or stimulate one another. The choice is not between individuals and the group. Rather, freedom creates new concentrations of energy which allow individuals and the group to expend and store energy in a more flexible and economical way.

5. Segundo, *Grace and the Human Condition*, 26, 37.

6. This is especially true in a culture which has little role for public life and holds that the real satisfactions and fulfillments of our lives will come from our interpersonal relations alone. See Richard Sennett, *The Fall of Public Man* (New York: Alfred A. Knopf, 1976).

7. Farley, *Personal Commitments*, 12ff.

The impact of freedom which makes a difference is different from cultural freedom simply making a change.[8] It requires an equilibrium involving two more elements of Chardin's thought.

Diversification and unification

When freedom creates a difference which makes a difference, human beings as "centers" of radial energy are integrated into a whole in a better way. Two terms which describe this process are diversification and unification.

Diversification is the process of enabling the optimal number of human differences to develop in a group. The measure of how much diversification can exist in a group is regulated by the assessment of energy needed to maintain it in relationship to criteria such as these:

1) Can it meet its minimal needs for food, clothing, and shelter and provide the proper means for insuring their use and maintenance?

2) Can it maintain the proper amount of energy needed for it to plan and build its future?

3) Does it have the needed amount of energy for it to perform its role and service to the broader pattern of change which it contributes to the society and the world?

Energy calculation is a key ingredient in decisions that make a difference. Contrary to what popular culture dictates, freedom's power is not just to stand before unlimited options. Rather, the goal of freedom is to make a difference. That difference is measured by a second aspect of this process, unification.

Unification is the process by which diverse elements are brought together into the whole. Unification is required so that new complexity and "minority" experiences are integrated toward a fuller human development. Culture sees group life as a mere conglomerate of individuals, all seeking their own interests. A good group is one that has the least amount of restriction on

---

8. For communities, integral to discernment of "differences which make a difference" are criteria. Often these criteria will emerge from study of the community charism.

the operation of individual freedom. Culture does not hold unification as a high value. In fact, culture today militates against most forms of community.

Evolution has no pattern for this type of thinking. The natural world is based on ecosystems of interdependence. Evolutionary patterns suggest that social constraint forms an integral part of the true function of freedom. Yet, in the evolutionary pattern, the human person stands apart from other levels of nature through the unique character of its freedom.

At the human level, ultimately it is the force of love which keeps equilibrium in relationships. Through love, living, interacting, and dynamic change can hold together a life system of mutuality and purpose. The negentropy of love keeps the delicate balance between majorities and minorities and discerns necessary and unnecessary limitations.

Unlike other levels of evolution, humans do not live by the law of the survival of the fittest. Only love unites unique individuals without blotting out their differences. Only love creates a synthesis of centers, rather than an aggregate. Later we will examine obedience in religious life as an expression of the love of unification.

Regulation or de-regulation?

Freedom involves the ability to bond increasingly diversified elements into a unified whole. However, we realize at the human level that people are not only centers of energy; they are self-centered. Regulators are needed to facilitate the conditions that enable the adaptation of our conduct to the conduct of others.[9]

We find these regulators in nature. They enter into natural processes, trigger change, and prevent destructive instability in natural systems. At the human level, regulators loosen us up from the concerns of our own center in order to connect with the needs of others.

We create regulators at the human level. Here human beings differ from others in nature. Freedom distinguishes human be-

9. Segundo, *Faith and Ideologies*, 60.

ings in the analogy of nature. Unlike other species, we do not act from species interest alone. When nature reaches the human level, it explodes into as many centers as there are individual freedoms, and with these centers comes a new dynamic. The individual integrates the interests of the species only insofar as such activity shows up as simultaneously realizing and fulfilling a person. It must have meaning.[10]

The human species helps the individual find meaning but it cannot provide human meaning. No group can do this, nor can any regulator. Rather, each human being has to construct a meaningful life structure through personal risk.

People never take this risk out of species interest. Rather, they risk because they realize any investment or risk is a means to realize self. In order for any action to dynamize the energies of the individual, it must truly be the realization of the person. In other words, it must be done in freedom. In the human sphere, this use of freedom is unique to the human species, for it is called the freedom to love. When this freedom participates in the processes of regulation, it does so because it wants to.

Freedom is not just the cause of new things. Freedom is manifest in the emergence of a difference which makes a difference, for such differences are created by love.

As religious examine the freedom of their founders and foundresses, they find that it was the power of their love which desired to make a difference. They took the risk and displayed a new variety of freedom as love. This risk launched a whole new concentration of energy in the human family and the Church, the religious congregation.

Freedom occurs where we find this same economy of energy which stands before incalculable odds and effects a qualitative, creative change for love.

Freedom remains a power to create something new, even before entropy. Yet, because of entropy, when change occurs, it is so intertwined with innumerable contributions that the projective energies of action seem only to graciously release what time has so hidden. The "change" is simply received as gift.

10. *Ibid.*, 100

Chapter Six

Getting Direction

Evolutionary thought can provide no map for the future of religious life. It can only offer coordinates to interpret human existence and interaction. The compass needed by religious requires other points of reference. Religious must chart the way not only to corporate success but to spiritual integrity. The Christian mysteries of grace and sin, freedom, faith, and revelation ground religious life and offer direction for this journey in the Church.

Grace and the everyday

Grace is another name for God's revealing action in our evolutionary world. Grace is the most profound dimension of human history. It marks the union of God's life with ours. Grace is God's presence with us within time.

Grace is experienced in everyday existence. Living in grace is not a life apart but a new way of operating within ordinary time. Grace is such an integral part of human existence that it is difficult to separate grace as an experience in itself. Conceptually we can compare grace with nature. Their differences, however, can only be noted intellectually since grace and nature in reality are intertwined.

Nature is all that conditions human life. It is our biological, psychological, and sociological reality.[1] When we study our personality type, we inquire about our nature. The study attempts to name characteristics "given" at the core of our personality.

1. Nature here is used in contrast to grace.

Yet, there is more to the human personality than its nature. A person can be studied biologically, psychologically, and sociologically, but their person is not captured. Persons cannot be rationalized, systematized, or analyzed because transcendence, union with God's own mystery, is core to being human.

Nature is part of entropy. It is a force that tries to "fit" each person into the order of the universe. Middle age is a good experience of nature. The natural order is unaware that tennis and jogging are still desired by the middle-aged person with sore muscles. Nature claims its own in death.

Nature functions in the unconscious as racist, elitist, and sexist stereotypes. These mechanisms are "given" in a cultural setting and absorbed unknowingly. Nature not only works on us, but in us. Nature is not just external; we belong to nature's mechanism.

Evolutionary language expresses the difference between grace and nature by using the quantitative and qualitative measures of its processes. Grace is qualitative, sin is quantitative. Sin shares in the pull of entropy. Grace is the qualitative presence of Christ's victory opposed to the quantitative, or more apparent, force of sin at every level of human existence.[2]

Grace is not added onto ordinary life, nor something which ends the human struggle with sin. Grace is not like super unleaded gasoline pumped into our human tanks so they can function more effectively. Grace is not a new layer of existence that covers up the old, nor is it new energy.

Grace and sin

Grace is best understood in terms of the human condition in which our freedom exists. Freedom is limited by personality weaknesses, background, and life problems. Yet, it is also in a type of bondage due to sin. This bondage occurs at a deep level, so it is easy to deny.[3] Human experience testifies that at a fundamental level something blocks us from loving.

---

2. Juan Luis Segundo, *The Historical Jesus of the Synoptics,* trans. by John Drury (New York: Orbis Books, 1985) 494.

3. Patrick McCormick, *Sin As Addiction* (New York: Paulist Press, 1989).

The grace of Jesus Christ touches this hardness and transforms it. Grace is the gift of God's relationship to us. Grace moves us from a situation where we are caught in the destructive hold of sin to one where there is the possibility of loving, despite the power of sin. Human beings can work to receive this gift. Yet, it is something they do not do for themselves. Salvation in this sense is a gift, a gift of grace which qualitatively changes personal existence.

Grace and our world

Grace enters our fundamental experience of the world. It stirs our hopes and elicits our faith. An essential experience of being alive today is one of indignation. Through various media, observation, and listening to others, we are aware that things are not in order.

Good people, however, are unwilling to give evil an equal footing with good. Indignantly we say, this shouldn't be! This "no" to the world, as we find it, hides a deeper "yes." It discloses a better world of our hopes. This situation, yet unknown, engages our energies and imagination. We devise plans to carry out our intent to make changes in the world. We invest in this vision and act as if love is worth the effort.

We cannot prove this is true. Yet, from time to time, we have fragmentary experiences of meaning on small and large scales which nurture, establish, and sustain our hope.[4]

Both believers and nonbelievers have this contrast experience of a "no," and that of an open "yes." For some it is an experience of human faith; for others, one of religious faith. Both expressions of faith have a role in the life of the vows.

Faith

Grace is perceived only by the risk of faith. Faith takes over where complete assurance leaves off. Because of this, faith requires a "leap" or surrender. In faith we place our confidence in a center beyond ourselves. Paradoxically, we confirm in the self a new potential by confiding our life to what is unverifiable.

4. Edward Schillebeeckx, *Church: The Human Story of God* (New York: Crossroad, 1990) 22.

Faith can be human or religious. Anthropological or human faith is the act of risk by which we use our freedom to move out toward others in love. The opposite of faith is the turn toward ourselves in egotism and self-preoccupation.[5] Through basic human faith we form relationships, create values, and reach out to the problems of our lives and communities.

Faith, outlook, and values

Faith is not just a leap of the heart. It is also a way to look at life. A life ordered by the "bet" of faith can be compared and contrasted to others. The choices made by faith can be experienced as satisfactions and weighed alongside others.

Faith affects our outlook on life. One author puts it this way. Faith directs where we put the period in the sentence of life. The cynic puts the period after a negative event. The person of faith uses a comma, leaving room for the creation of a new possibility.

Growth in faith requires community. Human freedom is so socially structured that we have to believe others in order to grow. Life is not long enough to form values solely through trial and error. There is not time to test all possibilities in a personal way to measure whether each possible value is worth the effort.

We rely on the witness of others to choose values. We place faith in those with whom we have formed bonds. We observe how their values have brought them satisfaction. We then take on the practices that form those values in our own lives. Religious form values, not in isolation, but influenced by community, friends, family, and those in ministry.

Transcendent data

Faith gives us information about life. Faith, however, provides a different type of data than gathered in other ways. If we learned to ride a bike as a child, we can call on this data at middle age if we choose to ride a bike, say on a vacation. Even though we haven't ridden a bike for a long time, we have this experiential data stored for later use.

---

5. Merkle, *Committed by Choice,* 26ff.

Other decisions in life are more complicated. When we decide on a vocation, it is impossible at the beginning to know what is involved in a choice from personal experience. Robert Frost's poetic statement, "Two roads diverged in a yellow wood, and sorry I could not travel both, and be one traveller" attests to this.

To make this evaluation, I have to rely on data which is impossible for me to know experientially, as far as the long range satisfactions are concerned. This kind of decision requires transcendent data, that is, data relating to things which I experientially cannot know and which are beyond me.

This data is called transcendent, not because its knowledge is beyond the human capacity to know, but because it involves knowledge which cannot be grasped in its fullness experientially. Life is too short to live out all choices and see the long term satisfactions they can bring. However, this data is decisive for the acceptance or rejection of values. It informs us of the possibilities for satisfaction which those values can or cannot provide.[6]

Transcendent data and values

Knowledge of the worth of a value involves more than subjective preferences. To choose a value is to engage our faith. It requires risk. We ask, is this really worth my effort? We do this every time we choose a value or reinforce one.

Others cannot resolve our question. Yet voices such as "Mother said there would be days like this" or, as our foundress said, "All beginnings involve the cross," enter into our decision. We decide through faith to use these pieces of transcendent data or not.

Transcendent data, dreams, and order

Why do transcendent data engage us? They have meaning because they reflect our deepest hopes about life. Religious communities mirror transcendent data to their members. For example, religious enter with dreams of personal growth and the

6. For further discussion of transcendent data see Segundo, *Faith and Ideologies,* 23, 74–5, 84–5.

world they hope to build. The community reflects to the new members belief in those dreams and a way to accomplish them.

While each human being has the potential for the full range of constructive human values, the concrete realization of these values has to be mirrored and attested to by others (Phil 4:8, 9; 2 Peter 1:5-7).[7]

We structure our lives by use of transcendent data, as meanings which we cannot ultimately prove. They help us develop a scale of values and create priorities. These values influence our world-view and structure how we interpret events. Through faith we give our lives meaning and structure.

Values and thinking

The values formed by human faith are not just concepts. They are grounded in deeply affective experiences which influence thinking. Decisions are made by more than rational thinking alone. Verifiable information and facts are not our only sources. We gather data from our relationships. Relationships provide beliefs which exceed direct verification. Yet, this data influences us greatly.

Instead of empirical reality being the measure of these beliefs, they measure reality.[8] Relationships which involve the transfer of transcendent data largely determine how we perceive reality. Experience does little to alter the values formed by them.

We observe that the same reality can be seen as a triumph or a defeat—be it death, money, imprisonment. It isn't so much that I evaluate them as such; rather, I already perceive them that way because I have learned their value from others. These learnings form my faith.

Faith involves loyalty to something which draws on the whole of my life, affecting how I view everyday events.[9] I think of a

---

7. Anne E. Carr, *Transforming Grace: Christian Tradition and Women's Experience* (San Francisco: Harper and Row, 1988) 49–51, 117–33.

8. Juan Luis Segundo, *Faith and Ideologies,* 1–20.

9. Roger D. Haight, S.J., *Dynamics of Theology* (New York: Paulist Press, 1990) 15–31.

young doctor who went to Somalia to help with the famine-stricken victims. Some saw this as a stupid act, others as the best her profession could offer. People draw on different kinds of transcendent data in their evaluations.

Human faith involves risk. Without the powers of human faith, no religious could make vows or hear values embraced in religious life. But to understand religious life more precisely we have to turn to the role of religious faith.

Religious faith

Religious faith in the Christian community is the identification of the ultimate possibilities and limits of human life and the world with the revelation of Jesus Christ. While human growth is experienced through human faith, religious faith interprets the process in relationship to God.

Believers and nonbelievers share the experience of saying no to the world as they find it. Believers, however, see the face of God in this experience and name the unfolding of a better history as God's gift.[10]

Religious faith is more than God-talk. Fundamentally, religious faith has two characteristics. First, it is the commitment to transcendent data or beliefs which are decisive for the formation of values. Second, it is a fidelity to a "way" of living and a community who witnesses how to gain access to these values.[11]

Human faith and religious faith work together. The concreteness of faith is recorded in the Bible. In Exodus, there is a human process of liberation whereby the Israelites liberate themselves from the hands of the Egyptians, a real evil in their lives. Later, believers see that the Lord saved people from Egypt. Before events are seen in *the* light of religious faith, they are first experienced as meaningful events in themselves.

Religious faith grasps the religious significance of human action which in fact liberates, heals, or establishes communication. Religious faith makes clear how an experience relates to God's

10. Edward Schillebeeckx, *Church,* 6.
11. Segundo, *Faith and Ideologies,* 81.

promise to save. Religious faith impacts values decisively. A religious person is someone who allows the transcendent data of the gospel to continually transform their meaning structure.

The Church

The Church lives in the gap between human faith and religious faith. Christians speak about God on the basis of Jesus, whom they testify is the Christ. However, no one can make this leap between Jesus and the Christ except in the power of the Spirit. Faith in this sense is a grace, not just a personal decision.

Talk of Jesus is only possible in and through the mediation of the Church. The Church is the community of believers who convey the transcendent data of the gospel. We would not know Jesus without the witness of the Church. The Church also has a unique role in the whole process of evolution and in the unification of humanity. The Church is the historical instrument of the kingdom which lies in the future, a kingdom which will be brought to its completion by the final eschatological action of God (*Lumen gentium,* 8).

For Christians there is no Jesus outside the Church, just as there is no church confession of Jesus without the concreteness of Jesus' life and ministry. Religious give witness to these realities of religious faith in a unique way.

The vows

Christianity is defined by a paradox. God's life, infinite and full of mystery, lays hold of us through what is contingent and finite. God's life joins ours from within by gift. On the one hand, God's life is such that no natural intuition or accomplishment can create it. The great mystics repeatedly remind us of this. On the other hand, the ordinary and commonplace is the vehicle of the divine through the gifts of grace and creation.

The vows fall into this broad paradigm of religious experience. The vows are not just this-worldly promises, which spring from the moral will to live in a certain way. The decision to make religious vows is different than deciding to go on a diet or begin an exercise program. The vows are a promise to be open to the mystery of God but to do so through very concrete choices and decisions.

The vows are rooted in mystery. They flow from a belief that the mystery upon which human life rests, and the center to which the soul journeys, is in love with us and desires for us what we most deeply desire ourselves. This love relationship is seen in faith as the basic structure of reality. In it God reveals and touches our lives. We respond and enter more deeply into God, ourselves, and others. We build our world to reflect the quality of life we learn in this mysterious relationship. The vows belong to the mystical experience of the Church and express its holiness.

The vows are a response to a religious experience, and are an effort to give this experience expression. Without belief in this love relationship, the vows lack the ground which gives them life.

The struggle to give expression to a religious experience is always symbolic, never conclusive or complete. At a basic level, each Christian responds to his or her call to salvation through a concrete sign, membership in the Church. The Church itself is a symbol which concretizes human responses to God.

Religious vows are a further specification of response to God through the Church. They are a sign in the Church of a desire to follow Jesus without reservation. They are a life choice as a categorical choice. They are a choice which eliminates others. They symbolize the direction or state which will ground one's entire life.

Coming full circle

The vows are grounded in a human search that all people share, the search for meaning. This search opens all to mystery. Contemporary authors call this search by many names, the longing for wholeness, completion or fulfillment.[12] However, at its core, the search is rooted in the experience of finitude in a variety of forms: the sense of the fleeting and of death and an intuition of the permanent and everlasting; the longing for significance and self worth and the need for a deep confirmation; the experience of violence and injustice and desire for a better world; the knowledge of limits and sense of dependence with the subsequent search for Someone who is ultimately reliable.

12. Gerald May, *Addiction and Grace* (San Francisco: Harper, 1988) 1.

Faith experience is a personal search for an answer to these ultimate questions of life. The "answer as mystery" cannot be fabricated by us. Mystery is revealed as Other yet One who speaks to us. God as Word is not a word we create. It is a Word we receive inwardly and through the mediation of the community.

God's transcendence as other, yet in communion with us, is communicated in the history of the faith community. The faith that grounds the vows is more than personal plans for wholistic living or social justice. No law, whether the old law or a self-created one, can save or satisfy the desire for mystery.

Christian faith is concrete. It is more than a vague feeling of being loved by God and a desire to help people. Religious faith has a history and exists in a continuity of experience in the faith community. The content of Christian faith is a record of faith experience found valid in the community. It is not infinitely malleable.

Faith requires a way of life which corresponds to its beliefs. If God is transcendent, relationship with God is fostered by a "way" which opens one to God's ways. God invites all human beings to create ways of right living. Yet, the basic outlines of harmonious relationships with God, self, and others are in the history of the community and its scriptures.

The obedience of faith, in which we entrust our whole self freely to God, reveals to us the truth of God and the truth of ourselves (*Gaudium et Spes* 22). People do not lose themselves through such obedience but rather find their truest identity.

Faith and the vows

The vows are a "way" of life based on a faith response to God as mystery. As a "way" they are received from the faith community. The vows must have a concreteness sufficient to express the affirmation of God, self, and others made in faith. If God did not exist, the vows would not make sense. As a response to mystery, the vows are lived through the mediation of others, who symbolize the otherness of God.[13]

---

13. Religion today is viewed as personal and individual. The vowed life is countercultural in this sense. See Bellah, *Habits of the Heart,* chapter 9.

Most likely, people of other Christian traditions and other world religions experience a call to unreserved following of God. However, in Roman Catholicism there is a structure in which what is experienced as an internal call is given a social form.[14] How is this unique call distinguished from many other calls of the Christian life? We will look to this in the next chapter.

14. This structure also exists in other Christian denominations.

Chapter Seven

The Reach of Salvation

Contemporary spirituality encourages reflection upon the action of God in personal history. It is one thing to know God saves. It is another matter to know God saves me in the events of my life. That God saves is a fact of Christian existence. Realization that God saves me in my history is astonishing and life transforming.

A core sense of God's personal love is needed to make vows. The vows are a mutual reach. God reaches out in love. The religious responds to this love through the vows. The vows are an act of trust in the saving love of God already known in life. The vows are a promise to trust God's love in working out the struggles and opportunities of life in the future. The vows in this sense are a reach of salvation. God reaches to us in love, and we respond.

Experiencing salvation

Most do not experience salvation directly. Instead, salvation is experienced in being freed from various internal and situational evils which make up the fabric of everyday existence.[1] As we reflect upon personal history at one level, we recall important events in our lives. At a faith level, we see God's hand and care in them.

Salvation is not only God's offer of relationship but an initiative of God which is continually active in life. To make vows is to reach out to God's promise that God will be there to fulfill the desires of our whole life. Setting aside other means of fulfillment, the religious places confidence in God's relationship as primary

1. Segundo, *Grace and the Human Condition*, 35.

in the completion of their lives. Fundamentally a vow is a categorical act whereby a person reaches to appropriate the offer of salvation in their own life. The vows involve a mutual reach.

The reach for salvation

The search for salvation is a deeply personal inquiry. Salvation in general does not hold our interest. The most profound questions center on our own salvation, or that of people dear to us. Even childhood questions of whether stillborn babies are saved had a lot to do with an estimate of God's fairness or what kind of God we were dealing with.

All reach for salvation in hope that there is ultimate goodness and meaningfulness in life. Salvation is an absolute good which stands in opposition to absolute evil, life without a foundational relationship with God. Salvation grounds that life is in fact good and meaningful. Hope in salvation overcomes the fear that life is meaningless and death is its ultimate end.

Humans reach to salvation, not from some belief that God saves people in general. The reach of salvation occurs when we take our hand and place it in the hand of God, knowing that God's offer of relationship to us is not something we produce.

The search for salvation is implicit in the choice to make vows. The vows involve an openness to God who saves us. The vows are a trust in Jesus Christ as the ultimate promise and realization of God's closeness. Jesus' victory over evil in his cross and resurrection is not just information, but God's word regarding human life and my life. God's kingdom is life's deepest meaning and the future of my life and the world.

Whenever the circumstances of life contradict this hope, the religious can reach again for the hand of God. This reach does not produce salvation; it accepts a salvific relationship with God, continually made new. This relationship, mediated through Jesus, is experienced also as one with others, the world, and oneself.

The reach of salvation can only be done within the contours of real life.[2] God saves and humans respond within the potentials

2. Merkle, *Committed by Choice*, 26–31.

and flaws of personal history and within the possibilities and limits of the world at the turn of a millennium.

To make vows is to make an interpretation of life. Vows are an
answer to the life questions: who am I, where am I going, how do
I get there? This response is not theoretical or philosophical. It is
an affirmation that God sustains life at its center, and I bet my
one and only life on this belief.

Some observe how the dynamics of family background, place
of birth, meeting a significant person, taking a course, being missioned to this city rather than another, working through a health
issue all were means through which God has led and cared for
them. The life evoked by the vows is just this concrete.

God saves, not in some abstract way, but really and concretely.
Any threatening evil, sickness, error, sin, or death is part of the matter of salvation. Even at the social level, realities such as racism, sexism,
classism, and militarism are among the "matters" from which Christ
sets us free. Every aspect of human life is encompassed by the reality of salvation. It grounds the life and ministry of the religious.

It takes an entire lifetime to unfold the truth of God's salvation. As a lifelong commitment, the vowed life is structured to incorporate the revelation of this mystery throughout the adult life
cycle. The normal unfolding of life, individually and commu-
nally, is the ordinary context in which this mystery occurs. However, it is a mystery only discovered fully at the moment of death.
The hopeful passing on to the life of God in the life of the vows
is a passing on done ultimately at death. This ongoing conversion
of religious surrender is at the heart of the vowed life.

History and salvation

Salvation also has a cosmic and global dimension. Redemption
is God's plan to bring all men and women to a full humanization
which is their divinization. Through their life and ministry, religious participate in redemption as a force in the evolutionary
process.

By their vows, religious witness that God continues to save
from the first moment of creation to the end of the world. They
promise to participate in the action of redemption as a force that

continually fights against entropy and the disruption and degeneration it brings to everything that exists.

The vows affirm that redemptive action in our times involves the cross. The affirmation of humanity before inhumanity, of hope before the despair of the age, of care for those whose class, race, and gender renders them invisible in society all bring conflict.

Since redemption is more than a balancing factor in evolution, its victory is qualitative rather than quantitative. So often it seems like evil wins out. It is only through the eyes of faith that the qualitative victory of love and truth is affirmed. Through faith, love is recognized as stronger than the quantitative, or often more numerous, forces of evil which plague the world. To have this faith is to participate in the cross of Jesus.

Salvation is also universal. Salvation embraces all humans and is universally given through creation. The fact that God offers salvation to all does not make it less a miracle in the life of a religious.

God's salvific action is not limited by the boundaries of the ecclesial community. Yet, the religious centers his or her life in the Church as the visible sign of the presence of Christ the savior in the heart of each human being. From the foundation of the Church, religious reach out. They respond to ever greater circles of need within and beyond present ecclesial boundaries.

Choice and choices

The reach for salvation is a choice which responds to a basic life question. What kind of person am I going to be? The inner freedom used to make this choice is the power not only to choose this or that, but to chose "to be."[3] We do not make choices at this level every day. However, a major choice, such as the choice to make vows as a religious, evokes this deep level of our person.[4]

Theologians call this choice one of transcendental freedom. "Transcendental" suggests that the object of choice transcends the categories of everyday life. At one level, we choose a vocation.

3. This theme is developed by Paul Tillich in *The Courage to Be* (New Haven: Yale University Press, 1952).

4. Merkle, *Committed by Choice*, 28–29.

At another, we reach out to the mystery at the heart of life, God, and define ourselves as persons in relationship to it.

The choice is transcendental in another way. Through it we say something about the meaning of life and the purpose of our life. The act of making vows is serious enough that it opens us to Life itself. We will call such a transcendental choice, a Choice with a capital "C."

The life of the vows is also more than a once and for all choice. The vows are a way of living. They involve choices among alternative courses of action. I can marry or I can live a single life in community. I can enter into a profession independently, or I can minister professionally as a member of a religious community. I can plan my personal financial future, or I can live corporately in a shared future in my religious community.

These choices involve acting in one way and not acting in another. They are categorical choices. We will name this type of choice with a small "c." The vows are also a categorical choice. To live the life of the vows is to make choices regarding how one will act from among alternatives throughout a lifetime.

Theologians call these choices categorical choices because they involve the choice of doing one thing rather than another in time and space. We take a situation in which many options are open to us and change it into one in which all others are put aside except the one we acted upon.

All human action involves choice with a small "c." I cannot prepare dinner and go for a walk at exactly the same time. It is a choice of one or the other. Even preparing dinner and reading a book, two activities that can be blended, ultimately involve at some point, putting the book aside and stirring the stew—or developing a taste for burnt meat.

The Choice where I define myself as a person and the choice between alternative courses of action are related. We never make a Choice outside the choosing between the alternatives of choice.[5]

5. Josef Fuchs comments, "Morality ultimately consists in the entire person's self actualization before the Absolute through the categorical moral acts," in *Personal Responsibility and Christian Morality* (Washington, D.C.: Georgetown University Press, 1983) 25.

In the spiritual tradition this experience is echoed. It is said love has no specific act. We never simply love. We always love through a way of loving. We are patient, we are kind, we listen when we would rather not, we call a friend rather than wait to be called. It is the choice of love that expresses the Choice of love.

Likewise, religious life as a way of life is a choice that expresses the fundamental Choice of love. But how do we make such a choice? It is to this question we now turn.

Conscience

Through conscience we overcome the tension between Choice and choice in our lives. Conscience is often thought of as something we have, like a tool of decision-making. Modern theologians, however, refer to conscience as something we are. Conscience is "a dynamic thrust towards authenticity and self-transcendence at the core of a person's consciousness." It is an inner demand for responsible decision-making which is in accord with reasonable judgment.[6]

Conscience engages the whole person, not just thinking. It involves attitudes and values, the heart and the mind, all interacting at various levels of consciousness. One aspect of Conscience is the awareness that we can be called to account for our behavior, not just by our co-workers and friends, but by our inner self, in religious terms, by God. Conscience, in this sense, is our secret core, our inner sanctuary (*Gaudium et spes* 16). It is our sense of responsibility before God for what we do. We will name this aspect of conscience, Conscience with a capital "C."

Through Conscience we take responsibility for living a good life in the comprehensive sense. We seek to become good persons and carry out right actions. As an essential part of the reach for salvation, we seek moral truth. This is the truth about a genuinely good life in the here and now. We recognize it as a truth through which God saves and we respond. When we ask ourselves, "Did I do the right thing?" we are operating at this level of our Conscience.

6. Sean Fagan, S.M., "Conscience" in *The New Dictionary of Theology*, 226–30.

Discernment of vocation is a search for truth at a fundamental level. The search is authentic whether totally conscious or not. Conscience is a stirring in our hearts where Choice comes to awareness.

Choice is never something acted on directly. We cannot think of ourselves with the degree of self-awareness that we see ourselves as objects and give ourselves to God. We make gifts of ourselves symbolically in an action. While most explain choice of religious life as something they felt "God wanted them to do," these deeper issues were present.

To discern a vocation, or affirm it in the course of life, involves two things. We express ourselves deeply as persons, in self commitment. Second, we express this choice through something that is truly valuable in the here and now. This leads us to another level of conscience.

A second level of conscience seeks to do the right thing in the practical world of alternatives before us. We will name this experience of conscience with a small "c." We see "conscience" acting in the various responses to Jesus in the gospel. He said, "Follow me" to many people. Some followed and some did not.

The people in the gospel used their conscience to weigh the matters before them. The decision to follow Jesus affected many practical matters: houses, family responsibilities, and land (Matt 19:27-29). Alternatives had to be examined and considered.

Some had to decide just how they were going to follow Jesus. A few, such as Joseph of Arimathea, followed secretly (John 19:38). Others were with Jesus so much that they were recognized as "being in his company" (Mark 14:66-71). Women who followed Jesus had to step outside cultural expectations to respond to him (Luke 23:49; Matt 15:41).[7] It is this type of concreteness that conscience addresses. Through conscience we make a categorical choice, a choice among alternatives, but a choice which has moral overtones. The choice to have a Coke instead of a Pepsi does not carry moral overtones, despite what commercials tell us. Actions which are means of self expression before God and which sym-

---

7. Elizabeth Johnson, *She Who Is* (New York: Crossroad, 1992) 158ff.

bolize right living do carry the weight of a moral choice. They involve acts, chosen freely, that are constructive or destructive of human life and growth in community. Moral choices involve more than licit or illicit actions according to common moral standards. Moral choice involves response to the "more" to which God calls us. It engages us in the movement from being good to being better.

Conscience with a capital "C" cannot act without conscience with a small "c." For instance, if the desire of my Conscience is to live in harmony with nature, my conscience might tell me I have to overcome my laziness about recycling. Without the concreteness of conscience which suggests courses of action, the desires of Conscience remain inoperative. Conscience and conscience come together to produce a decision of conscience. We ultimately decide to take one course of action rather than another. Through the decision to act we create our lives and respond to God.

Often we are only aware of the decision to act one way or another. The decision to act, however, provides access to the mystery and meaning of life sought at a deep level. Here Conscience lives. In the walk to the recycling bin, I know what it means to live in harmony with nature at a new level.[8]

Conscience and faith

Conscience is operative in the reach to salvation. Conscience involves more than our head applying principles to decisions for action. Conscience also involves the heart and the faith we bring to decisions. The head and the heart function in an interactive whole. Human faith and religious faith mutually affect one another.

We can see this in the practice of faith, hope, and love. Many as children prayed the "acts" of faith, hope, and love in school. Why were these chosen as core values of evangelization?

Faith, hope, love, following of Christ, openness to God are not just ideals but ways of behavior. Religious faith testifies they are

8. Timothy E. O'Connell, *Principles for a Catholic Morality* (New York: The Seabury Press, 1978) 62–3, chapter 8.

ways of behavior made possible by Christ. As we engage in faith, hope, and love we are being drawn into a life beyond ourselves, a life which we cannot produce. The vowed life is such a life.

Acting in faith, hope, and love is possible because we have already received salvation. However, faith, hope, and love are also the process by which the meaning of this salvation is learned. Through faith, hope, and love we blend human and religious faith and integrate head and heart. This is the road to becoming fully human and doing God's will. It is also the journey of putting on Christ.[9]

Human faith, while maintaining its proper character, becomes a religious faith in making vows. Religious faith gives vows their core motivation. The concerns of our human faith are not left behind. We bring our dreams and hopes for human fulfillment to the vows. Yet the core values of our religious faith blend with them in an inseparable way.

How does this occur? The religious accepts the transcendent data or beliefs from the faith community, decisive for values in a particular congregation, through faith. They adhere to a tradition of witnesses regarding the experiencing and acquisition of those data through hope and love. Through faith, hope, and love the religious adopts a framework of living for a lifetime within community. Through the vows which provide the framework for their response, the religious participates in the mutual reach of salvation.

---

9. Pope John Paul II reflects on faith, hope, and love in *The Coming of the Third Millennium*. See John Paul II, *Tertio Millennio Adveniente: Apostolic Letter for the Jubilee of the Year 2000. Origins* 24:24 (November 24, 1994).

PART III
FOUNDATIONS OF THE VOWS

Chapter Eight

A Different Touch

When we hear a new pianist play Bach, what makes them different than all those who have played Bach before? It may be that the difference between the Christian lives of religious, married, and single people is just this elusive. Each has a different "touch" in the Christian life.

Yet, religious life as an adult life-style in the Church has an identity. Fundamentally, religious life is a response to the person of Jesus and the life of the gospel through a committed life-style in the Church.[1] Alone, this broad description is insufficient. Just as the style of a pianist cannot be isolated by one factor, religious life involves a number of distinguishing characteristics. If combined in a proper context, these features make up a unique school of Christian "performance." Core to the identity of religious life is the role of religious faith in shaping the course and integration of one's life. Religious life involves a profession of religious faith that has profound effect on life choices.

Life choices

A particular issue in the Church today is how the call of religious life is different than the call to discipleship adopted by any serious Christian. We observe many forms of adult living in the Church. Many members seek to live the gospel in deep ways. Former ways of identifying religious life as a life apart, withdrawn

---

1. There are other forms of religious life in other world religions.

from the world, are no longer tenable. Religious walk a common road with all people of good will. They share a journey with all members of the Church.

Yet, religious life is not everything or every good thing. Choice cannot be escaped in the life of an adult. One adopts one framework of life, setting aside others. The image of life as a smorgasbord captures the dilemma faced when deciding a life vocation. If one tries to eat the whole table, a type of indigestion sets in. Some things must be chosen and others left aside.

In order to discern the special "touch" of religious life, we must identify common elements it shares with other Christian vocations and indicate factors which are unique to it. Let us begin by consideration of the road which religious share with all people of good will.

The common life

The power of grace is not something new with the Church, nor is it given only in the Christian era. All people are given the gift of personhood which flows from God's gift of relationship to them in grace. This comes with birth, the gift of creation. With this gift is given the call to love. Love defines not only the true destiny of each human life but also its moral call. Being human, living in God's image, and learning to love all, form the single human and moral "road" all people share.

As a religious sits in an emergency room in a hospital, she knows the common humanity she shares with all. Religious face the vulnerability of bad health and aging with the rest of humanity. They must learn how to relate as adults in their families and work through important relationships. Religious struggle alongside others to acquire competence in a profession. Daily, religious experience the common life of humankind as they enter into varied tasks. For instance, they join others in a walkathon for multiple sclerosis or support the parish bingo.

Vows do not make religious automatic adults. They struggle with the same letting go and growing up that forms the fabric of adulthood. Maturity does not come any more graciously to religious than to others. They walk, at times haltingly, the same road toward maturity as others. They, too, learn to love step by step, seeking meaning as they go.

Knowledge of this road comes not from books but from continued probing and expansion of human life itself in both its negative and positive experiences. Religious have no special knowledge of good and evil. All men and women, through their creation in God's image, are capable of knowing the good and their destiny and purpose in life. This power is a divine possibility yet one so intrinsically bound to human life that no person can be considered without it.

When religious say their lives are "no different" than those of other people in the society, they reflect this experience of the "common life." As religious move away from living in an institutional framework, their shared struggle with other adults becomes more obvious. Some discover the "common life" through deeper contact with their families and friends. Others, through ministry experiences, meet daily life in society in new ways.

Religious have mid-life crises, sexual struggles, bouts with depression, and addictive and co-dependent behaviors which they share with all humanity. A moment of grace in religious life is to take up the spiritual pilgrimage of "homecoming" to human existence. To do this requires great courage for it demands the putting aside a false sense of self as above these struggles. Religious are called to respond to grace responsibly, simply, and effectively in areas shared in the "common life."

Human and religious faith are called forth on this path. Human faith risks to assume responsibility for life. Yet, religious faith finds God's grace in the transformations we undergo. The two are one in experience. We experience God in the common life, lived with religious faith. God walks beside us on the road of our human existence and prepares new paths for us.

In the stirrings of conscience, all human beings experience the call to be human in germ form. Here, the initial whisper of vocation is also first heard. Everyone who listens to his or her conscience finds alongside themselves the hand and voice of God.[2]

2. Kathleen Fischer and Thomas Hart, *Christian Foundations. An Introduction to Faith in Our Times* (New York: Paulist Press, 1995).

They are elevated to that place where God touches their person and communicates with them. A relationship with God is recognized, if only vaguely, and participation in eternal life begins, if only in an initial way.

The first vocation given to each human being is to be the person they are called to be. Fulfillment of this human vocation continues throughout life through commitment to others in love. A religious vocation is marked by the primary call to be human and to be oneself.

Grounded in the community called the Church

Theology since Vatican Council II has indicated that baptism is the ground of religious life. Baptism gives all Christians a distinct identity on the road of life. This identity marks religious life.

While Christians do not have another process or road by which to enter into a salvific relationship with God, or a monopoly on grace, they are given other "signs" along this road. Through baptism they are illuminated by the grace of revelation, and an integral change in existence occurs.[3] Through baptism they are invited into Christ's death and resurrection and made members of the faith community. Revelation brings a new access to the meaning of Jesus' victory over sin.

Revelation offers to them an expanded consciousness of the journey they share with all. Revelation teaches them how to follow with a heightened conscience and a greater hope for the road they share with all of humanity.[4]

Christians are given a consciousness of the meaning of the road they share with all humanity, a consciousness which for all others is only spontaneous. One author puts it this way: "Christians walk the same road as all humanity but to them has been revealed what is the origin and term of this march."[5] The way of

---

3.   Karl Rahner, *The Practice of Faith* (New York: Crossroads, 1983) 44ff.

4.   Josef Fuchs, *Human Values and Christian Morality* (Dublin: Gill and Macmillan, 1970) 124ff.

5.   Juan Luis Segundo, "La función de la Iglesia" *Diálogo,* I, no. 2, 10.

Christianity marks where we came from, where we are going, and how to get there. Religious life is a special journey along this way.

Religious define their lives through the Scriptures. Religious discern the Word of God as individuals and communities. In the Word is their role and identity in the Church and world.

All Christians, and religious, live their moral lives in the Church through faith and sacraments. The content of the faith and sacraments makes conscious the transcendent data of the message of Jesus Christ.

Faith and sacraments also assist Christians to know how to love. They enable the power to love. This effects a different quality of knowledge in the Christian. Christians know more than that God has a plan. They know how God's plan acts. It follows the paschal mystery of Jesus Christ. The sacraments ritualize and effect this reality.

For religious today, especially women, there are struggles over participation in the sacraments. For some, controversy over the ordination of women causes alienation regarding the sacraments, especially the Eucharist. For others, the fact that a central element of their religious life is debated within their communities is a source of sorrow and alienation.

Religious life, even in our times, remains a shared life in the eucharistic community. The eucharistic celebration ritualizes the mystery of the Christian life in its other manifestations. Paradoxically, religious bring to the Eucharist conflicts over the sacraments today. In the Eucharist they are challenged to willingly embrace the death and resurrection these conflicts involve and find strength to work them through on all levels.

The transcendent data of Jesus is learned also through the gifts of faith, hope, and love in the Christian community. Faith provides a certainty which stimulates love. Hope holds out a future which transcends the possibilities and limits of the present. Hope points to the ultimate goal of existence as the project of this life: union with God and the coming of the Kingdom.

The gift of love renders a power to love. Revelation witnesses to love's permanence and its strength and fidelity. Through the gifts of faith, hope, and love, the Christian is called in a special way to go beyond a mere consciousness of sin and avoidance of it to an ethic to build the Kingdom. Through them, the Christian is called to mission.

Religious life involves these common elements of the Christian life. Different religious will blend and harmonize the mystery of Christian living in unique ways, but these structures and practices will be the elements of their composition.

Communal conscience

Finally, the Christian life is distinguished by a special quality of conscience. Christianity is a religion of love. The Church is called to build the communion of all people in love. The Christian conscience is geared toward the creation of this communion.

Christians have a special relationship to Christ through their communal conscience in the Church. Theirs is a more discerning conscience, centered in listening to God in Scripture and the sacraments. It is to be a more certain conscience confirmed and directed by dogma. The gift of Christian conscience, however, finds its ultimate significance in its service to the world and in its power to stimulate and sustain loving action.

Knowledge of Jesus Christ is meant to bring a revolution in morality. The Christian conscience is directed at the construction of the existence of one's brother and sister. It is meant to build the earth and better the world. While the Christian shares with all people of good will the duty to serve others and to develop the world, the Christian "privilege" in conscience is a special responsibility. Christian responsibility is grounded in the responsibility of the Church in the world to be a special conscience for the whole of humanity. Religious share this conscience for mission and act on it individually and as congregations.

The Church fosters the conscience of humanity, focused on human dignity. Christians experience their moral life through sharing in the life of the Church. The Christian carries out his or her responsibility to the whole of humanity often through the Church. Through the reciprocity of consciences, the Christian contributes to and receives the necessary witness to keep alive the transcendent data needed for faith, for discernment, and for a life of service. While most Christians give this witness in a secular arena, the Church is the primary community of conscience in their lives. Religious life is marked by this shared conscience.

Here religious life emerges with a ripple of its own touch. The religious also share in the communal conscience of their religious community. Religious witness and express gospel living through the specific calls of their congregational charism. They do so as permanently vowed members who take responsibility for and give public witness to this shared conscience.[6]

The challenges which spring from religious charism are not additional to the common responsibilities of the Church and those of good will. Actions which flow from religious charism point to and express this responsibility. The charism of a religious congregation is a focus on the gospel life to which the whole Church is called. It functions in the conscience of a religious congregation as a lens on the gospel and a witness they offer to the Church and world.

Through their public adhesion to the person of Jesus Christ, religious and their congregations participate in the discipleship which the whole Church shares. They express the human desire to love. Their lives invite all to hear the gospel without reserve. They rely on the whole Church and people of good will for support in their lives. Yet the summons of a religious is distinct.

The call

It is difficult to discern the "touch" of religious life today. Because of this, we will look to the level of moral call, to identify its uniqueness. Hearing a call and choosing to follow it is a central movement of the Christian life. Religious life is first a vocational call. It involves many "calls" over a lifetime, yet initially it is a summons from God. How do we distinguish various calls in the Christian life?

Moral theologians describe four types of ethical choices which form the moral experience of Christians.[7] Naming these "calls" or choices in the Christian life sheds light on the call of the religious.

6. Associate members share this responsibility in a different way.

7. Richard A McCormick, "Does Religious Faith Add to Ethical Perception?" in *Readings in Moral Theology, No. 2, The Distinctiveness of Christian Ethics.* Edited by Charles E. Curran and Richard A. McCormick, S.J. (New York: Paulist Press, 1980) 156–73.

The first are *essential* choices. These involve the ethical duties which apply to all people. Calls to preserve and maintain the dignity of persons, not to kill or steal, and to keep promises are essential moral calls. They are required of all. All people of good will strive to keep these demands. Religious also hear these calls in daily life. As they join with others in an ecology project to help preserve the earth, they respond to an essential moral call.

The second type of moral choices are *existential* choices. These involve a good that individuals should realize because of the circumstances in which they find themselves. A person witnesses an auto accident and is needed to testify. An existential moral call enters their life.

Not all people arrive at the same ethical decision when hearing an existential call. During the Gulf War there was a difference of opinion regarding its morality. People heard different moral calls springing from the same existential event. Some felt the war was justified, other saw it as unjust. Religious, too, were divided over this issue.

Existential calls require moral sensitivity in order to be heard. Not everyone hears them. We experience an erosion of moral responsibility in the society if too many people fail to take up existential moral calls.

Religious communities also experience existential moral calls. The Holocaust museum in Washington, D.C., displays photos of communities in Europe who hid Jewish children in their boarding schools during World War II. The human dilemma presented itself, the communities were there, and they responded. Religious and their communities discern existential moral calls daily.

A third type of moral call is an *essential Christian call.* These are calls to a Christian because he or she belongs to a community to which the non-Christian does not belong. The code of the Church community is an essential Christian call. These are moral demands placed on Christians as Christians.

The entire life of the gospel belongs to this summons. It is difficult to classify the moral calls which come specifically to Christians as Christians. Many of the gospel calls reflect the challenge to be human which all people share. Revelation and the witness of the community make these demands more evident for the Christian, or motivate response to them.

A moral call is marked as explicitly Christian, not by the content of the call, which is often shared by all, but by its motivation. The essential call of the Christian is to belong to Christ. The desire to belong to Christ, whether conscious or unconscious, marks Christian morality. We express this desire through the life of the commandments, the beatitudes, the virtues, and the building of the Kingdom through the paschal mystery.

The Christian, for example, may feed the hungry as many others in society do. Christians do so, however, because they are brothers and sisters in Christ. Through imitation of the compassion of Jesus, feeding the hungry takes on the special motivation of the following of Christ.

Love to the point of the cross is a Christian call, but many argue that anyone who seriously loves discovers the cross and suffering. Christians, however, find in the suffering that love requires, the cross, the experience of Christ. When they embrace the cross they do so in imitation of Jesus, finding their strength in him.

Christian morality is understood through faith in Jesus. The life of the beatitudes is a New Testament reflection on what it means to know the Risen Christ. Without Jesus the beatitudes do not make sense. Since Christians have different relationships with Jesus, their ability to hear Christian essential calls will also differ.

Prayer life, personal and communal spiritual health, and the understanding of Christian life all affect the discernment of and response to Christian essential calls. Religious will respond to essential Christian moral calls from the same variety of dispositions and motivations as that of any Christian. The following of Christ is a gradual process. Hearing Christian essential calls in the life of a religious is a constant challenge.

Religious communities will also vary in their capacity to respond to essential moral calls. We have numerous examples in Church history where religious communities were key in witnessing to essential Christian virtues at a time of crisis in their cultures.

But at other times communities were not only weak in their vocation but failed in matters of essential Christian living. This situation stimulated the great reform movements in religious life.

Religious recognize that one of the deepest challenges of communal life today is to truly live a gospel existence. One religious commented, "At times in community we are not even Christian, let alone 'religious.'" This person is aware of the integrity necessary to hear essential Christian calls.

Essential Christian moral calls are ultimately rooted in the moral ramifications of baptism. The socio-ecclesial duties which baptism calls forth comprise many of these calls. As baptism immerses us into the life of Christ, the essential calls of the Christian life become the warp and woof of the fabric of Christian existence. Any understanding of the vowed life is first rooted in the radical life in Christ to which baptism calls all Christians. If the core style of Christian existence is characteristic of religious life, what then gives it its special touch? Let us turn to this question in the next chapter.

Chapter Nine

Touched by God

I remember walking with a friend one day in a woods in Kentucky. We were looking for a woman who had become a hermit. I wanted to meet her. My friend remarked, "You know, most people go bike-riding or walking along the river on Saturday. We go looking for hermits!" Becoming a hermit is a special Christian call. Not everyone does it, or even thinks about it.

Becoming a hermit falls into the category of a final type of moral call, *existential Christian choices*. These are choices a Christian makes because they seem in accord with the gospel imperatives as Christians experience them in their lives now. Not all existential calls are as unusual as one to become a hermit. Traditionally, the gospel counsels are seen as existential Christian calls.

Existential calls in the Christian life are best understood alongside essential calls. Essential calls are addressed to all. They are standing moral codes, like the Ten Commandments. Yet, moral codes are not always present in our imaginations. They become evident in concrete situations. The commandment not to steal stands on the edge of my consciousness until a situation presents itself where there is a moral conflict about stealing.

One way essential and existential calls differ is that the discernment of an essential call is not subtle for a normally good person. There is public consensus around essential calls. Stealing, for example, is prosecuted by law. Existential calls are different. They never contradict essential calls, yet they go beyond them. Not everyone hears them, agrees with what they are, or acknowledges they exist.

Existential Christian calls are unique moral calls which come to Christians individually.[1] Simply put, an existential call is experienced as an imperative, "this concrete thing needs to be done by me." To the degree we create the person we become by our individual choices, these calls are important in the moral life. They explain individual differences in Christian experience. The counsels fit into this paradigm of the Christian life.

Counsels

The term counsel is rarely used in the New Testament. Patristic writers use it to differentiate between what has been commanded, the Ten Commandments, and what goes beyond them. St. Thomas uses counsel to refer to elements of religious life and virtues whose performance are not obligatory.[2] Here counsel refers to the various moral calls which comprise the life in the Spirit in the New Testament.[3]

A counsel is an exhortation to a choice which can further and deepen one's choice of God. The counsels are not commands, but rather warnings or pieces of advice about ways of acting that can remove obstacles to response to the Kingdom. The counsels reflect Jesus' own attitudes and are modeled in his life and ministry.

For example, we are warned against riches insofar as attachment to them can divert us from the call of the Kingdom. Forgiveness is encouraged because to take up an unforgiving stance closes off God's grace. To be unforgiving is to refuse to be like God who forgives.[4] We are to judge not, so as not to be judged.

1. See: Karl Rahner, "On the Question of a Formal Existential Ethic," *Theological Investigations* II (New York: Crossroads, 1990) 217–34.

2. John M. Lozano, C.M.F. *Discipleship: Towards an Understanding of Religious Life* (Chicago: Claret Center for Resources in Spirituality, 1980) 132–4.

3. See the classic, C. H. Dodd, *Gospel and Law* (New York: Columbia University Press, 1951) 54ff., for a description of the ethical maxims of the gospel as calls to existential action. See also Frank J. Matera, *New Testament Ethics. The Legacies of Jesus and Paul* (Louisville: Westminster John Knox Press, 1996).

4. See Donald Senior, "Biblical Foundations for Religious Life" in *Living in the Meantime,* edited by Paul J. Philibert (New York: Paulist Press, 1994) 59.

People obsessed with the faults of others can use this practice to escape their own calls and responsibilities.

The counsels are existential calls. They do not provide a blueprint for morality. One cannot list all the counsels in the gospel as a list of commandments and then set out to fulfill them faithfully.

Why can this not be done? The counsels are commands for the moment. They cannot be carried out all at once. The counsels contradict one another if juxtaposed as rules. For instance, in one part of the gospel Jesus says to turn the other cheek. In another, the Christian is to confront their opponent, in imitation of Jesus who tells Peter to get behind him.

Whether one is forgiving one's enemy, not storing up riches, or settling differences directly, the end result of the counsels is the same. A response to a counsel represents a desire to respond totally to the Kingdom in the following of Jesus.

Acceptance of the call of a counsel expresses a desire greater than building a perfect character. Desire for self perfection is good pagan morality, but not the call of the New Testament. To follow a counsel expresses a desire to belong to Christ. This is an act of Christian morality, for love of Jesus motivates it. The decision to follow Jesus is expressed in the practical choice of following the counsel.

A counsel is a distinctive moral call in that it often focuses on "freedom from" behavior, behavior which frees us to love. It encourages behavior which acts against those things that potentially dull us to the call of the gospel. However, we follow the counsels, not for their own sakes, but to live out the "freedom to" call which the gospel involves.[5]

Counsels are Christian existential moral calls. They represent moral demands which are not universally required in the Christian life. Their practice enables the reception of other calls of the Spirit.

Margaret Farley in her book *Personal Commitments* offers us another view of the counsels. She does not speak of the counsels directly, but discusses "conditions for presence," ways of remaining present and faithful to our commitments.

---

5. Merkle, *Committed by Choice*, 91ff.

The way to keep love alive is to try to keep seeing. Love is seen at times only dimly. Often, the only hope of continuing to see is to keep looking. Believing itself involves keeping watch, seeing through hope and through memory. When we cannot see directly, we see better by attending more carefully, more consistently. Through looking we heighten our capacity to see.[6]

The gospel counsels are such conditions of presence to Jesus, the Church, and his people. They are ways to keep connected with and engaged in our commitment to follow Jesus. They are not essential choices for the Christian, as is the law. Instead they symbolize a state of readiness to respond to the call of the Spirit as it comes.[7] Through the counsels, the Spirit transforms us in the new life which is Christ.

Following a counsel

The story of the rich young man illustrates the nature of the call of a counsel. The rich young man kept the law "from his youth." He answered the essential moral calls faithfully. Jesus places before him another call, to sell what he has and give to the poor, and to follow him. Obviously, for the rich young man, the selling of his goods and a deeper following of Jesus are linked.

For the rich young man, the value in the moral call which Jesus placed before him was not just in giving up goods. The value was in the following of Jesus, for which the young man's goods were an obstacle. We notice that everyone Jesus called was not asked to sell goods in the same way.

People were called to various forms of renunciation in the gospel. The apostles had to leave their nets. Others had to give up a permanent house. All were called to enter into the renunciation which love requires. Luke 18:22 warns against "riches," not because there is anything wrong with material things, but because they are an obstacle to a deeper love of Jesus.[8] Yet, riches are different for different people.

6. Margaret Farley, *Personal Commitments* (San Francisco: Harper and Row, 1966) 54.

7. See Matera, *New Testament Ethics*, 169–73.

8. Aloysius Pieris, *An Asian Theology of Liberation* (New York: Orbis Books, 1988) 15ff.

The counsels do not provide a blueprint for the Christian life. The selling of goods in itself is not a prerequisite for the Kingdom. The call to sell goods is existential: sometimes it is necessary, and sometimes it is not fitting. The counsel advises that there is always a conflict between God and "mammon" in life. A desire to grow in love of Jesus requires an alertness to the need to let go in order to follow Jesus more deeply.

The first religious?

The parable of the rich young man has been used to typify the call to religious life. Yet, it says something about the life of every Christian. There are calls beyond the essentials which invite each one to live the Kingdom in a new way. These calls are given to all Christians by the Holy Spirit. The Spirit of God is the one who calls us to what is needed on the path of conversion "at the right time."

All Christians experience these existential calls. All sense from time to time that "this concrete thing needs to be done by me." Christians experience the Kingdom as "kairos," the moment of the coming of the Holy Spirit. They participate in the coming of the Kingdom through the circumstances of their lives. Each receives a special call when the good of others requires it. God "uses" each person for the good in building the Kingdom.

All adults must sell what they have. Children grow up and leave the home; parents and children must let go. A sane approach to ministry requires curtailing a schedule. Christians are called to reach out to a new need or to develop a talent required by the community. Response requires they let go of something else.

If everyone receives these invitations, what makes them Christian calls? The "law of Christ" adds nothing particular to the essential moral calls of human living.[9] Yet, Christians share in a new dynamism and power as they carry them out because of Christ.

What is distinctive in the Christian life is a new way of being human. Christians hear moral calls with religious faith. Their intention is based on love of God. Through discipleship and com-

9. J. M. Aubert, "*La Spécificité de la morale Chrétienne selon Saint Thomas,*" *Supplément* 92 (1970) 55–73.

panionship with Jesus, they share a divine life while living a human life.

How, then, are the vows existential Christian calls? There are many gospel counsels: to be meek, peace-loving, and forgiving. However, historically, the counsels of poverty, chastity, and obedience have been linked to religious life because they touch on three central areas of human living: sexuality, possessions, and power.[10] All Christians practice the counsels of poverty, chastity, and obedience some way in their lives.

However, religious vow poverty, chastity, and obedience as a framework of living, making a lifelong intention to live them because of love of Jesus. The religious takes these existential choices in the Christian life and makes them essential choices. To understand the difference in intention which marks the religious lifestyle, we need to recall the two aspects of moral choices. All make a "choice" of a specific action to make a "Choice" which expresses the self in reference to the Absolute.

Touching the Divine

When two people marry, it is their commitment or intention to love one another totally for a lifetime which defines their lifestyle. This choice eliminates other choices. Their promise is one of sexual exclusivity and permanence. The mutuality of their promise to one another creates the bond of marriage. Their sexual love for one another consummates this lifelong promise. Through this choice, married Christians make a Choice, consciously or not, of how they respond to God's love in their lives. Instead of moving away from love in egotism and self absorption, they are moving out of themselves toward each other and to God.

To choose to make religious vows is a different response than marriage. It is a response primarily to God's reality in our lives. Because religious vows set aside usual avenues of fulfillment, the "Choice" aspect of vowed commitment is highlighted.

---

10. The custom of designating traits of religious life as counsels became general only from the thirteenth century on. See Lozano, *Discipleship,* 138ff.

The choice of poverty, chastity, and obedience symbolizes the intention that Choice is without reserve. Through the gospel counsels the religious takes on a framework of life which has as its main intention response to God above all things.

Jesus sought the Kingdom and the will of his Father as the focal point of his life. He did not focus his life on a commitment to another in marriage. He was an itinerant preacher and devoted his life to the building up of the community of Israel.

For those who choose Christian marriage, the singlemindedness of Jesus gives impetus to the total commitment of their love. For those who choose celibacy for the Kingdom, the example of Jesus connects this choice to attention to God's call and to love of neighbor. It is not that religious imitate Jesus and married people do not. Both imitate the singlemindedness of Jesus in different ways.

The intention of the religious is what marks the distinctiveness of their life-style. Their intention is to give their lives to God without reserve. The vows are not ends in themselves, but a means or framework to express this intention of love. As a valuable choice, vows contain within them a potential toward and contact with the Absolute, a Choice. As with the rich young man, it is not the action itself, the selling of goods, which was important. It is the openness to the presence of God created by the action which gives it meaning.

To understand religious commitment in this manner requires faith. Religious faith is the belief that as we reach out to move beyond ourselves in love, we touch the hand of God who takes our desire and fills it with God's own presence.

For a religious, the role of religious faith is accentuated as confirmation of his or her desire for love through a partnered relationship and family is set aside. The transcendent data of his or her heart directly affect structures of daily living. While religious life is rich with the hundredfold of people, lands, and houses promised in the gospel, it still cannot be explained without God.

The ongoing experience of religious life is an experience of grace. In the vowed life, the call and address of God is not perceived as a thing or as an object which we understand or grasp. If that were true, pursuit of God could be just another personal project of our lives, like a diet or social commitment.

Instead, grace is experienced as a horizon of transcendence. We recognize it in our capacity for an active openness to the infinite and Absolute. In the ongoing life of the vows, desire for "the more" grows and deepens, even amid the struggle and confusion of the cross. This is the growth of a religious vocation. Its orientation to God comes from within us, yet it is indistinguishable from the stirrings of the transcendence of the human spirit. It is one we name with religious faith as having its beginning, meaning, and goal in Jesus.[11]

The profession of vows manifests the mystery of grace symbolized by religious life. Grace is more than the positive effect of God. Grace is God's self. The capacity to respond to the grace of vocation is not just a passive ability to receive grace. Rather, it is an active seeking and desiring from within. A religious is engaged primarily by this desire as it is directly related to its Source, God's own self.

A transformation of energy

The compelling desire of a religious is to allow the energy and drive of his or her desire for God to be the organizing factor of his or her life. The religious does not experience this as a call for the moment. The religious promises that not only the present, but the future, will be characterized by attention to the call to seek God above all things.

The commitment of a religious is a consecration, a claiming of our deepest desire for God, beneath, above, and beyond all other things.[12] All Christians are called to love God above all things; that is the great commandment. The commitment of a religious, however, is one where he or she adopts a framework of life which focuses primarily on an assent to God's transforming grace and on witness to its presence in the world. To focus our understanding of the distinctive touch of religious life, let us examine it as a life framework.

---

11. Roger Haight, S.J., *The Experience and Language of Grace* (New York: Paulist Press, 1979) 126.

12. Gerald G. May, *Addiction and Grace* (San Francisco: Harper, 1988) 149.

Chapter Ten

A Framework for Loving

The three vows of poverty, chastity, and obedience form a single framework of life. It is a way of life defined by the gift of one's life to God in love. The vows open the religious to a trust in God's companionship and become the channels of their love. As a choice, the vowed life flows from an experience of being touched in some way by God's loving embrace. The vows express a desire to allow God's spirit to penetrate every facet of life.

The three vows of poverty, chastity, and obedience lived in a community within the Church is a framework not just for living, but for loving. By vow we give our love a future.[1] Love's desire in the vows is more than for the moment. Rather, the vows are a promise that future decisions will be shaped by choices made at the moment.

As a framework of life, the vows make ongoing demands. In this they are a cohesive structure of life which have an internal consistency.[2] The vows situate religious life as a "way" of loving. While we cannot predict the future, we vow that our decisions will follow a certain path. We limit our freedom and our options in order to give our love direction and purpose.

A framework for love stipulates what will be expected as signs of love, as deeds of love, and as efforts to make love continue to grow.[3] Through the vows, religious assume the way of life shaped

1. Farley, *Personal Commitments,* 36, 90, 98ff.
2. Doris Gottemoeller, "Befriending the Wind," *Review for Religious* (Nov.–Dec. 1994, Vol. 53. No. 6) 806–19.
3. Farley, *Personal Commitments,* 36ff.

by their community charism. They give up the ability to follow any path for the freedom to follow this path or framework for love. Paradoxically, freedom is gradually and steadily "lost" as it is used. To choose one framework for love involves leaving others aside.

Each vow involves a commitment to do something and a promise to refrain from doing something else. One chooses to vow celibate chastity and not to marry. One opts to hold all things in common and not to amass personal material security. A religious puts his or her life and talents at the disposal of a communal effort and relinquishes a type of self-direction. Canonically, religious life is defined in this generic form.[4]

As gospel counsels, the vows trigger an ever increasing alertness to the mystery and action of God in one's life and society. Living the framework of the vows is meant to create a freedom to embrace the whole complex of gospel imperatives. The consistency of life they are meant to form comes from the heart of the gospel ethic to be like Jesus, which is their basis.

The vow of obedience involves a trusting openness to God's loving direction. The vow of poverty commits us to the freedom necessary to respond to God. The vow of celibate chastity frees us to respond to a passionate bond with God which overflows in an ever expanding commitment to the needs of others in mission.[5] These gospel counsels, however, are placed in a framework of life lived in a specific religious community.

Someone may take up the concerns of a religious yet not enter into the internal consistency of religious life. A person may choose not to marry, may engage in a common good work and live simply, but this is not the same as religious consecration.

The consecration of a religious is religious, that is, it is an act of surrender to God. It is an action of the heart which unifies reli-

---

4. See Canons 559, 600, 601. *Code of Canon Law* (Washington, D.C.: Canon Law Society of America, 1983).

5. See Donald Senior, C.P., "Biblical Foundations of Religious Life" in *Living in the Meantime: Concerning the Transformation of Religious Life.* Edited by Paul J. Philibert, O.P. (New York: Paulist Press, 1994) 54–72.

gious life as a framework of living. This inner movement of the heart is "held" in some way, by public vow or through the permission of ecclesial authority. Essentially, religious commitment involves the gift of one's life to God in ongoing conversion. Walter Conn comments that in religious conversion religious interests move from the periphery to the center of one's consciousness and become one's habitual, dynamic center of energy.[6] While religious undergo many types of conversions in a lifetime, religious conversion is central to their life-style.

Essential to a religious consecration is trust in God. The heart of religious commitment is more than a trust in one's autonomous self. Having a good self-concept and sense of self-reliance are necessary to make vows. However, religious consecration involves relativizing and de-centering the self and allowing God to take over the center of the self. It involves giving up a type of control over one's life which now is not necessary. The traditional term for this is abandonment.

Religious consecration is not the destruction of a healthy sense of autonomy. It is a preservation and transformation of it by taking it up into a new horizon of love and the concerns of that love, the concerns of the Kingdom.

The three vows concretely deal with life experiences which involve a sense of self: sexuality, relationship with material things, and use of power. Religious consecration fosters a de-centering of a false self and the development of one's true self by concrete choices in these three areas of human living. In this process, the religious meets God, learns to love, and becomes fulfilled.

The conversion to Christ involved through the vows is more than moving from bad habits to good habits. It is becoming a totally new person in Christ. The vows are an ongoing act of attention to the basic desire for God in one's life and an act of love to place this desire above all others. God's own self is joined to the openness of the religious, and a new gift of energy and life comes to them personally and to the Church.

---

6. Walter Conn, *Christian Conversion: A Developmental Interpretation of Autonomy and Surrender* (New York: Paulist Press, 1986) 190.

Religious life is not a life in which someone pursues an interest about God. Rather it is a framework of living intended to facilitate an openness to God, where the Spirit of God becomes present in the life of the religious. While this is true in the life of every Christian, the religious publicly witnesses to this event. Through the integration of his or her own life, the religious testifies that God truly does fill the desires of the heart and makes us fruitful.

Traditional theology said that the religious had a prefigurement of the beatific vision. Today we would say God presents Godself to the religious through an active being present which informs and floods the person with a growing consciousness of God's presence. The religious in turn chooses a life-style in which attention to the Absolute and to God's action in history can be fostered.

A framework for adult Christian living

Religious life is a framework for adult Christian living. It is characterized by the bond arising from the gift of one's life to God. While comparisons between religious life and Christian marriage in the past have proven odious, a fruitful comparison can be made between them as two frameworks of adult Christian living.

Christian marriage provides a framework for giving love a future. Spouses commit to do all they can to foster the bond between them, to honor the sexual exclusivity of married fidelity, and to develop and grow in generative and personal love.

Religious life is also a framework for giving love a future which has comparable responsibilities, commitments, and internal consistencies. We can understand this framework on four levels.

On a primary level, religious life is an act of religious faith by which one consecrates one's life to God in the Church through a religious community. Entering religious life implies there is a certain transfer of "transcendent data," information about life and how to live that we cannot entirely prove. This data is decisive for growth in faith and is received through the tradition of the community and the Church.

Religious life also involves an adherence to a tradition of witnesses regarding how one experiences and acquires those data. At this level, religious life is the acceptance of a way which is defined both by the Church community and the tradition of one's congregation. A religious is one who says yes to this way of life of faith and takes it on as his or her own.

At the second level, where framework structures our relationships into recognizable life-styles of "marriage," "religious congregation," and "single life," religious life is a framework for living where one's bond with God is characterized by a complete gift of self through the vows of poverty, chastity, and obedience.[7]

The moral responsibility taken on by religious vows is the promise to give oneself to God without reserve. The bond of a religious vow is also exclusive. One promises consecrated chastity within a religious congregation and commitment to build community, not the community of one's own family but the new community begun by baptism. Religious life is generative. Active religious make a public commitment, a promise to participate in Jesus' redemptive mission to defeat "death" and entropy" in all its forms. Whether death be of ignorance, sickness, alienation, homelessness, racism, or poverty, active religious commit themselves to a socially recognized apostolic work according to the charism of the community.[8]

At a third level, the framework for religious life takes on various cultural and historical forms. We see religious life institutionalized differently at various times in history and also culturally diverse in other parts of the world.

At this level, the framework of religious life can be critically reflected upon and submitted to the same processes of cultural critique as applied to the wider culture. Is the framework of religious life in tune with the culture? Has the culture so defined religious life that its transcendent identity is lost? Changes and adaptations can be made according to how these questions are answered.

---

7. Farley, *Personal Commitments*, 90.

8. For the contemplative and retired religious, the witness of prayer is their service to the Church and the world.

For instance, there can be a patriarchal model of religious obedience as well as one where expression of obedience implies the fostering of mutuality. The question is more how obedience has been inculturated than the nature of obedience itself. There is a letting go implied in mutuality which can be materially indistinguishable from the surrender traditionally associated with religious obedience. Both involve the experience of the de-centering of self.

Unhealthy expressions of the religious vows do affect their relevancy. It is unrealistic to think the vows can be understood if they are not lived authentically. It takes great energy and discipline to let go of false practices and to assume better ones.

The reform movements witnessed in the last thirty years have tried to express the primary nature of religious life in the modern world. Yet, the primary framework of religious life can be lived in many forms, both "progressive" and "conservative." It is human nature to award our own cultural frameworks an importance which we do not give to the essentials.[9] A blindness, "our way or the highway" among religious can prevent true reform across a congregation.

The recent witness of Eastern European religious remind us of this. They have lived among their families for years, with no habits, under conditions of secrecy, needing to hide the Eucharist in their homes, yet have preserved religious life for the next generation. They testify that the deeper framework of religious life transcends current ideological battles and our imaginations. We, on the other hand, can easily identify cultural forms of religious life as its essence. We can be paralyzed by progressive views as well as conservative ones. The question is, will we preserve religious life for the next generation?

The final level of the framework of religious life is the particular structure worked out by individuals and communities. This framework may change in the life of an individual. At one point

9. See Karl Rahner, "Structural Change in the Church of the Future" in *Concern for the Church. Theological Investigations* XX (New York: Crossroads, 1986) 130ff.

a religious could live and work in a large institution, at another time with members of other communities on an Indian reservation. A third time could find him in a parish, or her living alone, yet meeting with regularity with other religious for prayer and sharing. At another time, she or he could live with a small group.

All these frameworks can be expressions, for the time, of the more essential framework of one's religious life. Their suitability depends on how they are assessed as consistent or inconsistent with the way of life of the group. Ultimately they are chosen and abandoned to the degree they help or hinder one's essential commitment within the broader commitments of one's congregation.

Summary

The framework and promise of the three vows expresses our trust in God and is the means by which we make our statement of love irrevocable. We seek to initiate in the present a new form of relationship with God, with the community, and with the Church. It is a relationship defined concretely enough that it will endure in the future, either in the form of fidelity or its opposite.

The vows neither add to nor contradict our baptism; they specify it. Through the vows we give a new law to our love. By giving our word, we yield to God, to the community, and to the Church, a claim over us. When we make vows, we may only have a glimmer of an understanding of their full import on our lives. Yet implicit in the initial promise is a commitment of our entire lives. Margaret Farley puts it this way, "Commitment is love's way of being whole while it still grows into wholeness."[10]

Religious take three of the counsels, which all Christians must observe from time to time, and make of them a way of life. They take what is an existential call in the life of every Christian and make it an essential call of their lives. The vowed life becomes a way of living which will enable them to allow their desire for God to integrate their entire lives.

---

10. Farley, *Personal Commitments*, 34. We have drawn heavily on this important study in this chapter. See especially chapter 3.

All loving is a door to transcendence, our capacity for an active openness to the infinite and absolute. Yet, we experience transcendence in the "corner of our eye" as we engage in the world of everyday relationships. Only in the everyday do we come in contact with infinity. In reaching out in love, we are an "awaiter" of God's word addressed to us in this world and its history.[11]

By vow religious commit themselves to a life with a different touch in loving. Their touch of love unites with God's as a way God's transcendence is shown in a world filled with sin and entropy and new creation and possibilities. Religious take up the tasks of love because of God, and commit themselves especially to those tasks which their moment of history calls forth.

Religious in the past have been early to detect these needed areas of love. They have been, as the psalm tells us, "awaiters of the dawn." Religious have been among those early in the pursuit of new means of hope for those trapped by the sufferings of their age. We believe today that religious are still called to embody this hope. A new dawn does await those who sit in the shadow of death and its power at this turn of a millennium. Religious of today continue to take our place among those who work for this Kingdom. Let us look at how religious in the nineteenth century changed their framework of life to meet their new challenges. We hope that in better understanding them, we can gain insight for our own future.

11. Haight, *The Experience and Language of Grace,* 120.

PART IV
HISTORY

Chapter Eleven

Hearts for a New Age

Religious life is changing, but not for the first time. The change experienced today is just one in the history of religious life. An evolutionary outlook can bring a focus to these changes. Evolutionary thinking would suggest that what exists today is a more developed version of an earlier and simpler form of religious life.

The primary framework of religious life, its simplest form, has not changed at all. It remains a desire to give one's life entirely to God. Religious life through the ages has been an historical and symbolic concretization of this desire in the Church. As a life framework, religious life is designed to make this desire concrete and to provide a path to realize it.

At other levels of framework, however, there have been various forms of religious life in the history of the Church. It would be wonderful if we could put a changing form of religious life from the past under a microscope and study it. Just like a scientist, we could observe cells dividing and new organisms being formed. We could look for patterns of change that provide insight into our lives today. We could ask the following questions as we observe.

Why did they change as they did? What did they take from the old in their new form? Why was their new form more adaptive to their environment than the old? Why did some groups die? Answers to these questions could provide insights for our present situation and coordinates for our future. An exact scientific study is not possible. Yet, a look to the past can be instructive, even if the insights it gives can only be partial and suggestive.

We cannot go back to the beginning of religious life to trace the change it has sustained. There are fine historical studies which have already done that well.[1] As a thought experiment, though, we can inquire into changes in religious life during just one period, the nineteenth century.

Why the nineteenth century? Changes in secular and democratic culture impacted religious life in a dramatic way. Many apostolic orders with simple vows, as well as other forms of consecrated life, evolved at this time. Religious life changed more dramatically in the nineteenth century than it had since the thirteenth century. It seems fair to say we are still reeling internally in religious orders from the issues raised in this important time in the Church.

Religious of the nineteenth century inherited a pattern of "old" religious life. As religious responded to the Industrial Revolution, their adaptations were both discontinuous and continuous with past forms of religious living. Some of "old" religious life survived the turmoil of the nineteenth century, but other parts were discarded. To understand these shifts, let us look at what was startlingly "new" at that time.

Institutes of simple vows

One new form of consecrated life which has developed in the last two hundred years is the institute of simple vows. These institutes were different from religious life as conceived prior to the nineteenth century. The Code of Canon Law prior to 1917 understood "religious" as those who took solemn vows, lived enclosure, and were under the jurisdiction of the bishop.

The nineteenth century called for a new type of religious. Much of the Western world was engaged in the turmoil of the Industrial Revolution. There were many new and unmet needs because of rapid changes in major institutions of the society.

"Religious" in the nineteenth century left their life apart and became actively involved in works of mercy, especially teaching

---

1. See Raymond Hostie, S.J., *Vie et mort des ordres religieux.* A book in English which utilizes this study is Lawrence Cada, S.M., et al, *Shaping the Coming Age of Religious Life* (New York: The Seabury Press, 1979).

and hospital work. Solemn vows, rules of enclosure, and the restriction for mission based on accountability to the jurisdiction of a local bishop were not suitable to the "new mission."

"Old" forms of religious living limited congregational outreach. But besides these practical issues, enclosed religious were associated with the old regime and often not accepted in society. Religious were frequently persecuted. Convents were burned down and religious were driven from cities.

The tension between new needs and old forms of religious life, however, gave birth to a new expression of consecrated living. It took a period which extended over one hundred years for congregations of simple vows, or "new institutes," to be born.[2] From the perspective of the twentieth century, these "new" congregations may not seem that different. However, they were, at least in their origins.

The process

Today, in the world of instant communication and sophisticated processes of ecclesiastical administration, we imagine new groups of religious forming in the Church in a logical way. If a group wanted to start a new religious congregation now they would refer to the codified canonical process by which they are approved.

However, in the nineteenth century, processes were not that formal. All during the 1800s new groups of "religious" were formed. They began informally, like pious societies, and functioned without formal ecclesial approbation. Since the juridical mentality surrounding religious life was one of enclosure, the Church was not sure what to do with this new phenomenon in religious life. The Church at the time did not have criteria to judge the authenticity of new religious groups other than the older vision.

---

2. Here I am following the research of Eutimio Sastre Santos, C.M.F., *El ordenamiento de los institutos de votos simples según las Normas de la Santa Sede (1854–1958)* (Roma-Madrid: Urbaniana University Press, 1993) 72.

Since to be a religious in the 1800s meant to be "removed" from the world, the new congregations had a different spirit from that of the canonical code. This required a new mentality to give them "birth" ecclesially. This did not happen overnight.

In the nineteenth century we can observe a process in which new congregations of simple vows formed over a period of one hundred years, while the main body of canon law only officially recognized the traditional enclosed style of religious life as "religious." It was not until the change in canon law in 1917 that religious with simple vows were recognized on a par with those of solemn vows.[3]

The development of institutes of simple vows, from the perspective of their canonical codification, had a beginning (1854), a middle period (1900–1917), and an end (1958). This one hundred-year period traces the birth and decline of one framework for living religious life. During this period, three different forms of consecrated life appeared in the Church: institutes of simple vows, societies of common life without public vows, and secular institutes. A more radical dialogue between religious life and society produced, not the death of religious life, but newness in its expression and forms.

Church law

Church law was important in fostering this newness. During the hundred-year period, the law helped religious life through its capacity to promote gospel living and a clarity of life-style. The relationship of canon law to religious life also had a negative side. Many congregations have in their history, misunderstandings, struggles, and outright battles with church authorities over the direction of their identity. Also, in the latter periods of this process, the law forced congregations across the world into a uniformity which overshadowed their spirits.

There was a paradox in the law's relationship to religious life in this hundred-year period. The law sought to protect the identity of religious congregations, yet in the process, over-codification

---

3. Sastre Santos, *El ordenamiento de los institutos de votos simples,* 59.

obscured it.[4] The nineteenth century points to the struggle between the healthy need for code and the stifling effect of legalism in religious life.[5]

At Vatican II, the Church encouraged religious to step back from this period of institutionalization and reclaim the significance of their original charisms in a new period of secular history. Religious today are still engaged in this search. A closer look at the period 1854–1958, however, discloses steps in the process by which the Church attempted to deal with a new phenomenon in religious life and the time it took to clarify differences between frameworks of religious living.

1854–1958

Since canon law saw religious life as enclosed, there was no canon law which recognized the framework of living religious life which new groups presented to bishops. Bishops solved this dilemma by approving new groups one at a time, almost on an experimental basis. Generally these groups were seen as pious societies which shared an order of life that was recognizable to those living outside the group. This approval gave the new group the potential to take root in the Church.

The new societies grew, expanded to many dioceses, and engaged in the work of the Church for some years before a canonical process for approval, beyond that of the local level, emerged. It was not until 1854 that an administrative procedure was established for the approval of "new institutes," the *Methodus* of 1854.

This process produced an approval which went beyond the local bishop, to that of the Holy See. Before 1854, bishops had some rules of thumb they used to approve new groups. However, none had been codified. Groups simply followed the rule of life written by their foundresses and founders, and approved by their bishops.

4. Sastre Santos, "*Institución y <crisis de identidad> en un Instituto de perfección*," *Claretianium*. XXIII, 1983, 211–70.

5. Popular thinking sees legalism as making religion more difficult than it has to be. But traditionally, legalism is an escape from the true challenge of religion. Human laws replace the call of the gospel.

There were so many new groups forming in the Church that the "ad hoc" process used over the years was no longer adequate. In order to respond to the reality of this new phenomenon in the Church, the Roman office of Bishops and Regulars, which preceded the current Sacred Congregation for Religious and Institutes of Consecrated Life, issued *Methodus*, a document which stipulated how local bishops were to proceed in the approval of new institutes, requesting now their submission to Rome.[6]

This began the formation of a new Code of Canon Law which would reflect the real lives of the new institutes of simple vows, instead of reflecting the life-style of enclosed religious only. New religious were no longer "exceptions." However, the process of formation of canon law did not happen overnight. It took fifty years to develop.

It was not until 1901 that a particular code which pertained specifically to institutes of simple vows, *Conditae a Christo*, and *Normae* was formulated.[7] By 1917 these particular norms pertaining to institutes of simple vows were joined to the common canon law for religious, those with solemn vows, and a new Code of Canon Law was formulated in 1917. By 1958 revisions of constitutions were requested so that all congregations would be in conformity with canon law.

Secular Institutes

During this period, an embryonic form of another expression of consecrated life began, that of secular institutes.[8] While as early as the sixteenth century Angela Merici wanted her Ursuline order without habit or life in common, it wasn't until 1889 that we see a recognition of a consecrated form of life lived entirely in secular society. This was expressed officially in *Ecclesia Catholica*.[9]

6. Sastre Santos, *El ordenamiento de los institutos de votos simples,* 53ff.

7. *Ibid.,* 115.

8. Sharon Holland, I.H.M., *The Concept of Consecration in Secular Institutes* (Rome: *Pontificia Universitas Gregoriana. Facultas Juris Canonici.* 1981). I will draw often on this important work in my comments.

9. *S.C. Episcoporum et Regularum* decre., *Ecclesia Catholica,* 11 August 1989, *AAS,* 23 (1890–91) 634–6.

Groups that formed according to this style of life were recognized initially as sodalities, not as religious.[10] These groups also grew out of the new needs of the Industrial Revolution. Members were consecrated to God, but the new association made no distinction between their works and those of a member of ordinary society.

There was no collective mission, as in the new congregations of simple vows. The activity of members of these new secular institutes was understood as the activity of an individual person.[11] The association directed and confirmed each member in a certain professional activity, rather than directed them to the collective work of the association as such.

We may wonder why this form of life demanded a new association. People at that time, as today, could become active members of a parish and live a good Christian life. Why was this not enough? Members of the new associations of secular institutes wanted to be consecrated to God. They desired a more explicit framework of Christian living from that in the common state of being baptized. They gave up some of the freedom that would be theirs as baptized laity in order to bind themselves in a new way to God. They promised celibacy.

Members of secular institutes evidenced that desire which characterizes the primary framework of consecrated life, a desire to give one's life entirely to God.[12] They desired to experience God, not only in the shared knowledge of doing good, which comes from authentic Christian living, but in the knowledge of

10. A leader in this early movement was Agostino Gemelli. See M. Ciccarelli, *"Padre Gemilli e gli Instituti secolari,"* *Studi Francescani*, 57 (1960) 7, as quoted in Holland.

11. Holland, *The Concept of Consecration*, 27.

12. One may wonder how this act of consecration would be different from a consecration to Mary in a sodality or spiritual association. The difference lies at the level of framework of life which it affects. Consecration here refers to a desire to bind oneself to Christ in a manner which would preclude the taking up of another life-style such as marriage. Consecration in a spiritual association is aimed at bringing an intentional faith dimension to one's state of life, not defining a vocational stance.

union which comes from a conscious and focused surrender to God. They wanted to take on a life-style that would highlight this openness to union with God. The consecration they sought was religious, a giving over of their lives to God.

Members of the new institutes had an intention different from that of the baptized because they wanted to enter into a new conscious bond with God which would have permanent ramifications in the framework of their lives. Commitment is an act of the will by which one is bound to another. The totality of their promise to God was expressed through the decision to be celibate. The commitment they wished to express was so total it precluded marriage.

Members of both secular associations and of "new" religious congregations of simple vows desired total consecration to God in the new situation of the society of the Industrial Revolution. Both acknowledged a bond with God which permanently characterized their lives. It is obvious that neither group was satisfied to make their commitment to God in the privacy of their hearts alone. Both sought to give some type of external form to their intention.

We may wonder why aspiring members of the embryonic secular institutes did not join the new institutes with simple vows. The new religious certainly were less structured than those living solemn vows. We find, however, each took different means to serve God. They adopted different secondary frameworks for living out their desire to make the gift of their lives to God and service to the mission of the Church primary in their lives.

Incorporation

"New" religious and members of secular institutes wanted to be incorporated into a group of others who shared their religious experience of desire for total dedication to God. Those with simple vows did this through a common life. Those of the new secular institutes did so through incorporation into a new society and by commitment to the life of the same society.[13]

13. Holland, *The Concept of Consecration,* 25

Neither group wanted their membership to be temporary. Both wanted the society that received them to be approved by the Church and be formally rooted in the life of the Church. They desired a new ecclesial bond, but we might ask, why? While it is hard to reconstruct intentions from this distance, we can venture to interpret a few.

No one needed a new ecclesial group to live an active Christian sacramental life, or a life of personal prayer, penance, service, or charity. What they desired was an additional framework of living beyond this common life of the Church. They requested *recognition* from the Church for a new way of being a member of the Church, one which would be lived out with others.

Characteristic of the "new way" was total dedication to God by means of the gospel, according to a specific charism. Commitment was permanent and the group was comprised of others who had similar lifelong commitments.

What made these groups different from informal gatherings of sincere Christians is that they sought to form something beyond themselves, beyond the sum of their reciprocal relationships. They intended that the group live longer than the life of the present members. Instead of basing their group life on mutual friendship alone, they wanted a relationship that was transpersonal.[14] They began an institution, a society characterized by a shared experience of commitment.

They asked the Church to use its own ministry of recognizing the movements of the Spirit to help them solidify a new way of being a Christian in the Church in the Industrial Society. The Church was enjoined to help them create a form of life which was clear enough that others could join. They sought a continuity, coherence, consistency, and firmness in their new identity which would make their group not only in service to their spiritual needs but a path that others could follow.

---

14. This in essence is the definition of an institution. See Sastos Sastre C.F.M., *"Institución y <crisis de identidad>,"* 222.

A change of life

Commitment to God was central to the framework of life in both groups, but this commitment had several characteristics. It was radical. Commitment evoked a change from one way of living to another. "Before" and "after" commitment could be seen as different periods in life, a movement from one framework of life to another. After consecration the lives of new members could not be explained in the same terms as before. Something qualitative happened on their own journey with God and this change was marked by new ways of proceeding in the way they conducted their lives.

A second characteristic of the commitment was that it was future-oriented. The act of love of God which they made was meant to go beyond the present moment to the future. It was not the case that people committed themselves to this framework of living until something better came along. Inherent in the promise was an anticipation that before the inevitable changes in attitude, circumstances, and feelings which the future would bring, one's course in life was set. The commitment was made anticipating that such changes would occur, and their resolution was answered in principle. While both groups shared a desire for a commitment that would affect the future, they differed as to the secondary framework they adopted to express their commitment.

Some committed themselves through vows, the gospel counsels of poverty, chastity, and obedience. The vows were the means by which commitment was expressed, but the vows were not the commitment. The commitment was the bond, the intentional giving over of one's life to God. Through the act of commitment, the vows became inseparable from this intention of the heart. They were the framework by which their intention took form. Since commitment is deeper than the vows, groups could choose a framework of life which best suited their calling, the result being that some chose other forms of commitment.

The third characteristic of their commitment was that it was explicitly religious. They desired to form a new relationship with God through the surrender of their will. The desire to give one's whole life to God is in essence a surrender. God initiates this desire. God, in fact, consecrates and we respond.

Traditionally the counsels of poverty, chastity, and obedience have been singled out from the others offered in the gospel as signs of such a transformation of life. However, both groups did not choose the vows as the framework to express their consecration.

Vows

Some early members of secular institutes expressed their new commitment through the vows of poverty, chastity, and obedience; others did not.[15] Others promised to observe the counsels of the gospel but did not make specific vows. Religious of simple vows did use the traditional three vows as an expression of their commitment. However, they did so understanding them in a different historical and cultural framework than "religious" at the time.

For members of some secular institutes *incorporation,* not the vows, became the focus of their form of life. It was through the efforts they made to be incorporated into a society committed to a life of the gospel counsels and approved by church authority that they expressed their commitment to God.

Because the essence of consecration is the intention of belonging to God totally, forms other than public vows gradually became recognized as means to express totality of commitment.[16] A private commitment of celibate chastity also expresses total commitment. For members of some secular institutes, incorporation or investment in a society of shared commitment and the intent to live the gospel counsels consciously in the "world," rather than apart from it, better expressed the goals of their lives.

Other members of secular groups did make vows, but they did so privately. Here we see that public or private vows were taken according to the goals of the particular groups. Religious with simple vows desired a public witness. Members of secular institutes wanted to live their witness in the world, not by taking up a social place in society identified as religious.[17]

15. Holland, *The Concept of Consecration,* 23.
16. *Ibid.,* 14.
17. Public profession sets one apart, as sacred space is set apart from the everyday. It makes one's insertion in the world a witness to the Absolute, which is beyond yet the ground of the world of everyday.

Some members of secular institutes lived their vows privately within the society, often living alone or within their families. A third group lived a common life but without public vows.[18]

Key to all three types of consecration in the nineteenth century was a desire to be dedicated totally to God. All three forms shared the primary framework of consecrated life. History shows that consecration was the intention from the beginning of the new secular groups. The clear acceptance of consecration in the practice of the counsels as the real basis for all consecrated life in the Church, however, came only one hundred years later at Vatican II.[19] We can see, though, that new forms of consecrated living, based on true religious experience, did not weaken religious life. New forms which were based on its primary framework, the desire to give one's life entirely to God, gave new life to religious living as a calling in the Church.

Summary

In the nineteenth century we have two new styles of religious commitment, "new" religious and the beginnings of what we know today as secular institutes. There were theological, juridical, and economical questions which surrounded this new life in the Church. Some of the questions raised at that time have yet to be answered. Is "leaving the world" the mark of a religious life? How do we distinguish religious life as a form of consecrated living? How can one be invested in the secular mission and yet be religiously consecrated? What are the external marks of the change of life which entrance into religious life represents?

The history of the process by which institutes of simple vows and other forms of consecrated life is really not over. Many congregations after Vatican II revised their constitutions. Even after revising their constitutions, however, many congregations struggle with who they are in the new situation of the Church and the world. To understand why this paradox occurs, let us continue to examine the next two periods in the institutionalization of congregations of simple vows.

18. Sastre Santos, C.M.F., *El ordenamiento de los institutos de votos simples,* 56.
19. Holland, *The Concept of Consecration,* 34.

Chapter Twelve

New Forms of Energy

Why did new forms of religious life appear in the nineteenth century? Reduction of a complex situation to one factor is odious. Yet, it seems fair to say, that new needs in the Church and the world influenced their formation. Even congregations which existed before the nineteenth century changed. Waves of political, social, and cultural crises during the 1800s impacted religious life.

The historical documents point to the new issues which arose during this century. Letters of petition from the United States to Rome requested dispensations for cloistered religious to open the doors of their monasteries to begin schools. Canon lawyers debated whether religious with the rule of enclosure could use their houses to nurse the sick. Could their homes include a hospital?

The limitations of the period surface as well. Black congregations of religious were formed in the United States. The racial biases of many white orders would not accept blacks as sisters and brothers. These small glimpses of nineteenth-century life point to a century in transition. Religious stretched to meet new needs and were stretched by them as well.

New needs

Rapid changes in society created profound human need. While old forms of social assistance and patronage had collapsed, new structures to meet the social, educational, medical, and religious needs of industrialized societies were yet to be created. The nineteenth century produced a new type of religious as one way to meet this crisis.

During the 1800s, the Church expanded its geographical reach and its ministerial presence. Publicly, the Church was linked to the old regime. The Church had to struggle for new identity and defend its relevance in a shifting society.

The Church had new problems. It raised the social question. It stopped thinking of society in ideal terms only, and began to contrast the ideal and the real. Both church and society had a new sense of responsibility for the social structures in which they lived.[1] How was the Church going to respond?

The Church struggled for authenticity before forces that declared its irrelevancy. Liberal society relegated the Church and spirituality only to private life. It claimed religion had no role in economics or politics. Marxism declared religion an opium of the people. The Church was a distraction to the challenge of survival of the new industrial proletariat. It faced a dual challenge. It had to meet the needs of a new society, and defend its own credibility. It was a time not unlike our own.

The new religious

Into this scene enters a new religious, religious of simple vows. They were different from "regular" religious. Their new framework of life allowed them to engage in collective works of social significance: education, social services, and health care.[2] They rejected the upward mobility of liberal society by differentiating their activity from other forms of work in the society. They were active in the society yet were removed by social position and strata. They were "placed" by obedience in the works of their congregation.

Their works were not those of the new profitable capitalistic corporations. We do, however, have evidence of scattered experiments with founding "Christian factories" to give the poor employment and a sense of Christian community.[3] Congregational

---

1. Donal Dorr, *Option for the Poor: A Hundred Years of Catholic Social Teaching* (Maryknoll, N.Y.: Orbis Books, 1992) 13–59.

2. Holland, *The Concept of Consecration*, 27.

3. Paul Misner, *Social Catholicism in Europe: From the Onset of Industrialization to the First World War* (New York: Crossroads, 1991) 133ff.

works in the nineteenth century were, in today's terms, "non-profit." The new religious were different in substance from older forms of religious life. They left their enclosure and publicly performed the spiritual and corporal works of mercy.

The core framework of a life of simple vows was the profession of public vows received by the Church. Religious wore some form of distinctive clothing so they could be identified publicly. They lived in housing which gave them a place apart, and practiced a form of real and physical detachment from the "world." They did not live with their families.[4]

Religious of simple vows shifted their ordinary social relationships. They withdrew from many events and interests of their society in order to foster the vision and will which their commitment involved. They invested in the new societies which they created, and which the Church approved and welcomed. In this way they provided new energy to a church in crisis.

Secular institutes

New energy for the Church and society was provided also by members of new secular associations. Their life-style was secular and consecrated. The Church did not know what to do with this new form of religious consecration. Many wanted the members of the new associations to be put into a form of religious life. People who disagreed argued that if this were done, people with secular vocations might lose sight of their unique vocation.[5]

Others wanted to classify "seculars" as the faithful, or as members of an association of the faithful, like the Blue Army. Supporters again argued that this did not respect the fact that

4. We have evidence that religious, before the Council of Baltimore at least in America, were allowed to visit their families with more frequency and freedom than after the council. It is argued that the formation of the parochial school system in the United States actually changed the life-style of many religious communities. See Mary Evans, *The Role of the Nun in 19th Century America* (New York: Arno Press, 1978); Mary J. Oates, "Organized Voluntarism: The Catholic Sisters in Massachusetts, 1870–1940," *American Quarterly* XXX, Winter, 1978.

5. Holland, *The Concept of Consecration*, 30.

members of the new associations wanted a new and different relationship with the Church.

Since they were not religious, the vows of "seculars" were not received in the name of the Church nor did they have the privileges of religious. Members of secular institutes, for example, were financially responsible for themselves. Their associations were usually not financially committed to them for continuing care in old age.

People debated how secular institutes were different from other church associations. There were several distinctions between them. Members were not married. They did not share the majority experience of the faithful. Their bond was the shared experience of a new consecration.

Most associations of the faithful gathered around a single aspect of the Christian life. Pax Christi is dedicated to peacemaking or the Blue Army is a spiritual association dedicated to devotion to Mary. Other associations of the faithful regulated only some activities of their members. The new "secular" association involved their whole lives and all of their activities.

These new associations also asked for the authority to govern their groups internally. As laity they did not have the power of jurisdiction. They wanted a different form of authority from that of an association of the faithful. There the bishop held a great deal of authority and appointed a moderator chaplain. The new institutes wanted internal authority so they could direct their association toward its unique goal, total consecration to God from within secular society.

New institutes of simple vows and beginning forms of secular institutes were new calls to committed life which did not "fit" into the current framework of Christian life-styles. In the years that followed, the new energy of their initial spirit was modified by society, theological conditions in the Church, and the juridical process which brought them to the renewal efforts of Vatican II.

1901–1958

The identity of institutes of simple vows was clarified in the Church by reconciling the code used to approve the new institutes in course for almost a century and the more formal code used to approve regular institutes. This was done under the canon law reform of 1917.

The possibility was entertained to revise the Code in 1917 and reserve it to regular religious, and use just one canon to refer to groups with simple vows. The canon would simply say these groups had their own code. This idea was rejected.[6]

Instead, the Code of 1917 tried to reconcile the two frameworks of religious life. It held that "new religious" and "regulars" had public vows as their common bond. This was the key criterion for defining "religious" life in the years to come. After 1900, the term "religious" was used for those with solemn vows as well as those with simple vows. The notion of public vows distinguished religious from members of secular associations in the eyes of the Church.

The attempt to reconcile the code of life of enclosed religious and the new spirit and life-style of religious with simple vows was difficult. Institutes approved before the Code of 1917 struggled to express the identity of their Institute and maintain religious life as lived in the "regular orders." This mixed life was upheld by the law which governed their lives.[7]

1917–1950

Following the Code of 1917 there was a third period in the institutionalization of institutes of simple vows. From 1917 to 1950 the constitutions of congregations were revised again to conform to the Code of 1917. Congregations faced the problem of how to protect their particular identity while conforming to a new universal law which imposed on them a type of uniformity they had not previously encountered.

Scholars claim that at the time of the Code of 1917, the law governing institutes of simple vows could have been merged with secular institutes instead of cloistered religious, but it was not.[8] This

6. Sastre Santos, *El ordenamiento de los institutos de votos simples*, 56.

7. *Ibid.*, 133.

8. *Ibid.*, 60–1.

would have made institutes of simple vows more like secular institutes than like traditional religious. However, the opposite occurred.

Increasingly, more elements of "regular" religious life were incorporated into the constitutions of groups that began as new institutes, but with a different spirit. Those not founded to live in community were in communal houses. Those who did not pray the office were required to do so. Those who previously visited their families and the homes of those they served were restricted to the convent, in a type of semi-enclosure.

The result was twofold. A great homogenization of religious orders occurred.[9] Congregational practices were more monastic in style and not reflective of the original spirit of congregations. This was one factor which created the need at Vatican II to ask religious congregations to go back again to their founding spirit to retrieve their distinctive identity.

Approval of secular institutes

What happened to secular institutes? In 1947 they were formally approved by the Church.[10] Secular institutes were distinguished from religious orders by the absence of public vows of religion and the fact that common life was not imposed.

The framework of living in secular institutes was set down by this time. Members of secular institutes enter into a commitment of poverty, according to their constitutions, chastity, and obedience through a bond which is lasting, mutually held among members, and complete. While secular institutes do not have common houses, they may have common centers which serve as residences for superiors, places for training or retreat, and resi-

---

9. Casual conversation with older women religious today reflect this change in the application of canon law. Older women religious will claim that sisters older than they had in many ways a less rigid style of religious life presented to them. Religious life in the '40s and early '50s reflected a peak of uniformity and emphasis on code than had been practiced earlier in the century.

10. *Provida Mater Ecclesia* (February 2, 1947) A.A.S. 39 (1947) 114–24; *Primo feliciter* (Mar. 12, 1948) A.A.S. 40 (1948) 283–6; *Cum Sanctissimus* (Mar. 19, 1948) A.A.S. 40 (1948) 293–7.

dences for those who need it, e.g., for health reasons or by personal wish. They are different from associations of the faithful in that they involve total consecration of life by way of the counsels in an approved Institute.[11]

Consecration, or total commitment, in secular institutes must be adapted to secular life. The ministry of members of secular institutes is exercised in the world and originates in the world. Their vows are private, hence they do not "leave the world" by any act which publicly centers them into a socially recognized state of life, as do religious.[12] Their consecration is lived from within secular reality.

Harvesting energy

A characteristic of apostolic religious living since Vatican II is a turn to secular society as the context of its commitment. Rules of semi-enclosure once linked religious life to "regular" religious life and clearly distinguished it from secular institutes. Today, they no longer mark the cultural framework of religious life in most instances.

Constitutional revisions have not totally answered the question of the identity of religious life. While constitutions say religious live in community, many religious do not. While constitutions say religious orders have corporate ministries, many are hard pressed to express their ministry as they once did. Constitutions, in some instances, do not reflect the life as it is lived in religious congregations today. This is due to the transitional nature of the times. Religious life is never perfectly lived, nor is there a proper fit between canon law and lived reality in rapidly changing times. The Church allows periods of experimentation to respond to this problem.

As religious look toward the religious life of the future, can reflection on the nineteenth century provide any coordinates for this search? Should religious orders become secular institutes? Is

11. Holland, *The Concept of Consecration*, 46.
12. Merkle, *Committed by Choice*, 79.

there something different in the vocation of religious that needs to be maintained in the future?

As a thought experiment, what would happen if we used the evolutionary terms *tangential* and *radial relationships* to explore the differences between the commitment of religious and members of secular institutes? Let us see what light they may provide.

Tangential relationships are those of everyday life. They refer to the "ordinary" ways people create life, work, raise their families, live in neighborhoods. Radial relationships are those where centers meet. They lead people to go beyond automatic and prescribed relationships with others. They move out of their present circle of association to create broader and more inclusive bonds with others.

In terms of their commitment, members of secular institutes seek to live their commitment primarily in the tangential relationships of life. They form an association to bring a transformative effect on their families and workplace, but they do this from within these established forms of life. They do so tangentially.

Religious, on the other hand, make the context of their life and ministry radial relationships. They live and minister out of the coming together of their centers as individuals into the new center of their community. This is more than the tangentiality of an association. It involves the radial relationship of community.[13]

This costs energy, but it also creates a different kind of life and ministerial energy: that which comes from a synthesis of centers. The commitment of a religious involves a disposition to incorporate his or her energy into this corporate project. This is characteristic of the "new energy" religious bring to the Church.

If our thought experiment is right, it explains why many congregations today are struggling with how to express this corporate aspect of their life and ministry. Intuitively we know it remains a characteristic of religious commitment.[14]

13. Patricia Wittberg explores some broad differences between groups in *Creating A Future for Religious Life* (New York: Paulist Press, 1991). We are using different models for analogy here, but there are many helpful distinctions which Wittberg uses to differentiate forms of association that do apply to this discussion.

14. David J. Nygren and Miriam D. Ukeritis, "The Religious Life Futures Project: Executive Summary," *Review for Religious*, 52:1 (Jan.–Feb., 1993) 6–55.

Membership in a secular institute involves a total consecration to God and others. The energy of a secular institute, however, is directed in a different way. They are an association in the Church which has an internal ordering that is accountable to both the interdiocesan and universal church. However, the new energy they provide is that of a secular commitment that does not stand apart from everyday society. Another thought experiment may give us insight into the nature of this commitment.

Mass and minority experience

Mass and minority portray how individuals and groups interact in the social process in light of the types of relationships available to them. Mass experience refers to general patterns of behavior, agreed upon social customs, and a type of collective mentality. Minority behavior or experience is reserved for a few. Because it is different from mass experience, it requires more energy. Minority behavior involves a more complex centering of energy, and leads to a higher synthesis. It is only because "mass" conditions are stable that minority experience is possible.

Mass and minority experience in consecration

The consecrated lives of religious and members of secular institutes are minority experiences in the Church. As groups, however, their ministerial energy flows differently. Both religious orders and secular institutes experience and participate in both mass and minority phenomena as they minister in the Church.

In 1947 the Church recognized that "secular" consecration was not just a supplement to religious life. Instead, secular institutes were a new form of a minority experience in the Church. Their distinctive minority status stemmed from the fact that their consecration was not only in the world, but *by means of the world.*[15]

While religious and members of secular institutes share a minority function in the Church, seculars remain a minority in their life framework. In order to touch the tangential or daily relationships of secular life, they invest their energy in the daily work of

15. *Primo feliciter,* II. See also Sharon Holland, *The Concept of Consecration,* 55.

the society. They do not try to form any synthesis of their common efforts as a ministerial focus. Their consecration is expressed not only in the world, but by means of the world. They immerse themselves as individuals in the usual work of the society.

Religious, also a minority, minister to the whole by creating a new mass, their congregation. They do this by way of their charism. By public vows religious direct some of their energy into the tasks of forming a congregational thrust as a focus of ministerial energy. This public radial relationship among themselves is a touchstone of their vocation and a means through which they minister.

Through public vows religious form a new public mass by the shared expression of their "way," a congregational life of the vows. Minimally they are publicly known as those who live simply, love chastely as celibates, and collaborate for a common purpose.

The deepest characteristic of their "mass," however, is the public expression of their charism as blended with the life of the counsels. They form a visible and codified way of life which captures in some way a form of socially reinforced behavior or practices. This is their common expression of the life of the vows, their "way," which for active religious is integrated into their public ministry.

The mass religious create is meant to have the benefits of any mass. It should reinforce, direct, and conserve energy. As religious today consider the new energy they hope for in religious life, our thought experiment raises the question of energy expenditure.

Members today question a loss of energy within congregations. This questioning seems more serious than acknowledging that people are busy. Rather, some religious question how their way of living in a secular society feeds burnout, overextension, lack of ministerial impact, and fragmentation within the community. Are religious today simply victims of their culture? Is there a missing ingredient in our framework of life that needs examination?

As we look at some of the elements which released new energy in religious life and the Church in the nineteenth century, we see that religious created a new mass, and secular institutes created new minorities. In the 1800s, a mass was created, but its characteristics had different historical and cultural elements than the previous frameworks of religious life.

The choice before religious today might not be between new energy on the one hand and the absence of a mass or group component to their lives on the other. The choice is whether to accept the challenge to create socially cohesive patterns of practice within secular society. The criteria which direct formation of these practices rest on their ability to conserve energy and release it for significant goals for their own lives and for the Church and society.[16]

If our thought experiment is correct and religious life is to create a new "mass," then new frameworks of living can be tested by the criteria of whether they do in fact conserve and focus energy for the goals of religious life. Religious should have time for experiences together which reinforce their common values, build relationships, and challenge them to continue on their common journey of faith to minister effectively and creatively in a fragmented society.[17]

Our reflections on radial and tangential relationships and mass and minority experience are thought experiments. They are meant to give insight into these two forms of life, while open to the fact that the analogy may not be exact at every point. However, discussion of these differences can help us to clarify questions regarding the evolving frameworks of consecrated life today. If new groups did meet the evolutionary challenge of the nineteenth century, can they provide us with any insight into coordinates for our own future?

16. Larry Rasmussen comments, "Focal practices . . . are those actions intrinsic to a way of life that center, sustain, and order that way of living." *Moral Fragments and Moral Community*, 154.

17. *Ibid.*, 153. Rasmussen states that focal practices are not simply experiences that temporarily light up our life like a good song. They are the engaging, reenacted actions of a certain ritual quality.

Chapter Thirteen

Toward a New Synthesis

Religious of the nineteenth century developed a new way to live the vows. They translated the idealism, self-sacrifice, and devotion to Christ of religious life into a framework for their times. Religious life was both a "way" of personal transformation and a way to bring change in the world. They renounced the world as religious before them. Their renunciation, however, was not an abandonment of the world, but of an absolutizing relationship to it.

Religious of the 1800s embraced the values of their age. Yet, they witnessed that the goals and ideals of their times were not absolute.[1] Positive aspects of nineteenth-century culture can be found in their lives and ministry. At the same time, they stood against what was false in their culture. They reached out to those abandoned by the self interests of their age.

They translated religious life into a new form by integrating a "way" of personal transformation and service to the world. Four core patterns are evident in the complex strands of this history.[2] Their lives involved a "way of transformation"; they formed a new community of baptism; they engaged in the defeat of death according to their times; and they generated and were sustained by ecclesial energy.

1. See Merkle, *Committed by Choice*, 96.
2. For insight into the nineteenth century in relationship to a broader view of the history of religious life, see JoAnn Kay McNamara, *Sisters in Arms: Catholic Nuns Through Two Millennia* (Boston: Harvard University Press, 1996) 565–630.

A way of transformation

Religious communities of the nineteenth century were a "way" of transformation. They believed in the transcendent data of the gospel and followed a way which gave access to that data. Each "way" had positive and negative characteristics. They promoted "freedom from" habits and mentalities and a "freedom to" live the values of the gospel. Each "way" suggested leaving things which society claimed were not distractions. Each way promoted behavior which the age claimed unprofitable. By creation of their "way," religious engaged in ideological critique. They made clear that their way was not "business as usual" in their culture.

Thought in the nineteenth century held that the human person was perfectible. For religious, the transformed self was not an absolute goal. Religious did strive for perfection. Perfection often was interpreted through lingering scholastic frameworks. These encouraged the pursuit of "perfect" actions, such as perfect charity and perfect acts of contrition.

However, nineteenth-century spirituality went beyond scholastic frameworks. The "leaving behind" of religious life was to create a new "will" or a desire for God's will which was dynamically transforming the world.[3] God in the 1800s, among other things, was a God creating a kingdom. Nineteenth-century religious developed their spirituality in a mix of old and new practices. All was not clear nor was practice clearly that of one century.

Religious sought salvation in a century when people believed they could save themselves. Religious went against the mentality of their age. They renounced material things and redirected sexual and relational energy to seek and do God's will. Their choices gave new expression to the meaning of the gospel in a very secular age.

Their way of transformation was not isolated from mission.[4] Amid lingering monastic frameworks, union with God's will

3. Gerald A. McCool, *Catholic Theology in the Nineteenth Century* (New York: The Seabury Press, 1977) 190–200.

4. Here we will address apostolic orders because there were so many new ones, especially of women, that developed at this time. We do this, however, valuing the "mission" of prayer of contemplative religious.

drew them to union with a loving presence and action in the world.

Monastic spirituality gradually was transformed into one suited to the apostolate. Monastic discipline became apostolic mobility, acceptance of the hardships of community and ministry, learning new cultures, and the discipline of work.

Religious life mirrored a broader struggle in the Church to reconcile the natural and supernatural orders. Enclosed religious were still seen as "true" religious. Yet, congregations struggled to balance monastic practices and apostolic work. Religious blended the apostolic practice of social service and the renouncement of the world of monastic practice.

Love of God, delight in virtue, and service to others were the goals of the vowed life. Their ministry was a witness, not just a social service. They linked mission and their "way" of living. Religious of the 1800s not only did good work, they depended on God. They combined two inseparable marks of Christian holiness: reliance on God which gives rise to true courage and independence, and love of neighbor in the face of the rationalism and skepticism of their age.[5]

There was no recipe for this innovative approach to religious life. It involved a search not unlike our own today.

Facing the ideal and the real

The ideals of religious life had to be refound in the new situation of nineteenth century culture. In cultural transition, there is a tension between the ideal and the real. Those things once thought ideal no longer have the same meaning in the times. Some values are discarded, some continue, and others are re-expressed in new cultural forms.

Religious life, as enclosed life, did not conform to demands of the times. For our purposes, "ideal" will mean the image used as a model of religious life. The term "real" will mean what religious actually did and/or were called to do by the Church and society.

Religious, for the most part, were not asked to stay in monasteries. They were needed to start schools. They were on battle-

5. Kathleen Fischer and Thomas Hart, *Christian Foundations*, 146. See also McCool, *Catholic Theology in the 19th Century*, chapter 1.

fields nursing the wounded, in the streets collecting orphans. They ran parishes. They created hospitals. These helped industrial workers with subsistent wages recover their health and get back to work to support their families. Nineteenth-century religious were affected by a rapidly changing culture. Not everything was clear. Yet, they did respond.

Facing a tension between the ideal and the real could have resulted in hesitant, immobile, and fearful behavior.[6] Yet, religious faced the challenge. They closed the gap between the ideal and real in their times by incarnating their faith in a way of life that produced what was socially needed. Their life was a "way." It was organized to take the transcendent data of their lives and translate it into practices. These practices affirmed their values and made acquisition of them key to their way of living.

Practices

Practices are actions which are both a means to a good life and a socially situated good life itself. Practices differ from good experiences in that they re-occur. We may go to a conference or a retreat and find it lifted our spirits. A practice, on the other hand, is ongoing. Attending a yearly retreat is a practice. Making a retreat once is a good experience with no commitment to the future.

Practices engage us. As repeated actions, they help us acquire values. Practices are ritual actions which embody what is right in a context.[7] A practice of nineteenth-century religious life was the readiness to be sent to any mission. This readiness expressed the "faith" of religious life in those times. Religious were missioned consistently throughout their lives in this way.

Practices not only embody transcendent data but are means to acquire it. The way of life of a community is constituted by its practices. Practices form character both of the group and its members. They are meaningful because they are understood as means to acquire community values and to express community values. Sharing in common practices fashions character and gives

6. Donald Capps, *The Depleted Self* (Minneapolis: Fortress Press, 1993) 87.
7. Rasmussen, *Moral Fragments*, 154.

distinguishable shape to a way of life. A common practice among religious today is the sharing of income.

Practices are similar to actions which comprise a sport. One day I observed a young boy sliding into a pillow thrown onto the ground. He would run, fall to the ground, and slide into the pillow. He would repeat this action over and over again. Taken alone, this behavior is not easily understood. Unless one knew he was preparing to play baseball, this behavior was silly. However, knowing the game, the behavior made sense. Today the practice of sharing income is meaningless outside the expression of a total way of life.

Practices form a matrix of behavior which is meaningful as a whole, as a way. In isolation, their meaning is not understood. Monastic practices stayed in religious life long after monasticism was its main framework. These practices were gradually dropped as they no longer effectively formed character in an apostolic life. The vows shape practices of religious life. Nineteenth-century religious adapted them for apostolic life.

Practices, as praxis, also shape thought. What we do affects how we think.[8] Practices are at the heart of moral communities. In order to hold certain moral values, one must experience them. The group has to live their stated values in order to be a moral community.[9] Practices are essential for this task.

Practices are subject to moral judgment. People assess which practices are helpful for their lives and which are not. They may ask what practices communicate about their way of life or what kind of community their practices form. They may inquire about the type of power relationship practices embody. They might ask if their practices are in sync with the culture. Practices answer the question, what is the best way of life for us to lead? They make vision, obligations, values, and hopes concrete.

---

8. See Avery Dulles, *The Craft of Theology: From Symbol to System* (New York: Crossroad, 1992) 9. The relationship of praxis and insight is a popular theme of Latin American theologians. See Jon Sobrino, *Christology at the Crossroads* (New York: Orbis, 1978).

9. See Alasdair MacIntyre's discussion of practices in *After Virtue* (Notre Dame, In.: University of Notre Dame Press, 1981).

Practices cannot be coerced, but they can be reinforced by social sanctions. Membership involves fidelity to practices. They are the connective tissue that shapes participants. Practices often denote whether one is really playing the game, improving one's skill, or just sitting on the sidelines. Superficial or arbitrary understanding of practices creates a judgmental climate. New forms of "fidelity" are then difficult to recognize. Practices need to be grounded in healthy communal spirituality.

Religious life today is also a way of transformation. To follow this coordinate of direction, we need to link our "way" to practices. Effective practices today will connect a "way" of transformation and mission, as did religious of the nineteenth century.

Yet, modern society is based on a different conception of community from that of the nineteenth century. New practices must be based on a contemporary understanding of community. A false assumption today is that practices belong to the past. On the contrary, every community form needs them. The whole way of life educates and forms; it is not just episodic observances. Religious are challenged today to re-express their framework of life in a new cultural situation.

The new community of baptism

A second coordinate of direction provided by nineteenth-century religious is community. Religious of the 1800s lived the community of the gospels, as did many religious before them. They formed new ways of coming together and gave witness to the "new community" formed by baptism.

In the 1800s, religious created communities of caring, hospitality, and mission. They founded new institutions as images of God's intended community. They dedicated themselves to the practices which constitute community. They broke barriers of community and engaged in hospitality. They sought to welcome the world. They embraced a spiritual elitism that did not divide the world and the Church. It actually helped to unite them. Their spirituality was not divisive insofar as it was rooted in community.[10]

---

10. We note hospitality, acknowledging that enclosure often blocked efforts in this regard.

Baptism is a call to community. The communal mission of nineteenth-century religious gave new expression to the community of the Christian life. Today religious are challenged also to form community, but on new grounds.

Community of the nineteenth century was modern compared to monastic communities. Yet it was still a traditional community. Community solidarity in the 1800s was based on shared ethnicity, territorial identity, and common social class.[11]

Religious communities drew upon these traditional boundaries and went beyond them. Choir and lay sisters were joined. Brothers from different nationalities were merged. Religious had an international mission and a solidarity which transcended national lines. On the other hand, many nineteenth-century communities did have a common language, ethnic customs, and other markers of cultural identity as building blocks for community. It seems fair to say that nineteenth-century religious communities were transitional in that they had both traditional and modern elements.

Sociologists claim modern life waged war on traditional community. Modern times welcomed the freedom of an anonymous society. Oppressed by the small-mindedness and pettiness of small village life, people found new opportunities in the wider boundaries of modern living. Religious, too, experience these shifts in their experience of community.

Durkheim, Weber, Simmel, and Freud claim modern "beliefs" gave cultural and moral coherence to people's lives in the face of the unraveling of traditional community. Religious also seek shared beliefs to knit together a community not bound by the daily ties of living.

Changes in community also impacted identity. Traditionally, intact, long-haul communities create identity. However, modern society is built on a mobility of labor and capital, creating opportunities for exposure to wider worlds. This destroys the communal mechanisms and sanctions which cement communities into centers of identity and shared vision.

---

11. Rasmussen, *Moral Fragments*, 36. I will draw on Rasmussen's analysis in the following pages, adapting it to religious life.

Until Vatican II religious life remained relatively immune from broader cultural changes in community. Religious community was sufficiently withdrawn from the culture that its monastic style gave it the flavor of a traditional community, even though adapted to ministry.

However, after Vatican II this changed. Shared housing, living in the same locality as one's group, working in community institutions, engaging in similar educational opportunities and mission experience ended for many religious. Diverse experiences made the ideal of a shared community vision difficult. Its base in common experience was eroded. Pre-Vatican II religious life was in many ways a pre-capitalist life. Modern society dismantled that life, and with it, not community, but a model of community existence.

The modern model of community is based on a different ideal. The modern era produced a vision of a Great Society in which individuals fashioned their own lives, based on their preferences. Individuals name the relationships to which they hold themselves. Intact communities are not part of this vision, nor is public life and the common good.[12] Religious life, as it adapted itself to modern life, was affected by this change in mentality of the broader society.

In society, community was transformed from a place to an experience. Modern society defines itself around the economic world. Yet, it assumes that morals centered in a noneconomic life will humanize it. Moderns want to make money, but they assume people can be trusted, will be fair, and can tell the truth.

What modern society did not calculate is that intact communities provide the values, training, and skills to have a public life together. The modern paradox of community is that community is to provide the values for modern life; however, modern society does little to provide for the stability of these centers of human life. Historians claim that modern life lives off the moral capital of a more traditional society which preceded it.[13] The crisis in community is, what happens when this stable generation dies?

---

12. *Ibid.*, 37.
13. *Ibid.*, 45.

In religious life there is a parallel situation. Community life today assumes members already know how to live in community.[14] However, religious face a unique crisis. Some experienced members do not want to live in community, while younger members ask for community. The community variations, which many religious live today, work because they live off the "moral capital" of a more traditional way of life. How do we provide for formation of community in the new situation of today?

Life-style enclaves

People still need intimacy, identity, and support. Modern society meets these needs, not through community, but through life-style enclaves.[15] Life-style enclaves are not communities. They are groups of people who share similar patterns of consumption, leisure, and interests. A life-style enclave is a private community with its own goods and services, from a security system to shield it from others, to schools, pools, clubs, parks.

In enclaves, people have no common history, memory, or story. Enclaves do not call a group beyond itself. People simply gather around shared preferences, usually leisure and consumption. In enclaves there are group boundaries. People can keep others, who are not like them, away.

Community, on the other hand, is a place of manifold engagement.[16] Community is an inclusive whole where people live interdependently with one another, sharing both a private and a public life. In community, one generation initiates the next into a way of life. As center of manifold engagement, community gives each member a significant place in day-by-day participation. Manifold engagement creates important bonds which tie the members together.

---

14. This is often due to the "gap" between ministry expectations and the patterns in local living situations. Here we are using community to mean a shared living arrangement.

15. Merkle, *Committed by Choice*, 21. Here I draw on Bellah's *Habits of the Heart*.

16. Rasmussen, *Moral Fragments*, 139.

Manifold engagement can be contrasted to a life-style enclave.[17] Members of a life-style enclave are not interdependent nor do they act together except to insure the future of their life-style together. Their lives are essentially private. They gather principally around leisure and consumption.

Life-style enclaves assume a formed morality. They draw on whatever moral insights people bring with them to a loosely formed group. The enclave does not have shared practices beyond the structures of families or schools within it. It leaves all other decisions to the current mentalities common to a culture. It has no vision of life beyond that of the will of the members to keep choosing to live together. It provides no source for solidarity. Life-style enclaves are not centers of freedom; rather, they are groups of conformity who bind together, often to keep others out.

Community is a center of moral formation. Through intact small communities, people learn the staying power and trust to temper themselves, to serve, to sacrifice, to lead, to observe meaning-giving traditions, to develop character, to practice decision-making, to recover from mistakes, and to forgive. In small communities people learn how the world works.

Patterns of practice in community living today cannot be those of the nineteenth century. Yet, community is more than a discipline of religious life. Devising a modern image of community in religious life is key to its future. Community is central to religious life as a "way" of personal transformation and a way to bring change in the world. Yet, both must be translated for the culture of today. Religious are called not only to discern shared values but to name the conditions which develop those values and enable them in the next generation. As we receive this coordinate of direction from the nineteenth century, we ponder the next step.

17. *Ibid.*, 53. Again I will draw on Rasmussen's analysis and adapt it to the needs of religious community.

Chapter Fourteen

New Times for Community

Martin Luther King once asked, where do we go from here, chaos or community? King questioned the possibility of community in society. But he more seriously pondered the chance for a society without community. Religious today inquire about the state of the moral ecology of community. Is it an endangered species in religious life?

We cannot recreate the communities of the past. The rational quest of self interest alone will not create them. Coercive external authority cannot form them. Religious are called to build a new type of community, freer from the limitations of the past, yet able to form the humanity of the future.

Community is a center of multi-layered interactions among people. There, traditions and rituals are preserved and developed. Life skills are learned and called forth. Discipline is nurtured and expected. Fidelity and accountability to the community are practiced.[1] At its best, community is a way of life that shapes and defines members' identity. True community shows itself in an alliance for a common cause, a life beyond itself. If we desire a community which is different than the past, what would be its characteristics?

New times for community

Theorists claim that modern community is marked by a shared history, identity, mutuality, plurality, autonomy, participa-

1. Merkle, *Committed by Choice*, 127.

tion and integration.[2] Religious recognize these values in their own desires for community today.

A *shared history* assumes that customs, language, geography, shared events, and crises bond a community more than abstract ideals. A community shares a Story through which each member's story is interpreted. Since the moral principles of a community are latent in a community's shared culture, a community's history has to be multi-cultural. Yet, shared history alone is not sufficient to bond a community.

Aspects of a shared history can be pathological. A group has to face these weaknesses and move toward healing in order to have a future together.[3] Shared history and a sense of belonging are important for community, but the content of that belonging has to be open to moral criticism and ongoing reflection by all the members. For instance, most religious communities in the United States are marked by a long history of racism. The community of the future has to be built differently.

Identity refers to the kind of persons being formed by a community. The formation of identity in community involves a sense of "we" which does not destroy individuality nor is based on a hostile moral tribalism where "we" is seen always opposed to a "they." Identity in the modern era has to embrace a pluralism. Here individuality and identity are centered in a respect and loyalty which creates healthy boundaries.

Unlike former community ideals, there can be diversity in modern community. People can disagree when respect is present. They can even pursue varying interests if there is a way in the community for these diverse experiences to be received. However, identity usually requires that members be in each other's presence sufficiently to bond their attachment and involvements into a shared identity.

2. The following analysis is based on and adapted from the work of Rasmussen, *Moral Fragments*, pages 110ff., and his use of the work of Philip Selznick, *The Moral Commonwealth: Social Theory and the Promise of Community* (Berkeley: University of California Press, 1992) 183–90, 357–65.

3. Some religious communities today make "graced history retreats" and own their collective "grace history" as well as "sin history" as congregations.

Mutuality is the atmosphere of interdependence and reciprocity in a group. People sense they need one another in some way and gain from cooperating with each other. In the nineteenth century religious life needed new members to staff institutions and carry out an institutional ministry. Is there any relationship today between fewer entrants and a sense of community divorced from mission? A community that knows what it wants to do and why it has gathered can better attract new members and call forth its present members.

A community is connected by more than a contract. A real community has a type of open-ended caring and trust where obligations are shared and owned in an ongoing way. The mutuality of a community involves more than a voluntary involvement in a project or cause. It is a continuing relationship which is more than part-time. Mutuality in a religious community is a life relationship among core members and a selective participation of broader membership by those without vows. However, the relationship is always mutual, with both parties needing the other and assisting the other in some way.

Plurality is perhaps the most "modern" of the characteristics of community. It connotes that people will belong to more than one community at the same time. Modern community is not a totalizing one. Membership in a variety of groups does not threaten a group but enhances it. It extends the community into wider spheres of influence and brings to the community the well-being of family, occupational, recreational, ethnic, and religious groups other than its own. Plurality is held in relationship to the other values of community, identity, and mutuality. In this sense plural membership has to be balanced with sufficient presence to make community life a reality.

Autonomy is the ability of a community to develop responsible individuals while it incorporates them into a complex of relationships which gives them a social self or "we." Genuine autonomy is the capacity for self-direction that avoids both the illusion of unlimited choices within the group, and a brutal crushing effect of the group on the individual.

Autonomy fosters in the individual a sense of self which includes the group in its well-being and fosters in the group a sense of well-being that includes the flourishing of its members. Loyalty helps the group take the individuals seriously and supports the individuals to make the emotional investment necessary to incorporate the group into their self-identity.

Participation in community is marked by core participation in one's primary grouping and selective participation in others. In modern society both core and selective participation are necessary. Core participation is proper to primary groupings which engage in essential life processes of work, friendship, child-rearing, kinship, and, in religious life, participation in a framework for adult maturation and mission in the Church.

In religious community, core participation includes the primary activities of the "way." These involve a distinctive spirituality of the vows, community life, and ministry according to the charism. Core participation in a community is marked by an open-endedness, totality, and a sense of intrinsic worth rather than value based on accomplishments or skills alone.

Participation in modern community also involves selective participation in obligations with other groups. These are limited but real obligations. In selective participation, we can measure our investment with some degree of accuracy. We can maintain distance as well as fulfill important duties. In selective participation, we collaborate with others for common goals without the commitment inherent in communitarian relationships.

Unless one has a good sense of communitarian relationship, selective activities can take on a role they cannot fulfill. People can consume intense substitutes for community in work and other groups. Ideally, associational or selective participation supplements healthy communitarian relationships. Core participation in a primary group is necessary for a religious community and makes it a "way."

Integration is a quality of community that balances and mixes the others. No one value alone is a mark of healthy community. A healthy community is like a good poker hand. It is the relationship of the cards or qualities to one another that makes a winning hand or community. There is no one magic combination that must be present at all times. There are many possibilities that "work."

A shared history has to be balanced by a sense of pluralism or there will be a closed group. Autonomy needs a good sense of mutuality and participation. Identity alone is insufficient because growing identity must be open to change.

Integration is the capacity to keep a healthy tension between qualities of community in a manner which is unique to the group and the context. Some groups will stress one over the other. Essentially, integration will bring about intimacy in a community.

A community requires intimacy. Lack of intimacy will be experienced as no community. Yet the intimacy needed in a healthy community is not so close that others cannot bond with the group through selective or associational ties.

Community today is not based just on technical or organization skill but on a sense of responsibility, care, and commitment that both resides in characters already formed and forms characters entrusted to it. Tolerance, respect, and loyalty are insufficient to hold a community together unless these qualities are evident in a group which has sufficient face-to-face relationships so that people can experience trust and mutuality.

Evolutionary thinking suggests that frameworks for modern community have to obey the law of conservation of energy. Community must have enough tangential relationships that radial ones can occur. The nineteenth century linked the quest for community to an alliance for the good, or ministry. Community is not just a mark of religious life. Religious seek to create community with all with whom they minister. Availability, investment, witness, and credibility are essential to the heart of this integral ministry.

Religious life will continue to be marked by a unique quality of community. Because it has a communitarian ethic, it is a place where the experimentation with community needed in the society can occur. While community at this time is often viewed as expendable, social analysis shows the creation of community may be the most profound contribution of religious in the future.

Defeat of death

Religious "defeat death" as they share in the work of the redemption of Jesus Christ. Through their life and ministry, religious have participated in the power of Jesus' redemption in
every century. The Industrial Revolution set the stage for the apostolic work of nineteenth-century religious. Their focus was the
educational, health care, social, and religious needs in a time of
societal transition.

The framework of ministry used in nineteenth-century European and American society was generally institutional. Religious
founded schools, hospitals, orphanages, confraternities, social
agencies, worker circles, tabernacle societies, colleges and univer-
sities. These efforts extended to the "mission" regions of Africa,
Asia, the Pacific Rim, and South America. Various colonial relationships, or resistance to them, affected ministry and the creation of indigenous congregations.

Today religious minister to people different from the nineteenth-century worker. In many cases, it is the secularized person
who gets along quite well without God. In other situations, it is
the marginated, the newly pastorally transparent, the immigrant,
the dying, or the unemployed. It may be the new member of the
Church, waiting to be evangelized. Religious may minister to the
business executive looking for spiritual values, the addict, the
cancer victim, the religiously abandoned, or the abused. The
ministry of religious reaches people the official church may not
contact for a long time.

Today, as in the past, religious reach into the "abandoned
places" of society. While those places are often not captured by a
single target population or ministry, the coordinates provided by
the 1800s still point religious to them.

Separation from the world

The defeat of death, or sharing in the redemptive mystery of
Jesus Christ, expresses the consecration of a religious. Ministry
involves separation from the world. The ministerial style of a religious gives attention to God and God's ways of doing things. For

the contemporary religious, this separation will not be expressed in a flight to the desert or, for most, to a cloistered life.[4]

The separation is a stepping back from the "mammon" of modern society and the world's ways of proceeding. New expressions of separation are the fostering a critical consciousness, creation of alternative projects, communities and services, and participation in movements toward change. Religious foster an alternative professionalism in the works they undertake. They participate in the major professions of society and join with others in establishing good standards in them. They influence all professions to attend to the needs of the poor.

How religious do their ministry might be as important as what they do in the future. Today, society has modern systems in place to treat public education, health care, and social services in many countries. While they are flawed and need reform, they function in a way that was nonexistent in the 1800s.

Religious today find themselves working in these systems. Often they do not control them. They may even hold key positions, but their members are the minority. Can death be defeated in these systems?

Religious can foster an alternative vision in these ministries. Modern society affirms an expediency which is dead to reform. Postmodern society can be aimless, with no vision to call it beyond the present. Religious "separate" from the world when they do not use the same techniques. They are involved in the same systems, but not in the same manner.

Modern society does not lack the systems to meet its needs. It often lacks the focused leadership and vital moral vocabulary to change itself. The movements in society which provide an alternative vision deal with ecological concerns, concern for life in its beginning and its end, refugees, immigration, moral education, family survival, concerns of women, professional integrity, legal reform, world health issues, genocide, full employment, home-

---

4. We must note that cloistered religious also understand their own consecration as involving a commitment to a world in need of redemption, not a flight from it.

lessness, and poverty. These movements have centers outside religious life yet touch on systems in which religious participate.

Religious can be members of communities which gather these dreams. They can give them a place and a focus in the lives of more people. In the Dark Ages monasticism preserved the intellectual heritage from the early Church.[5] Religious today enter the cultural wars of society to provide the next generation a heritage of human and religious values which is their due. The future ministry of religious may be more "confessional" than imagined. Religious can foster a faith vision in society. If death in modern society is lack of vision, then its defeat will call religious beyond services even while they are engaged in them.

Ministry, as the defeat of death, gives direction to contemporary religious renewal. It requires discernment and social analysis. Among its characteristics are the following:

If modernity has misplaced its confidence in progress, then religious congregations foster communities that take suffering for granted. Communities can protect life beyond its economic value and build stability, unity, and harmony in their ministries. This is a harmony that remains firm in the face of the ambiguity, messiness, and disappointments of a culture in transition.[6]

Religious will engage in moral criticism. They can take a moral stance that relativizes other authorities. Because they have a sense of the sacred, they can peel moral legitimation from present cultural patterns and social forms. Religious ministry will seek integrity; one that discerns right and wrong, acts on one's discernment and says publicly why one is acting as it is.[7]

The public ministry of religious will help to rebuild an ethos of integrity in modern society. This ministry protects human dignity, promotes human rights, fosters the unity of society, and provides a sense of meaning to all areas of societal life (*Gaudium*

---

5. Roland Bainton, *Christendom: A Short History of Christianity and Its Impact on Western Civilization*. 2 vols. (New York: Harper and Row, 1966).

6. Rasmussen, *Moral Fragments*, 167.

7. Stephen L. Carter, *Integrity* (New York: Basic Books, 1996) chapter 1.

et Spes 40–42). Since it is a ministry that fosters the sacred in secular society, it is also a ministry of evangelization.

Models for ministry

Religious congregations will adopt different models for this ministry.[8] Some will use the educational-cultural model. They will direct energies toward influencing public philosophy, personal character, family values, and religious formation. Setting long-range goals, they will seek to form consciences and characters which will in turn influence public policy. The transgenerational character of religious congregations is well suited for this ministry.

Others will focus on legislative-policy models of ministry. They will incarnate church principles in the formation of their institutions. Because they enter the forum where policy and principles are mixed and related, they will discover new ways institutional ministry influences the public. Today religious congregations bring pressures, for example, on corporations for corporate responsibility. They witness in a new form to their identity as moral agents in the Church and society.

Congregations will engage in the prophetic-witness model. They will create clear counterpoint to existing societal practices and vision. They will offer members of church and society alternative institutions, movements, and programs. Religious will work with others, in rich as well as poor countries, to offer the choice of life in concrete ways. They will bear the cross this requires and witness to the spiritual values which inspire others to follow.

All models need one another. Religious life will embrace all models. Yet religious will also witness by being an anticipatory "way" for the society at large. Religious community itself can be a place of social experimentation by being a place that can give social form to a hoped-for future. To do this, religious will experiment with community itself.

---

8. J. Brian Hehir, "The Right and Competence of the Church in the American Case" in John A. Coleman, S.J., ed., *One Hundred Years of Catholic Social Thought* (New York: Orbis Books, 1991) 66–9.

Providing a "way" to defeat death

Religious communities will "defeat death" by being a type of a community which can combine communitarian ties and associational ties.[9] Different from the communities of the nineteenth century, religious communities of the twenty-first century will draw on the moral capital earned by modern living: freedom, democratic participation, equality, and mutuality. Yet they will also retain the monastic discipline of the capacity to welcome strangers. Religious will not recreate pre-modern communities but experiment with community itself according to the needs of their ministry.

Religious community can gather strangers and invite them to a shared space. This can provide others with an identity and purpose which they cannot find in the wider society. Religious community can provide an alternative to political or ideological movements that lack a moral framework for self criticism. Community can be a center of reflection for those engaged in many sectors of society.

Religious can offer a haven from the windstorm in which people walk in modern society. People today need places of reflection, retreat, discernment, and witness where the values needed for spiritual growth and societal transformation are made clear through shared practice and witness.[10] Religious today build a sanctuary not of stone, but one where those who are engaged in struggle can celebrate, reflect, and bond around their goals of resistance and the defeat of death in their lives.

Moral leadership requires more than pronouncements and statements. People need experiences which "capture" and historicize the values necessary to rebuild society today. Moral convic-

9. Rasmussen, *Moral Fragments*, 162.

10. In *The Historical Jesus of the Synoptics*, Juan Luis Segundo claims that relationships have to be maintained by communities which enflesh the principles needed for societal transformation. He does not use the word "practices," but the idea is the same. "Relations" (or practices) structure a process wherein people learn both a content and a "way" to learn further values. These are structures of interactive participation around a value. They, more than rules or laws, will lead people to a responsible humanity and will give them the vision to revalue history.

tion is sustained by experiences where critical values of solidarity, human dignity, and respect for creation are made clear.

Religious can provide not only food, shelter, and education to those without, but can help to sustain the type of moral community needed to bring the gospel to a culture in transition. Communities of core and selective participation can blend the person-centered and character-building atmosphere of a community with the harnessing of human energies for societal change.

Core and selective participation

The defeat of death by religious communities will take on a different direction from that in the nineteenth century. Community will be a blend of core members and those of selective participation. Core communities need others and those who engage in selective participation often need core communities. Selective participation alone specializes, mobilizes, and coordinates well, but it lacks the long-term commitment honored and fostered in a communitarian setting.

Religious communities need a clear identity around the meaning of core membership in order to invite others to selective participation. They maintain the necessary boundaries for their own identity and respect the fact that those with selective participation have core membership elsewhere. The more a religious community is a random association, the more it is headed for identity confusion and dissipation. It will not be a haven for others because its own house is not in order.

Religious communities of character require stable, ongoing associations of persons with special commitments to one another, a common purpose, and a common sense of life, people who can, through hospitality, combine close community with diverse interests and people.

People of selective participation will help a community not become closed and tribal, stagnant, and focused on itself. Communities will help those who have other primary communities join them selectively and draw from them an opportunity for involvement in the rituals, celebrations, and bonding which is not available to them in the broader culture.

These communities will be ones of mutual acceptance that respect and work from difference.[11] They are characterized by a common attachment and desire for key values and deep self-investment. Their identity is not complete identification, nor their unity conformity.

Ecclesial energy

The final coordinate for direction for religious today is that their center is in the Church. Historians of the Church claim that renewal movements generated by the Church in society have two characteristics. First, they are able to create community especially among lower socio-economic classes, those who are marginalized and disaffected people from the ranks of the privileged. Second, they are able to engage in the conceptual and ritual restatement and revisioning of traditions in times of great change.[12] The combination of these movements brings new religious vitality to the world.

Religious congregations today are challenged not only to survive into the future, but to claim and restate their soul, their sense of the sacred. Their sense of the sacred is the aspect of the gospel which is their reason to be. It is through this charism that each religious congregation will engage in bringing new vitality to society by engaging in the above tasks. Material survival is empty and contribution to society weak without this vital mark of renewal.

But the "soul" of each religious community is held in mutuality with the broader Church. The presence of the sacred is what the Church affirmed at the founding of the community. The Church affirmed that its "way" gave one access to the sacred and witnessed to its presence.

Openness to the Church community is an expression that the religious community depends on God and needs to be called beyond itself. Religious life remains rooted in the sacramental life of

11. Rasmussen, *Moral Fragments*, 131. Again I am adopting many of Rasmussen's insights, and the interpretation of others, and adapting these insights to religious life.

12. *Ibid.*, 144, quoting the work of Ernst Troeltsch in *The Social Teaching of the Christian Churches*, vol. 2 (Chicago and London: University of Chicago Press, 1981) 43–6.

the Church. Religious foster the sacramental life of the Church and rely on it for their spirituality. Since the 1800s they have shared intensely in the mystagological work of the Church.[13]

The Church helps a congregation to remember that the purpose of the congregation "transcends the purpose of the individuals that make them up" (Canon 114). Religious share a spiritual bond. The congregational structure protects it. Yet this bond is more than the collective wishes of the group. The "sacred" within a congregation calls it forth. This call is not based on the will of members alone. The group is summoned because God wills it and the Church needs it.

The spirit of the founder or foundress is normative for a community and the center is of its ecclesial identity. When multiple wills clash with one another, without this norm, they have no criteria for judgment.

In this case, a religious congregation as an institution ends, and so does its founding vision. Only corporate persons remain, that is, the physical body of the group. The community is a "communal person" with no identity.[14] A situation of moral hazard blocks the investment to collaborate and grow.

The risk of ecclesial engagement and cooperation is a "practice" through which a congregation witnesses to the presence of the sacred today. It assumes the discipline necessary to maintain its relationship with the Church and to promote its good. It is not only challenged by the Church, but it challenges the Church as well. It walks in and with the Church, despite the struggles of these transitional times.

Church and religious community exist in a relationship of mutuality. Church needs religious communities to enhance its life and mission. Religious congregations have their identity in the Church. Religious of the nineteenth century moved through a tu-

13. An interesting comment is made by the Protestant ethicist J. Philip Wogaman in his assessment of monastic spirituality. "The continued belief in the efficacy of the sacraments always qualified, to some extent, the reliance of monasticism upon its own 'works' for salvation." *Christian Ethics: A Historical Introduction* (Louisville, Kentucky: Westminster Press, 1993) 66.

14. Sastos Sastre, C.F.M., "Institución y <crisis de identidad>" 233ff.

multuous time in the Church. They not only survived the change but grew and increased the life and vitality of the Church in proportions never imagined. Religious of the twenty-first century are called to do nothing less.

Toward the future

As we look to the future, we see that the nineteenth century provides us with four coordinates of direction. Our lives are to be a "way" of transformation; they are to create the new community of baptism and defeat death in our times; and they are marked by an ongoing ecclesial identity.

Yet the distinct framework of living which expresses religious life is uniquely captured in the vows. The meaning of the vows cannot just repeat the nineteenth-century synthesis. The vows are real, but their context is different today.

The door of religious life of the future can be opened with new keys. Psychology, the social sciences, and current theology give us new tools to understand the vows and to grow in their spirit.

Through psychology we understand more about the human person and the developmental cycle. Through the social sciences we have new languages to articulate the significance of the vows in the broader society. Through theology we have renewed biblical and theological understandings to express the heart of the Christian experience in modern idioms.

In the next chapters we will use these "keys" to unlock the meaning of the vows and to examine the transformation of life which the vows evoke. Our reflection will not be the last word on the vows, but hopefully it will invite others to own their vowed life as it is lived. We invite all to engage in reflection on its future.

PART V
THE VOWS

Chapter Fifteen

Poverty: The Transformation of Desires

Gerald May begins a recent study on addiction and grace with the belief, "After twenty years of listening to the yearnings of people's hearts, I am convinced that all human beings have an inborn desire for God."[1] Desire for God gives life meaning. We experience this desire often in hidden ways. The longing for wholeness or fulfillment, the desire for integration, "being OK," are all reflections of our desire for God. Essentially, desire for God is the desire for love, the desire to love and be loved and to find the Source of love in our lives.

Many of us bury this longing under other interests. Something gets in the way of the all-encompassing and integrating desire of our hearts. Unaware of its importance, the longing we have for God disappears from awareness. Its energy is used by all kinds of forces which are not only unloving, but potentially self destructive. With St. Paul we say, "I do not understand my own actions. For I do not do what I want, but I do the very thing I hate" (Rom 7:15).

While it may seem strange to begin a reflection on religious poverty with a reference to addiction, learnings around addictive processes provide insight on poverty in contemporary experience. We have learned from the healing community about the underlying dynamic of letting go and reattaching energy. This is

1. Gerald May, *Addiction and Grace* (San Francisco: Harper, 1988).

not unlike the energy transfer that the vow of poverty is meant to unleash in our lives.

Why does desire for God and love fade in our lives? This desire causes suffering, so we take the energy from this deep desire and place it elsewhere, on safer things. Even for those who set out to love God above all things, a gradual misplacement of energy occurs. Over time, God seems rather elusive, and all things here are rather concrete and satisfying. Longing for what appears immediate, we repress the desire which calls for "more" involvement with God and love of others. We avoid its price, although this love is the most fulfilling.

From time to time we have a spiritual re-awakening. Our deeper and true desires take over our consciousness and lead us forward to God and love. Energy from our basic desire for God is always there, ready to be tapped. Reconnecting continually with our inner desire makes up the story of our spiritual journey.

Addiction and grace

There is a more sinister side of this story, the role of addiction in our lives. The energy we have for God does not remain dormant, in storage. Sometimes we shift its power and attach it to other things: substances, ideas, work, relationships.[2] May suggests that the derivation of attachment, which means "nailed to," reveals what our addictions do. They "nail" our desire for God to many things that are not God.

The image of having our energy "nailed" to something is a powerful description of the dynamic that underlies addiction. It is this human experience which ultimately the vow of poverty addresses. If I hold a picture to the wall, I can move it at will. If it is nailed to the wall, it hangs there without needing my permission.

Addictions and attachments in our lives work the same way. The energy we have for God, and for all good things in this world as they lead us to God and our true selves, is a God-given grace. We experience it in our call to "more." This energy gets nailed, as it were, to people, moods, power, food, drink, places, and an end-

2. *Ibid.,* 3.

less variety of things. It does not attach itself merely through our will, but remains attached by another form of energy.[3]

When "addictions" set in, we begin to lose freedom and control over our energy. Addiction and our attachments use our desire, leaving less and less available for love and other healthy pursuits. In the biblical tradition this dynamic is referred to as idolatry. We seek to fulfill our longing for God through objects of attachment. Addiction displaces and supplants God's love as the source and object of our deepest desire.[4]

Addiction is a state of compulsion, obsession, or preoccupation. It occurs whenever we are compelled to give energy to things that are not our true desires. It is important to see addiction as a normal process whereby the human spirit avoids its deepest desires. It is not just a clinical state, where we see it in an identifiable form. To varying extents, it is part of the human experience of every person.[5]

Addiction is reinforced in a consumer society. Our desire is attached to things we do not even need or want through the power of suggestion, competition, and mass advertising. Society tells us that our sense of self is grounded in things. It does not tell us the whole truth, that things can never give us our true identity.

To vow poverty in contemporary society is to acknowledge these personal and cultural realities. All Christians cope with them, for they form the context in which we live. Religious must sort through them, and move beyond them, to identify their desire for God as the integrating factor of their lives. They vow poverty as one means to live this out.

---

3. For an understanding of this experience as it is linked to sin, especially concupiscence, see Judith A. Merkle, "Sin" in *The New Dictionary of Catholic Social Thought,* ed. Judith A. Dwyer (Collegeville: The Liturgical Press, 1994) 883–8.

4. May, *Addiction and Grace,* 92.

5. McCormick, *Sin As Addiction, op.cit.* Here "addiction" is used as a modern paradigm to understand the mystery of sin.

Developing moral tastes

Moral theology describes this struggle for integrity of life in a different way. Human beings want, desire, and long for fulfillment. We seek justice, friendship, truth, goodness as aspects of a good life. These wants spring from deep inside and find their satisfaction in right living. They are our natural "tastes" for deep human values which will be ultimately satisfying.

Values are those things in life which people recognize as possessing an intrinsic worth.[6] Friends, for example, are not valuable because they get us something else, they are valuable in themselves. From a faith perspective, values are a window on God. Anything which is truly valuable is a reflection of God's own goodness, truth, and beauty.

Moral growth involves more than learning right from wrong. It also involves the search for what is truly valuable in life. Our values shift throughout the course of life. We develop and we change in fundamental ways of experiencing and thinking. We also do more than "think" our way into better ways of living. Our affections are transformed and our empathy aroused. We learn to love in broader circles and learn to care about an increasingly wider group of people.[7] Moral discernment is not only the application of the interpretation of value that one already knows. It is a continual search to know what true value is. The vow of poverty has a role in this human search and the process by which our values change.

Refining our moral tastes

As human beings grow and develop they recognize that what is important in life exists at different levels. Not all values are equal. We develop a hierarchy of values, separating passing desires from

6. Josef Fuchs, *Human Values and Christian Morality* (London: Gill and Macmillan, 1970) 112–47. Wade Clark Roof, *A Generation of Seekers: The Spiritual Journeys of the Baby Boom Generation* (San Francisco: Harper, 1993) speaks of this search for values in contemporary society.

7. Paul Molinari and Peter Gumpel, *Chapter VI of the Dogmatic Constitution "Lumen Gentium" on Religious Life* (Rome, 1987) 114.

things which are "worth our effort." We estimate the joy and satisfaction different values can bring. Sometimes we can draw on experience to make this judgement. Other times people tell us something will bring us joy and satisfaction, and we take their word for it and invest accordingly. Values worth pursuing are reinforced in the Christian community. Through gospel living we give and receive witness which helps to refine our moral tastes.

We can see this in the instance of a mother at the mall with her two young sons. She may buy the older an ice cream cone. For him, what is valuable is clear: to eat that cone with gusto. The mother may judge his little brother is too young for a cone and will get frustrated with handling it. So she may suggest that her elder son share some with his brother. What is this mother doing? She is trying to broaden her son's sense of the pleasures in life, from ice cream alone to the deeper human value of friendship and sharing.

These "higher" values of friendship and sharing reflect the deepest and best of the human spirit. They have to be taught. They require a climate of trust and mutuality to be learned. Our inner longing for friendship will not always lead us to altruism. Without some support in moral formation, our egotism keeps a strong hold on our choices.

The mother is trying to develop in her son a "taste for the good." Such a moral taste will lead him to take pleasure in sharing, just as he takes pleasure in ice cream. While equal pleasure in sharing may not come until later in life, the seed of learning a deeper human pleasure is here.

Life is a continual process of developing moral tastes. We learn to love, not just tolerate, the deeper values in life, and to derive pleasure from them. This pleasure costs the sacrifice of superficial pleasures of the lesser value. But one also learns the new face of love which is the reward of risk.

Deep gospel values such as "Blessed are the poor in spirit" could not be heard in the Christian community without the human experience of learning values which goes on spontaneously in the Christian community. If no one understood the human experience of risking and letting go which surrounds such scenes as the ice cream cone, no one would understand the beatitudes when they were read.

For the young boy who is insecure in his mother's love, sharing the cone may be a little much. He may need the cone as a symbol of his mother's love, and mother may have to wait to teach him this deeper lesson. The cone is not the issue. The issue is the role the cone has in his relationships and his growth as a person, personally and spiritually.[8]

We may ask what ice cream cones and little boys have to do with the vow of poverty. Religious struggle also with the relationship between material things and the whole range of values in their lives. While the deprivations of a simple life are at times difficult, or at least irritating, the vow of poverty is meant to be a means toward the values which are more important than an unreflective use of things. How does one calculate the promise of poverty? Can one make a type of "prenuptial" contract with the Lord, stipulating exactly how material things will be used and divided?

There is no exact blueprint for the practice of the vow of poverty. We fail if we materialize poverty to such an extent that we measure it solely in externals. We also fail if we spiritualize it so much that it becomes a constellation of vague attitudes which have little bearing on our behavior. Poverty in Jesus' life impacted his choices and ministry.[9] He let go or held on to things to the degree they served his mission that was rooted in a love relationship with his Father. He turned over even his own life as an expression

---

8. A type of moral reflection which focuses on the person rather than primarily on acts and consequences is called virtue ethics. The concern of this approach to the moral life is the acquisition and development of attitudes and practices that develop the person into a fuller moral person while also acting in a moral manner. This way of thinking seems helpful to understand religious life. See James F. Keenan, "Proposing Cardinal Virtues," *Theological Studies* 56 (Dec. 1995) 707–29.

9. For the role of affectivity, or transformation of desires, in moral growth see Margaret Farley, "New Patterns of Relationship: Beginnings of a Moral Revolution," *Introduction to Christian Ethics*, ed. Ronald P. Hamel and Kenneth R. Himes (New York: Paulist Press, 1989) 63–79.

of his love. Many today use the term simplicity rather than poverty because it seems better to reflect this sense of what is "fitting" and necessary for a love relationship.

The poverty of love

The gospel tells us that it is difficult for a person of "riches" to enter the Kingdom of God. This is certainly basic information for the religious. But it also tells us not to get too caught up in externals and miss the deeper calls of God. Scripture does not tell us exactly how to do this, but Jesus promises to send his Spirit to teach us what we need to know. All Christians need to reflect from time to time on their use of material things. Religious, however, also have structures in the framework of their life-style through which the Spirit can call them to continued authenticity in their use of material things.

Community, church, and needs of society refine the moral tastes of religious in regard to possessions. Religious poverty is lived authentically only in a matrix of relationships where letting go and holding on is given meaning in terms of mission, community building, personal and spiritual transformation, and societal change. Many religious of any experience have seen behavior which seems like clinical anal retentiveness passed off as religious poverty. The spirit of Jesus and of love is misunderstood here.

I remember a talk given to us as beginners by George Aschenbrenner, S.J., where he told us to give things to God out of love. If we could not do that, then we still needed them, and that was okay. The image was planted early that on one side of the poverty coin was "giving up" and on the other side was the entering into a love relationship with God and others. Essentially there is no more to it. But we will go on to see if we can continue to unlock the meaning of poverty with some contemporary keys of thought.

Kohut and Social Teaching

The human person needs things. We need things not just for physical survival but for psychological development. The psychologist Helmut Kohut tells us that a thing can be a self-object, a symbol of the self which has not yet consolidated sufficiently inside.[10] Not having enough things can rob us of necessary self-development. Replacing the deeper search for self with possession of things can hinder self-development. For religious today excessive attachment to material things can often be a signal that there are other unhealed issues in their personal life that need attention.

Catholic social teaching provides another key for understanding the human need for material things. It holds that each person has a right to private property. Private property is a human need because it provides the material means to express personality, set goals, and secure one's future. Inherent in the Church's teaching on private property is the concept that possessions are to be held in relationship to the common good.

Religious by vow hold things in common. Most religious, however, have a certain amount of property which they themselves use, a lot more than in former times. Through the vow of poverty religious are challenged to hold this "private property," in light of the good of the whole. Religious have the dual obligation to orient their possessions to the good of their religious community as well as to the Church and society.

The practice of poverty

Shortly after Vatican II, religious communities reinterpreted the practices associated with the vow of poverty in first world countries. Many moved away from the interpretation of the vow as everyone receiving the same. Religious entered into new ministries which created a need for the tools of their professions. They took over new positions, needing the cars, clothes, books, credit cards, and trappings to "fit" that situation. Housing needs shifted as more religious lived in smaller groups or alone.

The monastic style of a uniform practice of sharing gave way to a situation by situation judgment of what was needed. The

10. Michael Basch, *Doing Psychotherapy* (New York: Basic Books, 1980). Donald Capps, *The Depleted Self: Sin in a Narcissistic Age* (Minneapolis: Fortress Press, 1993). Alice Miller, *The Drama of the Gifted Child: The Search for the True Self* (New York: Basic Books, 1981).

close to subsistence style of living, which was common to the society in the nineteenth century, gave way to a living standard which was closer to family standards in postwar prosperity. Median family income from 1947–1973 doubled in U.S. society.[11] This same shift in the standard of living happened in many first world religious congregations.

Salaries of religious also changed. The tradition in some first world countries had been that every religious received the same salary, regardless of ministry. This policy was conducive to the building of the Church school system in the United States and was based on the underlying belief that all persons are inherently equal, though differently gifted and of different experience and competence. The diocesan administrator and the first-grade teacher received the same paycheck. This practice differed in communities with hospitals. However, today the salary range is mixed, with some receiving no salary and others receiving substantial ones. Equality is sought by holding salaries in common. All that one earns belongs to the congregation (Canon 668.3).

Today poverty in religious life often means in practice access to enough money to live modestly. One is required to work over the course of one's life, to earn enough so that the community can be independent from other groups and accomplish its mission. This means to live in such a way that each sister or brother can have the modicum of health care, leisure, knowledge, and so on that is needed for the full development of the body and mind and spirit, and the community as a whole can foster a mission outside itself to those in need.

Paul VI taught that no one has a right to keep what he or she does not need when others lack necessities (*Populorum Progressio*, 23). Religious community provides a unique means to make this goal of Christian living a focal point of one's personal and collective life. The fact that there is much diversity in congregations regarding use of material things makes this a greater chal-

---

11. Source: U.S. Census Bureau Statistics. See for example Edward N. Wolff, *Top Heavy: A Study of Increasing Inequality of Wealth in America* (New York: Twentieth Century Press, 1995).

lenge. Religious live their vow of poverty as they examine accumulation of institutional and personal "wealth" for its responsible direction to the mission and care of all the members of the congregation.

The vow of poverty is an expression of the religious' total commitment to service of God and neighbor. Concretely, it yields a claim to my property.[12] Canonically the vow stipulates that everything the religious accumulates from his or her work belongs to the congregation; one promises to hold all things in common, to forego financial independence from the group and contribute to the mission of the congregation, to live modestly and share the common material resources with those in need (Canons 600, 640).

It would be easy if the vow of poverty dealt only with things. But the vow means much more. Just as a married couple vow fidelity to one another "for richer or for poorer," the material aspect of this promise is a symbol of an all-inclusive commitment. The vow of a religious expresses this same totality.

Poverty is a key element in the framework of religious life. Along with obedience and celibate chastity, it has personal, social, and political-mystical ramifications. The practice of poverty is inseparable from chastity and obedience, for the three vows form a total "way" of life. Let us continue to unlock the meaning this holds.

12. Farley, *Personal Commitments*, 21.

Chapter Sixteen

Poverty: Beyond Isolation

Introduction: vows and life crisis

In our exploration of the vows we will call on the developmental theory of the psychologist Erik Erikson. Erikson's thought will be used to gain insight into the meaning of the vows for personal and spiritual growth. With this key, we will attempt to unlock aspects of the personal transformation which the vows evoke.

In the early 1950s Erikson saw the creation of the self occurring through the lifelong sequence of developmental stages. Each person goes through eight stages in life. In each stage is experienced a crisis or conflict whose resolution is crucial for continued development.

The eight stages are the following: trust-mistrust [ages 0–1], autonomy-shame and doubt [1–3], initiative-guilt [3–5], industry-inferiority [5–12], identity-identity confusion [12–18], intimacy-isolation [18–40], generativity-stagnation [40–65], and integrity-despair [65+].[1] The ages assigned are common times in which these issues arise. Yet, the crises are not restricted to these periods alone.

One works through each crisis by finding an appropriate ratio between the positive and negative poles of the struggle. In the crisis trust versus mistrust, the goal is not to eliminate mistrust, be-

---

1. Erik H. Erikson, *Childhood and Society,* 2nd rev. ed. (New York: W. W. Norton and Co., 1963) [1950]. Erikson later claims that women experience identity and intimacy in less distinct cycles and in a more interrelated way. *Identity, Youth and Crisis* (New York: W. W. Norton, 1968).

cause a healthy mistrust is needed in life. The crisis is resolved when trust predominates over mistrust and growth can occur.

Erikson awards each crisis to a particular time of life. The crisis characterizes the predominant psychodynamics of that age. At each crisis we must reorient our lives and relate to the world in new ways. This comes not just from social demands, but from physiological changes and the emotional, perceptual, and cognitive responses that these changes require. We are vulnerable at each transition because what has "worked" earlier is insufficient for the present challenge. Anxiety occurs as we leave one stage of nuclear conflict and move on to another.[2]

By working through each conflict vital strengths or virtues develop. These stem from effective negotiations of the crisis.[3] We can resolve a crisis adequately at the time but later experience a conflict from an earlier period of life. We then can revisit the conflict, but from a different perspective.

Development in Erikson follows an "epigenetic principle." All advances to the higher and later stages of development—toward independence, maturity and responsibility—carry forward and restate lower levels of development. Without the earlier development, the later is not truly better or stronger. Later stages become strong, rich, and stable by including and restating earlier levels of development.[4]

Religious life is a way of being adult and developing as a human being. It is not a series of practices or externals put on from the outside. Erikson can help to unlock the meaning of religious life as an integral way of living. Religious life offers a framework where not only the adult stages of development occur, but earlier stages are reworked and deepened. Our assumption is that the life of the vows engages the religious in a framework of iden-

---

2. Don S. Browning, *Religious Thought and Modern Psychologies* (Philadelphia: Fortress Press, 1978) 220.

3. Erik Erikson, *Insight and Responsibility* (New York: W. W. Norton and Co., 1964)111–57.

4. Browning, *Religious Thought and Modern Psychologies,* 204.

tity where earlier crises are reworked and in which adult maturation takes place.[5]

Religious life as a school of virtue?

Erikson's thought provides a new way to consider religious life
as a "school of virtue." Our treatment of virtue will differ, however, from past models of the spiritual life. In a classical understanding of the person, we asked of the person, "what is it?"
Virtues perfected the powers which we had, which in turn affected what we did (ST 1-2.q.56.1). In a contemporary understanding, virtues do not perfect powers or things inside of us, but
rather ways that we are. Contemporary thought views the person
as relational.[6] Our mode of being is to be in relationship. Virtue
perfects us "as we are," as humans, in our relating to God, self,
others, and the world around us.

Religious life is a framework which structures our relationships to God, self, others, and the world. Just as in other adult vocations, it involves face-to-face living and role expectations which
elicit mutuality, responsibility, trust, and communication. The
religious enters a matrix of relationships and roles which impact
the development of his or her person.

Religious also live in a specific religious congregation and cultural context. Both influence personal identity. Individual congregations offer a unique vision of the good person. Each culture
holds up certain qualities to be pursued and disvalues others.[7] All
these factors build the framework of religious life through which
a "way" or ideal of living, the image of a virtuous person, is clarified. Yet, the vows form a core to religious life. We will use Erikson's thought to examine how this core relates to human growth
and development.

---

5. Identity in Erikson's theory is not just an internal dynamic but involves the capacity to synthesize sexual, vocational, political, and ideological
commitments. See Browning, *Religious Thought and Modern Psychologies*,
210.

6. Merkle, *Committed by Choice*, 911ff.

7. Keenan, "Proposing Cardinal Virtues," 712–13.

The work of Donald Capps will assist us in this reflection. Capps furthers Erikson's analysis by noting that each stage of development involves a characteristic virtue-vice struggle.[8] Each person has a full range of virtue and vice capabilities. Yet, at certain times, and in specific crises, particular virtue-vice combinations characterize alternative courses of action available to them.[9]

We will engage in a thought experiment using Erikson and Capps by pairing life-cycle conflicts with particular vows. We will assume specific vows touch on the human issues which the life crises raise. Capps's work will shed light on the virtue-sin polarities involved in each crisis, and the human goodness developed by each vow.[10] This method will be used to reflect on the vows as ways of personal transformation.

We will also explore the implications of the vows for the creation of the new community of baptism and the defeat of death or ministry today. The vows will also be considered as practices of ecclesial life. Using these various means, we will relate the vows to issues of adulthood, the following of Christ, and meaning for society.

Poverty, the transformation we undergo in order to find the love we truly desire, is not only one vow, but characterizes the entire project of the vowed life. Let us turn to consider the vow of poverty in the life of a religious.

Holding on and letting go

Today people object to the idea of the vow of poverty, considering it old fashioned. A modern adult does not want to give up his or her "independence" or autonomy, they claim. Moderns assume that financial independence is key to this broader goal. Sociologist Robert Bellah notes that Americans link autonomy with

---

8. Donald Capps, *Deadly Sins and Saving Virtues* (Philadelphia: Fortress Press, 1987).

9. *Ibid.,* 25ff., 77ff.

10. The self-transcendence of religious life is not simply psychological but moral and mystical as well. Greed can be a moral block to self-transcendence in a religious whose psychological development is normal and in tact. Faith, hope, and love are infused virtues as well as human goodness. These nuances will be developed in course.

financial and social independence. Money is the key to freedom. The more money one makes, the more a person can withdraw from the influence of others.[11]

For Erikson, the struggle for autonomy begins long before we have checking accounts. He awards the psycho-social crisis of autonomy versus shame and doubt to early childhood.[12] Erikson claims this crisis emerges as we gain new physical control over our bodily processes. We learn that "holding on" and "letting go" are stances which can transfer to our dealings with people, specifically our parents. They no longer have all the power; we have a will, too. The autonomy we seek is the recognition that we have this right.

Genuine autonomy occurs when we do not allow our will to be broken, but at the same time do not always need to have our own way. While we "resolve" this crisis when we are young, most people revisit it throughout their lives.

The negative pole of the autonomy crisis is shame and doubt. Greater mobility lends to the possibility of failure. When we make bodily "mistakes," soil ourselves, spill things, fall down, we feel exposed and humiliated. We doubt ourselves and our abilities, and find the world less supportive than we had hoped.

Holding on and letting go transfer into our relationships. We learn to share not only things, but also to express our will and share power. Some modern theories view the construction of the personality as an attempt to restore equilibrium to a young self struggling with doubt in the face of this crisis.[13] Religious also share material resources in community through the vow of poverty. Holding on and letting go become dynamics of community life. The challenge of this vow, however, only begins with material things.

---

11. Robert Bellah, *Habits of Heart: Individualism and Commitment in American Life* (Berkeley: University of California Press, 1985). See also Merkle, *Committed by Choice,* 15ff.

12. As described in Capps, *Deadly Sins and Saving Virtues,* 29ff., 81ff.

13. Helen Palmer, *The Enneagram in Love and Work* (San Francisco: Harper, 1995) 7ff.

Will and anger

Internal resources are available to us as we tackle our developmental crises. The virtue-vice struggle in the autonomy versus shame and doubt crisis is between will and anger. The negative potential associated with this crisis is anger. Anger is an emotional response of agitation caused by displeasure. In this case, displeasure is focused against persons and situations that block our will.

Anger is a good emotion, but it also can be a deadly sin. Our discussion of the vices evoked in life-cycle crises will treat them as deadly sins, not as neutral emotions. The Christian community identifies a deadly sin as destructive human capacity which gives rise to other self-destructive behaviors.[14] The deadly sins are the roots of other sins.

Anger as a deadly sin is a drive toward vengeance which causes us to reject love or contacts with others who are essential for our growth. Anger is a state of personal bondage which leads to isolation.

Will is the positive quality and outcome of this crisis. Will is the determination to act on our desires, coupled with the acceptance that our freedom is limited. Will involves courage, the capacity to engage the world in spite of its capacity to inflict pain and evoke fear. Through will, we determine what desires are essential to our sense of self and our goals and what desires can be let go. We learn to exert judicious self-restraint in order to seek what we really want.

Will offsets anger, encouraging the self-restraint needed to cooperate. Will has courage, which offers an alternative way to cope with the injury to self-esteem that comes from humiliation and failure. Courage engages the world despite its hurts. It meets, greets, and defeats obstacles where anger blames and isolates.

Will and courage override the constriction or gridlock of anger, which is paralyzed by the opposing wills of others. Open to the world, will and courage engage with life. Capps shows us that

---

14. William E. May, "Sin" in *The New Dictionary of Theology* (Collegeville: The Liturgical Press, 1990) 966–7.

the crisis of autonomy versus doubt can be resolved in alternative ways, the way of will or the way of anger. We can reach for a healthy sense of self through will, having the "courage to be" in the face of obstacles, or we can escape in anger and blame, the red flags of self-doubt. How do these developmental understandings relate to religious poverty?

Religious poverty

A popular image of religious poverty is the scene from the life of St. Francis of Assisi where he takes off his robes of rank and lays them at the foot of his father. Here we see an act of autonomy. The apparent "shame" of poverty is taken on in order that a will for life beyond possessions can be expressed. In this act, Francis confirmed a deep sense of self.

Francis's action led to results. It began a journey which created a new community of friendship and service in the Church, far beyond his imagination. This step in his life with God remains one of the greatest spiritual treasures of the Church.

Today, vowed poverty is taken on by a religious as he or she turns in credit cards and signs over the title of the car. These symbolic first steps mark the beginning of a longer journey where the holding on and letting go of material things is redefined in terms of what is appropriate for one's mission, for service and building community.

Through poverty a religious enters into a countercultural practice of adult autonomy. By setting aside the legitimate pursuit of possessions in adult life, the religious seeks to free energy to find their identity in God and the values of the kingdom. They vow to let go of what cuts them off from others, from service of the needs of the Church, from building community, and from engaging in the defeat of death as it appears in their times.

By the vow of poverty the religious also promises to hold on to God.[15] "Freedom from" things is meant to be a "freedom to" love. Poverty involves the capacity not only to let go of what is unneces-

15. Johannes Metz, *Followers of Christ* (New York: Paulist Press, 1978) 47ff.

sary to this goal, but to hold onto what is important. A poor person finds his or her strength in God, and holds onto God and gospel values with all their might. Poverty is the readiness to follow Christ more than just "up to a point." Poverty accepts the "extra mile" of the Christian life, the consequences of an intense following of Jesus.[16] Ultimately, poverty is allowing God to fill one's life.

A religious who refuses to accept "business as usual" on a parish council, and works for a more inclusive policy regarding marginated members of the parish, shares an experience of "poverty" that belongs to many adult Christians. The rejection, pain, and discomfort which may come from this witness is borne so that the issue can be confronted. The "existential call" of the situation is met. Here religious share with all Christians the call to gospel poverty.

Religious life stimulates alertness to similar gospel action fed by a life stance, a habitual intention to refuse abundance in regard to material things. Religious vow poverty as a framework of Christian living within a specified congregation. Christians in other life-styles have other means: family obligations, marital bonds, civic commitments to keep alive the spirit of poverty in their lives.

By setting aside material possessions, the religious develops the capacity to set aside the possessions of good name, popularity, and position if the call of the gospel so requires. The positive outcome of the crisis of autonomy and self-doubt, will, is illustrated here. Through will, we determine what desires are essential to our sense of self and our goals, and what can be let go. A sense of self beyond legitimate possessions even of good name, popularity, and possessions is discovered as the religious seeks a deeper sense of self in gospel freedom.[17] The vow of poverty is not directed toward a

16. In the Ignatian tradition, this poverty is learned in degrees over a lifetime. The goal is continuing union with the poor Christ who emptied himself for us. See Gerald R. Grosh, S.J., "Models of Poverty," *Review for Religious* vol. 34, 1975, 550–58.

17. For women, because of cultural oppression, it is important that a healthy sense of self is first in place before this type of letting go occurs. If not, shame and its attendant anger (the result of not exerting enough will) are injested inappropriately.

stoic indifference toward material things. It is geared toward a deeper sense of self in Christ, one beyond legitimate possessions.

A religious may intentionally leave a ministry or give up a more comfortable living situation in order to begin a new work or meet a greater need. Here the framework of religious life itself enables a "letting go" and "holding on" which is distinctive to religious life. Service, needs of the Church, community, modesty in possessions become criteria which measure the holding on and letting go of a religious and color his or her relationship to material things.

Poverty is not just an attitude of the heart; it gives concrete direction to behavior. Each decision of a "due measure," evoked by the promise of the vow, expresses a love of God. Love, not the sense of renunciation for itself, engages the religious. While poverty involves setting some possessions aside, it also calls for a deep appreciation of all as gift. Nature, the arts, knowledge, friends, family are daily gifts of God, loving us and providing for our every need. It is love which is the deepest desire of the religious, the real goal of the will. While day-to-day living can obscure awareness of the love which grounds poverty, the religious returns to these deeper springs of meaning for frequent renewal.

The "riches" that come from this letting go are the life of Christ itself, a deposit of goodness from which others can draw in friendship, family love, ministry relationships, and the special communion of congregational life. Letting go and holding on to these more important things is the movement beyond isolation, the longing of the human heart. A second life crisis, however, also engages the religious and their promise of poverty.

Integrity versus despair

I remember a recent conversation with one of the senior members of my own community in which she recounted the diminishment and subsequent death of a close friend in community. She remarked, "She experienced real poverty those last months. All we say about giving up this or that is not poverty. She tasted poverty with faith in the deepest way."

The psycho-social crisis that comes at the end of life is evoked by the struggle with death. Death is the greatest "letting go" that any human being must face.[18] Erikson names this last crisis of life, integrity versus despair. This crisis is another key to unlock the meaning of the transformation of desires which poverty evokes.

The crisis of integrity and despair is a response to the loss and the inevitability of death which are characteristic of our later years. Lost opportunities, disappointments with others, the diminishments of old age, the curtailment of our autonomy, necessary dependencies, drying up of opportunities, and sickness are real. Poverty in old age is not an option, it is a way of life.[19]

Integrity is the human capacity for order and meaning in the midst of this diminishment. Integrity is the ability to be whole and centered in the face of decline. This can occur because we know our place in a larger sense of meaning. Integrity keeps us connected to people who have become important to us. It gives us perspective on our past, not as one of lost opportunities but as one which has made some contribution to others. Integrity is the link to a meaning system which takes our contribution and gives it a place in values which outlast our lifetime.

Integrity involves the acceptance of our one and only life course and the people who have become significant in it. We often think of integrity as a quality of personal character. But here it means a sensitivity to the order in life which is there for the seeing, if we want to see it. Erikson holds that our latter years call us to transcend the self we have developed through our lives and identify with the heart of life which holds everything together. In terms of religious faith, integrity is a new call to experience life as "no more I, but Christ in me."

Despair is the negative pole of this crisis, the looking back with regret on life. The regret of despair is different from the mourning which accompanies healthy loss. Regret arises from a contemptuous displeasure with others and with institutions, which ultimately is a projection of one's contempt for oneself.

There is much in old age which merits displeasure, but normal struggle with diminishments is different from despair. Despair is

18. Ernest Becker, *The Denial of Death* (New York: Free Press, 1973). Becker argues that the denial of death is a mainspring of human activity.

19. Capps, *Deadly Sins and Saving Virtues*, 63ff., 110ff.

in evidence when there are no constructive currents in one's life to offset one's disgust and displeasure. Efforts to cooperate, to care for others, to have positive thoughts, to express faith in the future are lacking. One is left with one's despair.

Some people defend against the real losses of old age through nostalgia or mythologizing their lives. The better defense is to see life in relation to the ongoing succession of those who have gone before us and those who will come after. This requires the letting go of resentments and the holding on to the deeper linkages which give life meaning.

Previous ability to let go and hold on is brought to this later crisis. Yet earlier learnings will be restructured and reframed before the new challenges of aging. It will not be the same letting go and holding on of another decade, but one which only the conditions of the later years can evoke. The crisis of integrity versus despair forms the new matrix in which gospel poverty continues to lead to vision and community, by-products of true poverty. The transformation of our desires in this crisis is expressed in a new capacity for wisdom and its ability to offset melancholy.

Wisdom and melancholy

Wisdom and melancholy battle to consume our energy during the last stage of our lives. Melancholy is more than sadness; it involves hate and ill will.[20] In contrast to mourning and the acceptance of loss to which it leads, melancholics, filled with resentment, want to avenge the loss. Most losses cannot be avenged, so this drive leads to a deep sense of frustration. Melancholy drives us to internalize our rage and direct it toward other people. In the grips of melancholy we repudiate people, systems of meaning, and pursuits or values which gave meaning to our earlier investments.

Wisdom offsets this melancholic pull. As "detached concern," wisdom is knowledge that comes from responsible renunciation. Wise people maintain their interest in the problems of everyday life. The older person enters into their solutions, however, less

---

20. For another description of melancholy, see Merkle, *Committed by Choice*, 68ff.

from self-interest and more from a viewpoint which views problems in their entirety, from the whole of life which one sees when death is approaching. It is not that older people have answers, but they have perspective which comes from having turned against disgust and despair and hopelessness as the answer to life's dilemmas. As they conduct themselves everyday, they witness to others that one can experience loss and still find meaning in life.

Wisdom gives a vigor of mind in the face of melancholy's twisted view of life which denounces and repudiates. Wisdom links one to the values that are transgenerational and worth the effort, even though in one lifetime, one can only taste their value, never consuming them in their entirety. In this sense, wisdom is the solace that mourning seeks. Wisdom responds to loss, the sense that one did not do everything, nor become everything. However, wisdom responds to loss with different conclusions than the melancholic spirit.

In the face of loss and diminishment, wisdom holds on to the truth that one's life has an essential wholeness, even though it hasn't been perfect. To the next generation, the person of wisdom communicates that life can be held together in spite of losses. While the melancholic are at odds with themselves, the wise witness to the essence of the spirit of poverty, that there is more to life than anything can take away (Rom 8:18).

Older religious witness in new ways to the transformation of desires which the vow of poverty evokes. They approach retirement, not with resentment, but linked to the same issues and concerns which have given meaning to their lives. Religious do not retire from religious life. Retirement in religious life is countercultural. It is measured, according to physical ability, by the support of service, attention to needs of the Church through prayer and action, community, modesty in possessions, and patience in need. All criteria have been active ingredients for living throughout religious life.

More importantly, the later years afford religious a chance to "hold on" to God and the goodness of life in the new spiritual journey of their mature years. Religious should be able to stop and smell the roses, witnessing to a peace beyond frantic activity and a self-worth beyond compulsive working. The shift of energies which the call to spiritual integration invites is a new expression of living the vow.

The practice of poverty in religious life finds an analogy in these two crises in Erikson's developmental schema. One part of the life of a religious is caught up with new expressions of the holding on and letting go of autonomy versus shame and doubt. While this crisis needs to be sufficiently resolved to have the freedom to make vows, its issues remain part of the path the religious embraces.

Religious struggle with integrity versus despair, facing the inevitable loss of life itself. Erikson's thought unlocks that decisions for will over anger and for integrity over resentment and rancor will continue to express the first promise to give all to God and count on God for everything. This promise, by the end of life, has made its way into subsequent levels of the self. The framework of community, service, the church and modesty in possessions have provided the limits whereby religious have become themselves by letting go of the possibility of becoming everything. Through poverty religious have focused their identity in Christ, who in becoming poor became rich in all that matters.

The goal of all "ways" of adult Christian living are the same, to belong to Christ. But for religious, the self-transcendence evoked by poverty leads them beyond the isolation of self-sufficiency, to find the love they have always desired. They, in this process, can be a sign of and witness to the "more" of life, which is more valuable than possessions.

Chapter Seventeen

New Times for Poverty

Poverty and the defeat of death

These are new times for the practice of vowed poverty. Today, anger instead of will reigns in a society obsessed with violence. Rancor and resentment for what one does not have holds sway in the culture. There is a blindness to the wisdom that life, the earth, and future generations are precious. People debate whether they can kill each other by euthanasia, while starvation riddles Africa and Asia.

Drug dealers in South America terrorize countries while parents in Vietnam sell their children into sexual slavery for food. Eastern Europe witnesses a savagery whose religious roots go back centuries.[1] First world countries wallow in secularism, while consumerism stifles the soul of freedom for which their forbearers died. Our practice of "freedom of choice" makes democracy impossible in many lands because our overconsumption robs them of economic opportunity. What does all this say to those with vowed poverty? What does it mean for the defeat of death in our times?

As religious seek to live poverty in new times, they witness to a gospel poverty that is embraced by all Christian vocations in different ways. At its core, poverty involves the search for true au-

---

1. Paul Mojzes, *Yugoslavian Inferno: Ethnoreligious Warfare in the Balkans* (New York: Continuum, 1994).

tonomy and integrity. To vow poverty is to set out on the spiritual journey of self mastery and longing in a unique way.[2]

The vow of poverty requires the human faith of self-mastery and longing. Yet, self-mastery and longing also express a religious faith which seeks to dwell in and manifest Jesus' own faith and spirit. Poverty is not just the stoic practice of individuals. Society needs faith also. Poverty is part of the faith needed by the whole society in the next millennium. A new spirit of poverty calls society to develop its potentials for self-mastery and longing.

The self-mastery of autonomy is needed in a society that has lost track of values beyond utilitarianism, the tendency to see the right as what works for personal wants. Self-mastery is the capacity to set goals beyond immediate satisfactions. Religious congregations also require self-mastery to develop the capacity to let go and hold onto what is needed to carry out a mission beyond themselves.

The beatitude of those who mourn, rather than resent, is the spirit of longing. The "longing" of integrity gives vision for countercultural decisions in a society of materialism and empty views of progress. The longing for justice comes from mourning and shares in the longing of the poor.

Through their vow of poverty religious partner with those who mourn and offer them more than sympathy. They draw from the responsible renunciation of wisdom, a new wisdom to create in the face of defeats and setbacks. They transform the energy they would have devoted to being keepers of things, to being keepers of hope for those without hope.

I think of a recent visit to my own community in South Africa. In the middle of a desolate township, our sisters had a center to teach sewing so women and men could make their own clothes cheaply but attractively. As I looked around I saw nothing but misery, dirt, and poverty. The center was the only nice thing as far as the eye could see. The hope in the people's eyes as they modeled their outfits explained to me in a new way what the vow of poverty was all about.

2. Capps, *Deadly Sins and Saving Virtues*, 125, 133.

Through the shared life of the congregation and the letting go of those sisters, they were able to hold on to something much more important, to defeat death in that township in a small way. The lunch we shared with the people and their own spirit of community was a richness I will never forget. The sisters knew that social analysis and structural change were needed in South Africa, and they, too, participated in standing with the poor at this level. Yet they were able to speak many languages of hope through their insertion in the daily needs of this township.

The new community of baptism

The "longing" which wisdom effects is a longing for a better world. Defeats and setbacks do not bring ultimate death for those who have learned responsible renunciation through wisdom. They know a greater network of meaning which supports human dignity, even when the values of society do not. This vision is the soul which religious congregations contribute to the human search for a better world.

The new community of baptism is the community which would not be, according to the laws of humankind. It is the community which transcends race, gender, economic level, and ideological barriers. Religious testify that such a community is possible, for it is possible among them.

We know that the presence of Christ in the Eucharist is evidenced in the *gathering* of the community, as well as in the sacred elements. So, too, a religious congregation witnesses to the action of the Spirit gathering them. They are diverse peoples, races, and ethnic backgrounds, yet united. The witness of community is a witness for the world.

A spirit of poverty in a congregation enables it to collaborate. The ability to "long" for a better world links the religious congregation to all people of good will. They share together the experience of saying "no" to the world as it is. Their "no," however, implies a "yes" to something more.[3] The new community of bap-

---

3. Schillebeeckx, *Church*, 6.

tism is a community of "desire," a desire to put love where it is not in the world, and to share in the redemptive work of Jesus.

A spirit of poverty builds community because the vow to let go and hold on, to overcome anger with will and courage, is a vow to depend on the grace of God. Such dependence transforms all ethical pursuits. Unlike the utilitarian mentality of the society, faith in God gives rise to mercy and reconciliation instead of vengeance and retribution.

The vow of poverty requires a freedom beyond that of the worldview of progress: my freedom, if need be, at the expense of yours. The freedom which is nurtured by the vow of poverty is one that retains a moral capacity to death. It is a freedom which can build community because it places its hope in something more than the moral capacities of others. It finds its hope in God who grounds the worth of all, even when we fail.

Because it relies on faith, poverty feeds memory, memory of those who suffer. It disengages energy which has been "nailed to" addictions to substances, people, power, and work. It supports a thinking process which goes beyond the logic of the society, which explains away all suffering. The poor in spirit face the irrationality of suffering through faith in God who ultimately has overcome suffering. Through faith, poverty brings to every concrete project an energy for commitment which outlasts rationality.[4] Poverty is the stuff of "transcendent data" which forms community in the face of fragmentation.

New time for poverty in our lives

Individuals and groups who reflect on the meaning of poverty today will discern new issues it raises in their lives. Individual charisms and contexts contribute to the unique circumstances for new expressions of poverty. Only a faith community can define these situations for themselves. However, I would like to suggest some general issues and questions which arise from our discussion of poverty thus far. Perhaps they will stimulate further discussion.

---

4. *Ibid.*, 28ff.

Conservation of energy

There is fear among some religious that energy is being placed into ministries which are no longer effective. If the essence of poverty is letting go and holding on to what is truly valuable, what meaning does this have for ministry today?

Congregations desire new life for their mission, yet are not sure how to create it with diminishing numbers and energies. Twin decisions to embrace a variety of ministries and let go of institutions have led some to question whether they are dissipating congregational energies, resulting in little ministerial impact. What is the relevance of communal sharing on our style of ministry? Are we doing anything together which we could not do alone? Are the old methods of common effort the only methods?

It is clear that poverty affects ministry when religious of various congregations combine their efforts to keep open an inner city school. But how do we find this unity of effort in other professional ministries? For instance, the trained psychologist today is involved in the hurts and abuses of our society in an unparalleled way. Yet, religious in these ministries often minister in isolated and unconnected ways to each other. What type of creative results would come if religious congregations pooled these efforts in an area, diocese, or religious congregation? What models could congregations share who have already tried this?

Inculturation

Inculturation of the faith is a key need in the wider Church today. This is especially true of the inculturation of religious life in a new society. Ethnic and racial diversity in the Church and in congregations has to make its impact. Yet inculturation also implies an openness to the new culture of post World War II generations. What needs to be let go of and held onto to make this happen?

Beyond conservatism and liberalism

There are questions about the direction of the inculturation of the vowed life. In some circles there is a call to renewal with a focus on ascetical discipline, common life, and traditional values.

This renewal calls for a withdrawal from the public sphere and a focus on internal transformation. Some would call this a conservative movement.

A liberal approach directs religious communities to maintain a vision of social justice, but keep their religious witness to individual piety and general humanism. The aim is to maintain a type of religious pluralism in communities.

Both trends abandon a balance characteristic of the vow of poverty. Both seek to de-institutionalize religious life: the liberals to afford more freedom, the conservatives to focus merely on transformation of life. Either way, religious life is de-publicized and takes a step toward irrelevance.

The conservative movement, even if it maintains regularized believing communities, removes religious witness from the public sphere, resulting in a loss of critical and prophetic power. The liberal suggestion loses a sense of transcendence. Christian witness even in politics is not only to do differently but to live differently, to live dependent on grace.[5]

Conservative religious life loses its relevance, while liberal religious life loses its transcendence when they translate poverty of spirit simply to conform to ideological preferences which have their basis in many factors other than the gospel.

Aloysius Pieris, the Asian liberation theologian, comments regarding voluntary poverty, "the few who renounce their possessions are not 'founded and rooted in Christ Jesus' if the many who have no possessions to renounce are not the beneficiaries of that renunciation."[6] Somehow the vow of poverty is to have relevance for the society.

Instead of the search of poverty, for real autonomy and integrity, both conservatives and liberals simply copy their political and philosophical counterparts in the broader society. Rather than inculturate the gospel, they spiritualize the culture that cannot save. Neither movement will adequately inculturate the charism

5. Johann Baptist Metz, *The Emergent Church*, 60.

6. Aloysius Pieris, S.J., *An Asian Theology of Liberation* (New York: Maryknoll, 1988) 21.

of religious life in the next millennium. Yet it is very difficult to step back from these movements. Each religious and congregation needs to ask, in what way am I caught in these trends?

Poverty and ecclesial renewal

What then is distinctive to religious poverty? What must congregations hold on to as they seek to inculturate the gospel and religious life in the next millennium? Many believers and non-believers will let go of material things and make sacrifices for a better world in the coming years. Religious, however, share with the Church a particular tradition in the manner in which they do this. They belong to a community of memory which is transgenerational within a believing tradition. Their poverty has roots in an identity which is beyond that of a single generation and is rooted in its founding memories and normative traditions.

Religious are bonded by common intentions, a bond stronger than group membership. They are individuals who share similar intentions about their lives and their relationships with others.[7] Intentions to live simply, to seek God above all things, to give themselves to the service of the Church and the poor bind them together and make their community distinctive. They share not only common activities but a worldview and a spiritual experience of common meaning.

The gospel promise of the rewards of poverty is a deep experience of Church. The poverty of religious is sustained by the wider Church as it draws its meaning from the life and death of Jesus Christ. The symbols and sacraments of the Church nurture and reinterpret the ongoing decision of religious to vow poverty as a means to live the gospel. The religious community commits itself to share in the call of the Church to follow Christ, not just as poor, but who is in the poor.

The poverty of religious is unique also because it is for the Church. Religious are called to keep alive in the Church its longing for the "more" in its own life. They live with the tensions of the Church and grow with the Church through its own contra-

---

7. Peter Hodgson, *Revisioning the Church* (Philadelphia: Fortress Press, 1988) 66.

dictions. In their persons religious bear the tensions between the structure and the people in the Church, the future and the present, the male and female polarities, its holiness and its facticity, its present institutionalization and its global transformation, its singularity and its pluralism, its universalism and its racism, its tradition and its renewal.

Religious orders are ecclesial in their ability to adopt long-term strategies and commitments toward making the effect of their poverty felt in the Church and by the poor of this world. They are together for life, supported by the Church to give their lives stability. But this special way of being church is for a purpose.

Many will commit themselves to service to the world's poor and to the construction of new systems of care to meet the needs of migration, malnutrition, over-population, disease, illiteracy, and displacement from trauma and violence which plague our world today. But religious congregations, because they are transgenerational, have the ability to make long-term commitments to these needs and to carry them out. They can strategize for the long haul. This may mean letting go of past ways of doing things and holding on to each other in new forms of collaboration. Religious can do this. The question remains, will they? Or as the rich young man, will they walk away sad because they have many things?

Political-mystical signs

The vow of poverty is a means to enter into the life of Christ within each religious, and which unites the community. At the level of anthropological faith, poverty touches the struggle between autonomy versus shame and doubt and integrity versus despair. It develops a spirit of self-mastery and longing.[8]

At the level of religious faith, the effect of the vow of poverty follows the structure of any following of Christ. It is mystical and political.[9] The personal and religious union with Christ never takes place simply in our consciousness. Union with Jesus is more

---

8. Capps, *Deadly Sins and Saving Virtues*, 123.
9. Metz, *Followers of Christ*, 42.

than a new consciousness. Rather, union takes place in a particular situation, ministry, community, family, friendship, health issue, or civic work. Reality never allows one to stand apart and practice poverty in thought alone. Rather, it plunges us into real life and seldom spares us its sufferings and contradictions.

Following Christ through poverty is more than a path toward a good ethical life, or a way of personal perfection. Rather, it is taking Jesus' way to God. We need to constantly look at Jesus to know how to do this, and realize that in this following we walk in the same confusion, contradictions, misunderstandings which mark his life.

To think of poverty as achieving a measure of moderate living, a norm of simplicity of life, the "right" amount of personal finances, or the proper decision whether or not to buy new furniture, misses the point. It is not that these may not be real manifestations of poverty. Poverty is material simplicity for sure, yet more.

Jesus outwitted death itself with a path of poverty and learned freedom to love giving what he had. This mystical poverty—whoever seeks to gain his life will lose it, but whoever loses his life will preserve it—impels us to continue to reinvest in real situations that can disappoint and disillusion. These are the real risks of life, not just going around with fewer dollars in our pocket. It leads to continued decisions to try again, never to give up on reconciliation, always to seek another way to connect. Poverty results in solidarity with "losers" according to the worldview of progress, and leads to the desire to make their need our own.

Gratitude and awareness of the holy

The radical nature of poverty dedicates us to a way, but not a way that is a self-initiated goal. It is a way that shows itself to those who seek it. How do we know we are on this way? Two characteristics of this search are a sense of gratitude and a growing awareness of the holy.

The search of religious life rarely provides a measuring stick of success. The experience is more that one is given enough light and hope for the next step. But what are signs that poverty influences the journey?

Grace or gratitude is a mark of one who seeks poverty. We are afraid of grace. We find that we reject kindness and the generosity of others, even though we claim we want it. We often do so out of a sense of inadequacy. Grace is the ability to accept what we cannot produce, the love of others and God. It is the ability to welcome the goodness of others, and to depend on them, even though they can disappoint us.

Gratitude is the mystical-political stance which is an alternative to resentment, resentment of others, of missed opportunities, of the world's imperfection. In poverty we learn to face life when it is full of pain and suffering as well as love. We learn to trust in God before the inherent contradictions of the human spirit and societal life. We are grateful for what we have.

We learn to be open to the goodwill of others, even though we have been disappointed. We overcome a sense of shame and doubt, and do not hide it through excessive material needs. We are grateful for the persons we are and the circumstances we have been given, instead of focusing on what might have been. In place of insisting on the finality of our own self-rejection, we discover our own blessed history, even in those things which have seemed as "loss."

Awareness of the holy is the discovery of what is really sacred in our lives. We learn that various diminishments do not rob us of what is in itself untouchable, God's life and wisdom and our invitation to live in it. Instead of despair, we learn we can depend on God. We learn to surrender, little by little, to the benevolent heart at the core of our lives, which is stronger than our inflated sense of self-possession and worth. We learn of our need of this love, which we cannot create. We gradually find we can depend on it in everything.

We begin to see the mystery in the ordinary, and when we cannot see, we wait for this vision in patience. Because of what we have suffered and lost and endured, we can live in the tension between what ought to be and what is, with our eyes open and with hope. For our hope is no longer just for ourselves but for life itself and all whom we meet. In our poverty, we have received what we thought we had lost, all. For all comes back to us and we learn to find God in all things.

This awareness of the holy is the essence of the witness of a religious in a secular society. For it is also an awareness of the dignity of each person, the true worth of creation, and the common future toward which the earth and its inhabitants must move. This awareness is born not of consciousness but of struggle. For as the masters of eastern religion have told us for centuries, mammon and God are incompatible. It is only those willing to enter into the baptism of renunciation who can live the new future to which God calls.

Poverty is not a test but a stance which allows us to see and act with the movement of the Kingdom. As we approach the next millennium, rethinking this charism of religious commitment, we are invited to drink again from its vitality and offer its newness to a world hardened by materialism and living the heartache of systemic poverty. Among other reasons, we choose voluntary poverty so that those for whom poverty is not chosen will have new life.

Chapter Eighteen

Obedience: An Affair of the Heart

In the past, obedience was considered as giving up one's will. It seems unlikely in modern times that anyone is seriously tempted to turn his or her will over to another. If an entrant came to a religious community with such an attitude today, most formation programs would suggest therapy.

The modern focus of obedience is not loss of freedom or turning one's will over to another, even though obedience practically involves a type of surrender of free choice. The question of obedience is what to do with freedom. What do I do with the freedom I have? How do I direct it? This is the issue for the modern person as he or she stands with the gospel in one hand and potentials and options in the other.[1] One is free. The question of obedience is how to use that freedom to love.

At a fundamental level, obedience is practical and necessary in the framework of religious life. It is at the heart of the affective bonding of a community. In human faith, people freely decide to join their wills to be and do something they cannot do alone. This free decision creates a sense of belonging and sharing in a common purpose beyond oneself.

Obedience sustains life-giving relationships which are particular to religious life. At the level of religious faith, religious bond their life with God's life through obedience, seeking God's will and Kingdom through their community and the Church. In this sense, obedience is fundamentally a surrender. The religious faith

1. Merkle, *Committed by Choice*, 91–2.

of obedience, however, expresses itself through the concrete networks created by human faith.

Most religious have no problem with God; it is all those other people in the community who test the promise of obedience. We are like Lucy in the Peanuts comic strip, who loves humanity but protests, "It's people I hate!" The concreteness of obedience as a life option opens the religious to the possibility of much fulfillment, along with attendant disappointment.

Obedience is the bonding of one's life to God's through the common seeking of the gospel done in the context of one's congregation. Obedience is not only a commitment to live within the framework of religious community, but a promise to keep working at it. Through obedience one inserts oneself into the life and mission of the congregation and the Church. It is a promise to stand with real people in imperfect situations.

The essence of obedience is sharing in the heart of Jesus who sought, above all else, to do the will of him who he called Father. Obedience is a matter of the heart because Jesus' decision to seek the will of the Father was not an intellectual pursuit. It was a heartfelt decision of love that integrated his entire life.

Religious obedience is one part of the framework of religious commitment, inseparable from poverty and celibate chastity. The three are one pursuit, union in love with God in a total way. Obedience takes on special meaning today as we reflect on the challenge of bonding with anyone or anything in a world characterized by individualism, violence, and mistrust.

The vow of obedience is an expression of religious faith. Yet it involves the growing trust, deeper commitment, and greater sensitivity to the life and the mission of the congregation which embody human faith. Because it is so divine and human at the same time, obedience cannot be separated from the disruption of this process. When one side fails, or situations of misunderstanding occur, there is a strain on the obedience relationship.

Disaffection

It is difficult to speak of obedience today without addressing disaffection. Some religious would describe their struggle in religious life not as one of obedience but of ongoing alienation from their communities or the institutional Church.

Since a religious congregation and the Church are comprised of people and structures, they both can support religious in their search for God's will, and at other times grandly let them down.[2] Disaffection is a disruption of the bonding which obedience is meant to foster.

Obedience and disaffection are both affairs of the heart. In one, the heart is in tune with the community. In the other, the bond with the group is strained or even broken. The tension between obedience and disaffection is deeply felt in religious life at various times.

As a form of alienation, disaffection has no significance in itself, rather it draws its meaning from its opposite. We are not alienated or disaffected from someone or something about which we do not care. Rather, disaffection is a felt separation from something which we see as essential or important to our wholeness or completion.[3]

When religious are disaffected from the Church or from their congregations, they feel cut off from a life force which is important to them. The feeling is one of anger or being "out of it."

We assume disaffection is not a state to embrace. Our language betrays that we believe people are better off if they can work through their disaffection. We say, "Oh, I'm glad she's worked that through," or "he seems to have moved beyond that."

Moving beyond feelings of isolation, separation, frustration, and powerlessness, classic images of disaffection, is a move toward a healthier stance in life. It is healthier because disaffection is the absence of something good. It is the disruption of a life-giving relationship.

Religious can be the cause of their own disaffection. They can fail in their commitments or give up "working at" their commu-

---

2. David J. Hassel, *Healing the Ache of Alienation: Praying Through and Beyond Bitterness* (New York: Paulist Press, 1990) chapter 2.

3. J. W. Fowler, "Alienation as a Human Experience," *From Alienation to At-One-Ness*, ed. F. Eigo (Philadelphia: Villanova Press, 1977) 2.

nal and ministerial relationships. However, we also see today the "faithful" person in a state of disaffection. Like Jesus as he wept over Jerusalem, religious struggle with triumphalistic, legalistic, and violent aspects of their church and communities.

"How often would I have gathered your children together as a hen gathers her brood under her wings, and you would not!" are feelings echoed in the experience of these religious. The words "how often," according to biblical commentators, suggest repeated efforts for reform made by Jesus in his preaching in the synagogues earlier in his Judean ministry.

Religious struggle with the same desperation we find in Jesus' words as they renew the Church and their communities. Their struggle is a fruit of their obedience. Yet disaffection, a disruption of the very bond which obedience is meant to foster, is a shadow experience of this effort. While obedience is a historical charism of religious life, it takes on new meaning as we confront the struggles of community living today.

Did not our hearts burn within us?

The disciples on the road to Emmaus reflect the struggle of obedience in the face of disaffection. Here we have two disciples, walking away from Jerusalem, talking to each other. Jesus himself draws near and walks with them. Yet Luke tells us, "Their eyes were kept from recognizing him" (Luke 24:16). This often is the experience of disaffection; we cannot see Jesus who is with us.

When Jesus asked them what they were talking about, "They stood still, looking sad." The reader can almost taste their sense of isolation, frustration, and powerlessness, experiences of disaffection. Jesus reminds them, and the disaffected of the early Christian community, "Was it not necessary that the Christ should suffer these things and enter into his glory?" (Luke 24:26)

The disciples were walking away from Jerusalem, from community. But after Jesus stays with them and breaks bread with them, their link with Jesus is renewed. "Did not our hearts burn within us?" Not only did the disciples experience renewed bonding with Jesus but they returned to their community. They "rose that same hour and returned to Jerusalem" (Luke 24:33). Later, they were missioned as members of that community.

The disciples typify the change from a disaffected state in the life of obedience. There is a movement from a sense of powerlessness and isolation to a sense of enablement and community. A feeling of enablement and community can exist even though the objective situation may remain unchanged at some levels, as it did for the disciples. The Jews were still hostile. Jesus was dead in a physical sense and no one knew the Church would survive. Yet it was undeniable that life was significantly different for these disciples before and after this event. They had undergone a healing.

The ongoing graces of enablement and community continue to mark the road from disaffection. Our foundress remarked that she was like a blind woman in search of God's will, always knowing she would have the grace and vision to take just the next step. This walk of faith, marked by moments in which our hearts burn within us, is the path of religious obedience today. Let us continue to inquire into the contours of this search.

Beyond the renunciation of the will

The theology of obedience has often been focused on response to someone who holds authority in a community or as a renunciation of one's own will and judgment.[4] Historically, obedience in this form was not a characteristic of religious life in its early period. Early monks obeyed as one would obey a mentor in order to learn a new form of life. Nowhere do we see a person understood as an intermediary between God and the religious.

Because obedience is an evangelical attitude, it has always been part of the tradition of religious life. St. Francis of Assisi linked obedience and mission, as friars were sent to various places to share in the Church's mission. St. Ignatius saw obedience as central to the order and charity of a community, an inevitable requirement of living together and being in mission together.[5]

4. John Lozano, *Life as a Parable* (New York: Paulist Press, 1986) 156.
5. John Lozano, *Discipleship: Toward an Understanding of Religious Life* (Chicago: Claret Center for Resources in Spirituality, 1980) 223ff.

The apostolic orders emphasized obedience as integral to the communion needed for witness within a community. It involved apostolic availability to carry out its mission, and collaboration with formal obedience structures in the Church in order to share in its service of evangelization. While we see various ways in which obedience has been woven into the framework of religious life, no one of them exhausts the gospel counsel.

The obedience of a religious is centered in Jesus' obedience to his Father, and in the obedience required of a disciple. Jesus' life is summed up in one line in the Our Father: "Your will be done on earth as it is in heaven" (Matt 6:10). Jesus' mission is not a project, a commitment to a particular ideology or way of self-perfection. It is to accomplish the will of his Father.

The obedience a religious seeks to emulate is not allegiance to a way of life or a philosophy of life. It is more than a commitment to a rule of perfection which can be accomplished apart from an ongoing relationship with Christ. Rather, the obedience of a religious is centered in a relationship. Obedience is both a bond with Jesus and a way to Jesus.

Why is obedience both a way and a bond? Christian faith is a response to the historical revelation of the person of Jesus, not merely to a philosophy of life. Religious faith turns to Jesus as the way to God. We look to Jesus' way of living to find God's will, in order to do it. We do not look to a preconceived framework or philosophy of living that does not change. Instead, we live in a relationship where in following Jesus we learn his ways and the next steps for our own lives.

The way of Jesus to God

Jesus' commitment to the will of the one whom he called Father had certain characteristics. He had concern for those outside the margins of social acceptance. Jesus' mission involved forgiveness and compassion, table-fellowship with those whom Jewish society thought were sinners and traitors. He proclaimed the Kingdom as both present and future, and claimed the Kingdom was made real through his own activity as healer, exorcist, and preacher. Jesus characterized his mission by demanding faith of those who wished to receive this Kingdom.

Jesus attended to the Law, yet went beyond it. Elizabeth Johnson reflects, "The parables show that the reign of God is going to be surprising; it is not going to be business as usual."[6] Jesus' own obedience was faithful to the law, yet turned expected ways of doing things upside down. The first were last, and the sabbath was set aside if someone needed healing. Jesus' own commitment to the Father overflowed in the demand for decisive action on the part of his disciples. They were called to decisions regarding his personal call to discipleship. They were asked pointedly, "Are you too going to go away?"

Jesus learned obedience from what he suffered (Heb 5:8). The opposition Jesus encountered in being faithful to God actually bound him closer to God. Foundresses and founders of religious congregations advise their followers to love the cross, not in itself, but because it leads to God. The wisdom of such advice lies in Jesus' own life.

Jesus' obedience was centered in prayer, a habit of living union with God. Jesus was known to be a joyful person; he emptied himself, yet was not depleted as a person. In the temptations in the desert we see Jesus encountering evil, yet faithful to the God whom he knew in the Old Testament. Even his suffering was not an occasion to be separated ultimately from him whom he called Father. Jesus' obedience was total, to the point of death. Yet his bond with God, fostered through obedience, outlasted death. The bond with God that the vow of obedience is meant to foster is one which follows this same life cycle of Jesus' life, death, and resurrection.

All Christians obey and are called to model themselves after the obedience of Jesus. By the vow of obedience, religious seek God through Jesus in their religious community and through its way of life. They vow to continue to deepen a relationship with Jesus, not just begin one. They vow through this relationship to seek God's will, not only in the essential and existential calls of

---

6. Elizabeth Johnson, *Consider Jesus* (New York: Crossroad, 1990) 53.

the Christian life, but also in the mission, communal life, and direction of their congregation.

Religious vow to obey through the framework of religious life, living the characteristics of Jesus' own commitment: concern for the marginated, compassion, and reconciliation, concrete works of service as manifestations of the Kingdom. They promise to live not just the letter of the law, but to seek its Spirit, receptive to new revelation, available for mission.

They commit themselves to persevere in difficulties, placing their confidence in God. The joy fostered through personal and communal union with God and service to the people of God grounds their discernment. Religious live obedience within the Church, as the community of those who follow Jesus as the way.

The Church sees the vow of obedience as all these things. Specifically by vow the religious promises to submit to superiors when they are acting in the community according to their authoritative role as specified in the constitutions (Canon 601). They promise to obediently participate in the mission and the communal life and direction of their congregation. Religious live out the gospel counsel to obey within the general framework of religious life as understood by the Church.

This framework of obedience is further specified at the level of congregation. St. Augustine remarked that if you wanted to discover the character of any people, you had only to observe what they love (*City of God* XIX.14). Obedient participation in the mission and the life of a congregation takes on the unique characteristic of the loves of one's group.

A member brings his or her dreams to a congregation and through obedience merges those dreams with that of the whole congregation. This mutual bonding is of the essence of obedience. Obedience in this sense is a process of affective bonding where the members grow in trust of the congregation and the congregation incorporates the member.[7] Let us explore some of the dynamics of this process.

7. For a treatment of obedience as affective bonding, see Judith A. Merkle, "Gathering the Fragments: New Times for Obedience," *Review for Religious* 55 (May–June 1996) 264–82.

Chapter Nineteen

Obedience: A Path of Becoming

In a weekly community meeting, a new member comments, "I guess obedience doesn't mean much anymore." Another sister initially agrees. She recalls years when assignments arrived in little brown envelopes. She knows those days are past. However, she thinks again, "Why then do we sit at these weekly discussions?" Obedience has changed. Yet has it? Is it not still a path of becoming in religious life?

Because of changing structures, the obedience of a religious can appear to be no more and no less than that of the Christian life in general. There is truth to this. Obedience touches on areas of personal growth that all Christian vocations elicit in one way or another. Yet, religious life is a framework of living where vowed obedience sets the religious on a unique path of becoming.

Trust versus mistrust

A young woman or man considering a call to religious life may object to the idea of obedience. They might claim they could never turn their life over to another! This popular misperception of obedience has a grain of truth. The path of obedience plunges one into the human dynamism of trust and mistrust in a new way. Over the course of a lifetime, obedience involves a trust-mistrust relationship with one's community, church, and wider relationships which are integrally connected to relationship with God.

Eric Erikson marks the conflict between trust and mistrust as the first crisis in the life cycle. It occurs in infancy. The infant who is dependent upon others for life's basic needs has to test whether caregivers are reliable or not. Through interaction with them, the infant forms his or her first notion of life. The infant learns whether life is dependable or filled with betrayal and abandonment, trying to defeat the infant in meeting basic needs.[1] The ideal resolution of the trust-mistrust conflict is a balance between the two. If caregivers are reasonably reliable, or "good enough," the infant will learn trust.

A person who enters religious life usually has resolved the trust-mistrust conflict in a fundamental way. People will differ as to how well they settled it. They will bring various needs for security to community, dependent upon its resolution. Someone whose trust has been betrayed repeatedly may bring higher expectations to community, or greater needs for consistency of life and response from others.

Since religious life is a new birth in one's life history, it stimulates a revisiting of the basic conflict of trust-mistrust. An entrant measures the trustworthiness of the congregation. Members test the dependability of each other and the group along the way, especially in periods of crisis. Disaffection reflects a rupture in a basic trust-mistrust relationship with one's congregation or the Church.

Obedience, as a faithful adherence to God's word and to one's inner truth and vocation, is mediated through this fundamental conflict. It also provides direction in its solution. Was not the obedience of Jesus essentially a basic trust in Abba, his Father, that elicited faithful action? Was it not the trust of the disciples in the conflict over the Eucharist that deepened their following of Jesus?

In response to Jesus' question to them, "Do you also wish to go away?" we hear in the gospel of John an answer of trust. "Lord, to whom shall we go? You have the words of eternal life: and we have believed and have come to know that you are the Holy One of God" (John 6:69). In the life of the religious, this paradigm of trust occurs many times.

---

1. Capps, *Deadly Sins and Saving Virtues*, 25ff.

Gluttony versus hope

The conflict of trust-mistrust elicits inner strengths of character. Trust-mistrust evokes the negative pole of gluttony, which can stagnate growth. It elicits as well a healing potential, hope. Hope is ultimately "saving," and leads to wholeness. Obedience plunges a religious into both possibilities.[2]

The goal of the trust-mistrust tension is not to trust everyone. The task is to develop appropriate trust in others, and in life, as essentially reliable. Learning trust involves a suitable mistrust of what is not trustworthy and ultimately brings harm. The trust which is the mark of this crisis is a trust in others and in ourselves. Gluttony is an act of mistrust as well as indiscriminate trust.

In infancy, we begin to learn to control urges. We do not bite or hit because these actions lead to the withdrawal of attention, or food and comfort. Caregivers do not always regard us with amusement and attention. Sometimes they say no. Even amid moments of withdrawal of attention, we learn to trust that they and we are reliable. We learn we can control ourselves, and they can meet our needs. Gluttony, however, is a desire for more attention, or its substitutes in food and drink, than is needed. We are gluttonous because we fear future deprivation.

Anticipation of future deprivation can make one overly demanding in the present. If love is withheld, people will grab all they can in the present in order to store it for tomorrow. In response, people withhold more. A vicious relational cycle begins which frustrates relationships and breeds mistrust.

Gluttony tries to collapse the future into the now. The need to satisfy present wants blinds one to any future. The gluttonous person is indiscriminate. Relationships are instrumental. Everything is subordinated to getting enough of the desired substance. Gluttony involves the indiscriminate trust in substances. The person thinks things can be taken into the body and not be harmful.

The virtue of the trust-mistrust conflict is hope. Hope is the capacity to believe that one's wishes can be fulfilled in spite of the

2. *Ibid.*, 25ff., 77ff.

dark urges and rages that mark the beginning of existence and continue throughout life.[3] Hope is grounded on early experiences of "good enough" care. Later, hope is a conviction regarding life which remains even when specific hopes are not met.

Through hope we refine our moral tastes. Even when something we hope for does not happen, we can begin to hope for another. Often on the spiritual journey, the later hope is more refined and more satisfying to deeper human needs.

Hope trusts that the world is basically reliable. Gluttony cannot hope for anything not linked to specific wants. Hope can maintain itself even before disappointment. It can focus on what is realizable when plans fail. Gluttony ignores the dangers of attending to the real consequences of its wants. It remains bound to immediate satisfaction. Unable to accept renunciation, gluttony cannot channel its desires to reach a new goal. Hope knows there will be a tomorrow, where good choices will bear fruit.

Hope is one aspect of vowed obedience. It is required in order to unite efforts with others toward a common goal, and feel one's own needs will be met in the process. For this reason, the trust-mistrust crisis described by Erikson provides a window to view the inner transformation of self and congregation which obedience evokes.

Issues surrounding gluttony and hope are common struggles of religious on the physical, congregational, and ecclesial levels of their lives. They involve their vow of obedience. Obedience, as seen through this lens, involves attention to reality.

Overweight, overwork, reliance on drugs and alcohol, dependency relationships, and sexual involvements are symptomatic of stresses and excesses of living in our times. They can be gluttonous reactions to issues of trust. Congregations, too, can adopt gluttonous patterns. They can focus so much on the immediate satisfaction of members that they fail to hope for and plan a future.

These gluttonous patterns can be offset by humble listening and facing reality. Obedience leads beyond these patterns and questions their effects on the congregation and the Church.

---

3. Erikson, *Insight and Responsibility*, 118.

Initiative versus guilt

The crisis of initiative versus guilt is evoked along the path of obedience. This crisis is especially significant as renewal opens the door for planning and decision-making not possible in the past. Religious today have unparalleled opportunities for initiative. Obedience involves how they use this power.

Erikson saw the psycho-social crisis of initiative versus guilt as centered in the young child's new capacities for language, loco-motion, and access to a broader range of goals. Initiative is a sense of ambition and purpose, the capacity to do things with zest. Guilt is the negative pole of this crisis, the anxiety produced when boundaries have been crossed.[4]

Mobility and access to positions and opportunities create for religious an analogous situation to Erikson's young child. Religious need to take initiative. Yet, initiative involves a capacity to cooperate with others, not just to take charge. Initiative, rather than conformity, draws one into the common enterprise which characterizes religious life.

The virtue-vice struggle of this crisis is between purpose/dedication and greed. Both potentials are developed through interaction with others. For Erikson, purpose and greed are outgrowths of the play age. When children play, they engage in purposeful activity, binding together their inner and outer worlds. They learn to cooperate and test the boundaries of the real world, using what appears to be a world without boundaries to test what really can be done.

The tension between initiative and guilt continues in adulthood. As we live with others, we test the limits and possibilities for initiative. Religious, too, must learn to include the wills of others in their choices. Religious life requires them to cooperate and blend their skills to accomplish a common task. As they engage in these tasks, both positive and negative potentials are evoked.

Purpose and dedication form the capacity to imagine and pursue a goal, face defeats, overcome fears. Dedication is the capac-

4. Capps, *Deadly Sins and Saving Virtues*, 34ff., 87ff.

ity to set aside certain tasks and focus on them. Children absorbed in a pursuit, whether it be pouring water or digging in a sandbox, can be focused on the task at hand. Through this purposeful play they enter into the world of reality, bridging the gap between desire and competence.

Purpose and dedication are also an outgrowth of a healthy religious life. Focus on union with God, mission, shared life in community, relationships, development of gifts and talents are carried out in the face of obstacles, setbacks, and limited opportunities. Purpose and dedication bridge the gap between desire and competence.

Greed is a desire to possess or acquire something in an amount far greater than is needed. Instead of testing the outer world and seeking to act in accordance with its laws and movements, greed seeks to make the world conform to its desires. It wants what it wants now. It thinks and acts impulsively.

Greed is deaf to the "inner voice" of conscience and the quiet movements of a discerning heart. Where gluttony strains the limits of the body, greed tests the social boundaries and patience of those with whom it associates. It sees what it can "get away with."

Greed is dynamically related to the negative pole of this life crisis: guilt. Healthy guilt is the awareness that one has trespassed legitimate boundaries. In contrast, unhealthy guilt squelches initiative. People can be so burdened by guilt that their legitimate desires are opposed. Genuine desire is curbed instead of transgressions and excesses of desire.

Guilt can be used as a mechanism of social control. Because religious congregations do coordinate common action, they can foster an unhealthy guilt. Greed for power or control can block legitimate outlets for initiative. Authority structures meant to promote accountability and shared opportunity can defeat those qualities if they are in the grips of guilt and greed.

Greed for power or attention obstructs action in a community. A negative climate can be maintained by the paralysis of guilt. Out of touch with their true desires, members do not take initiative and attempt to control authorities. They expect others to meet their needs, needs that never seem satisfied.

In religious life greed strains the fabric of affective bonding and spurns real accountability. Greed distorts thinking and dismisses information that does not conform to personal desires. It denies the rights and privileges of others.

While initiative envisions outcomes that are realistic, greed is based on illusions and delusions. Greed is a deadly sin because it distracts us from what is important, the very object of the vow and the practice of obedience.

The practice of guilt and greed are ways to avoid the challenge of initiative. Since greed wants everything, it lacks focus. Purpose and dedication seek the "one thing needed" and the rest in relationship to it. Greed collapses the future into the present, limiting its imagination to its own needs and desires. Purpose and dedication build bridges to the future. For this reason, the tension between purpose/dedication and greed is a dynamic of the vow of obedience.

Greed and purpose can characterize a community. Purpose plans, refines, and tests expectations in a collaborative enterprise. It fosters a congregational effort toward mission and quality of life. Unfortunately, greed is characteristic of a community when it unites around common comfort.

Since obedience goes beyond the relationship between subject and superior, it requires a different kind of discipline today. Obedience calls for a relationship of mutuality in which members and leadership commonly pursue the life of the congregation. All must enter into the self-emptying posed by the struggle between purpose and greed.

Industry versus inferiority

Erikson claims that the crisis of the school age is not bound to physical changes, as in earlier periods. The challenge of industry versus feelings of inferiority is created by need to be useful and productive. Industry is the capacity to sublimate personal disappointments in the interest of being productive. It involves taking pleasure in the completion of projects through attention and perseverance.[5]

5. *Ibid.*, 39ff., 91ff. In the following, as earlier, I rely on Capp's analysis and adapt it for issues of religious life.

For the child, the effort to be productive inevitably produces limits and failures. Someone is always smarter, runs faster, is innately skilled. Sooner or later we compare our abilities to others and come up short. Feelings of inferiority set in. Even if more serious issues of abuse, emotional deprivation, and adjustment problems are absent from our childhood, inferiority touches each life in some way.

Competence and envy are the virtue-vice poles of this crisis. Both are responses to the challenge of industry. Envy is a feeling of ill-will or discontent because of another's advantages or possessions. Envy involves the desire for these possessions for ourselves. Competence is more than the acquisition of skills. It is the discovery of what works in a given situation, whether it be a cooperative endeavor or mastery of a skill. Competence gives its own sense of self-verification. This comes from successful experience with the outside world. It involves dexterity, intelligence, and discipline.

Envy is a shortcut to industry. Instead of doing the hard work of competence and risking failure, we seek to feel competent by bringing the other down to our size. Envy is more than resentment at another's good fortune. We feel the other's accomplishments or advantages actually diminish our own. Envy can become internalized when we avoid productive situations altogether, or it can be externalized when we seek revenge against the envied party.[6]

The restrictions on a person caught in envy are not those of obedience. They are self-imposed and imagined. Where greed seems to lack a sense of boundaries in the real world, envy creates boundaries where there are none. Envious people convince themselves that there are boundaries that cannot be overcome or challenged. "I could not do that," "Oh, only *certain* people do those things," can be statements which cover up the unwillingness to put forth effort or risk failure. Obedience, on the other hand, is the willingness to respond to the lead of the Spirit, leading us to use and enjoy our real capacities.

---

6. For a study of the envied and envying, see Ann and Barry Ulanov, *Cinderella and Her Sisters* (Philadelphia: The Westminster Press, 1983).

Envy can wreck havoc on the collaborative enterprise of a shared life and mission. A congregation can promote envy or competence. A healthy community encourages the less advantaged to discover and use his or her gifts. Concomitantly, the advantaged also are supported to resist the efforts of envious community members to bring them down to size.

Envy can cripple members through submission to the paralysis of being envied. In such a climate, members must hide talents to be accepted. This community atmosphere is characterized by lack of obedience.

In community, most people share both sides of the envy equation. They are both competent in some things and inferior in others. Only through support of the different gifts of community members will the creative productivity of the group as a whole be unleashed (1 Cor 12:12-30).

Envy can be productive. It can be a signal that another has a skill or a quality that I want for myself. If used correctly and sublimated into competent action, it can be a signal to grow. Obedience involves coming to terms with one's gifts and using them as God calls. Instead of resentment of others, we promise in obedience to place ourselves and our gifts at the disposal of the Church and society.

The call of obedience involves the call from envy to competence. We see this in John 21:21-22. "When Peter saw him [the apostle Jesus loved], he said to Jesus, "Lord, what about this man?" Jesus said to him, "If it is my will that he remain until I come, what is that to you? Follow me!" The call to the competence of obedience prods us continually to leave self and follow Jesus in becoming who we are meant to be in his will for us. Rather than the paralysis of envy, obedience is a zeal for growth and the Kingdom.

For religious, the call to industry and competence in the Christian life is mediated through the framework of community, mission, friendship, family, and profession. Through these means religious discover their productivity by giving themselves to God and others.

The vow of obedience and the defeat of death

The transformation of desires elicited by obedience is meant to build the Kingdom. The vows are not just for individual transformation. They contribute to the entire community and create the Kingdom in a postmodern world. Vatican II made clear that the value of religious life is not only instrumental, that is, valuable because religious do good things in society and the Church.

Religious life is not a value just because it is a sign. It is a sign because it has a value, a sanctifying and redemptive value in the Church and society.[7] Obedience witnesses to a value deeper than activity, as religious enter into decisions and actions which plunge them into the redemptive activity of Jesus.

When religious choose hope over gluttony, they trust in God's redemptive presence in the world as the center of their motivation. By public vow they place this interpretation on their choice. They expect God to act. This vigilance connects religious to the Love which remains at the heart of the universe. Religious join with God through an obedient heart in prayer, during an encounter with a cancer patient, while in an inner city parish, in caring for AIDS babies, and during their work in the classroom.

They have hope because God is the reality beyond anxiety. Through a life of obedience, religious not only hope God will act; they learn to expect God to act. The remaining question is where and when. They listen for God individually and corporately with discerning hearts so they can be where God is in collaborative love.

To live life with purpose and to abandon greed is countercultural. It is to dedicate oneself to God's purposes in a world with vast economic disparities. Our society stands in need of this special type of initiative.

At the end of the last decade, the average pre-tax income for the top one percent of the population in the U.S. was $599,800, and for the top twenty percent, $109,400. The bottom twenty percent averaged $8,400, and the middle sixty percent ranged

---

7. Paul Molinari, *Chapter VI of the Dogmatic Constitution "Lumen Gentium" on Religious Life*, 159.

from $20,100 to $47,900. In other words, the total pretax income of 834,000 households was greater than that of 84,000,000 households. We had more poor at the beginning of the 90s than we have had since 1964.[8] It was a decade of the rich getting richer and the poor getting poorer. The gap has widened as we enter a new millennium.

Ours is a society which feeds on novelty, stimulation, new demands, and new markets. Greed is a virtue. Hedonism, permissiveness, and moral relativism smile on a life of purpose as a quaint vintage from the past. Our culture is not obedient. We are led to believe the world is left totally to our own crafting, a crafting based on raw liberty to get whatever we can "get away with."

Obedience in this climate of moral recession is countercultural before it even accomplishes the external purposes of the Kingdom. It witnesses concretely beyond the self and has meaning which transcends the immediate desires of an individual with ever-expanding needs. As religious live with purpose and initiative, they give flesh to the transcendent roots of their lives.

The post-modern temptation

The struggle between industry and inferiority takes on special significance for religious because of the "post-modern temptation." The post-modern temptation is the cultural pressure to resist any type of decision-making. It demands that everything stay open-ended. It is a shortcut before the problems of cultural transition. This attitude is fed by vast exposure to different people and ways of living. Pluralism gives way to relativism. No one way to live or act is better than others.

Peter Berger suggests that our technological, pluralistic, and secular world produces a dilemma for the Church as to how to respond. Religious share this predicament. It forms a context for the practice of obedience today.

---

8. "The 1980s: A Very Good Time for the Very Rich," *New York Times*, 5 March 1992. The source of this data is the Congressional Budget Office, as cited in Rasmussen, *Moral Fragments and Moral Community*, 93.

Berger finds three typical responses to confusion over religion in modern society.[9] People can refuse the world as it is and retire behind the conceptual and moral walls of a sectarian ghetto. Obedience, interpreted in this model, is rigid and isolating. Second, they can adapt uncritically to the secular world, merging sacred and secular to the point that they ask why they still remain in the Church. Obedience in this mentality disappears as a life value.

In a third option, people turn solely to their experience, unwilling to impose closure on anything by invoking an authority. Experience is the authority, and individual experience appeals to no legitimacy beyond itself. While this seems open-minded, the deep hunger for certainty implied in religion is not met. Identity is fostered through union with Life larger than the self. In this third option, experience has no larger framework through which to interpret itself.

Radical open-endedness is maintained through the rule; no authority can be invoked. To overcome resistance to all authority, some limit or leap has to be made and accepted. Obedience requires this leap and a surrender to a reality beyond oneself.

People fall into the post-modern option when they make no choices. This promotes personal and corporate drifting. The result is inferiority. Alienation and inherent anxiety result from the inability to submit to anything. Competence, on the other hand, confronts a society without boundaries. It overcomes this new face of inferiority and its crippling effects.

Religious witness to the defeat of death through the transforming effects of obedience in their lives. Obedience gives a new self-worth based on an identity valued by God. God weighs by different measures than does society. Religious handle the cognitive overload of these times by focus on charism and its calls. Religious then become a community of memory and identity in a society that is fragmented.

---

9. Piet Fransen, "Criticisms of Some Basic Theological Notions in Matters of Church Authority," *Journal of Ecumenical Studies* 19 (Spring, 1982) 50–7.

Before a world of drift and confusion, religious support healthy families and build intact schools and neighborhoods. They work to restore functioning towns and cities and promote balanced ways of life that endure over time because they are rooted in spiritual values. They enter a society without community to be community. They do this through the affective bonding of a shared identity, an identity rooted fundamentally in a personal call to follow Jesus and the gospel.

The new community of baptism

The new community of baptism transcends race, gender, economic level, and ideological barriers. Through obedience, religious testify that such a community is possible. They are called to it and build it among themselves. One way religious build this new community of baptism is by being trustworthy people. When they use authority, or participate in its processes, they act with integrity. Religious know they live obedience in modern times when authority itself is a problem.

Systems of "plausibility structures" are broken down today. We once had a coherent view of the world which explained reality from heaven to earth. Today, however, there is little consensus regarding fundamental relationships within the world. This affects how authority is perceived. This context is a new situation in which to live religious obedience.

In a simpler society, authority was the attribute of a person. It was attributed on the basis of personal characteristics or the position held. Persons and positions were not separated; authority came from birthright or was conferred. It was inalienable and not linked with competence. People held authority positions until they died. They were not re-elected and they did not retire. Church authority was interpreted in this cultural paradigm, including the authority we find in religious life.[10]

In the modern world people hold authority because of competence. This is called "functional authority." The job and the per-

10. See Frans-Xavier Kaufmann, "The Sociology of Knowledge and the Problem of Authority," *Journal of Ecumenical Studies* 19 (Spring 1982) 18–31. I will borrow from Kaufman's analysis.

son are separated. Ideally, if they are not competent, they are replaced. Trust is not in the person as much as it is in the organization in charge of appointing and replacing.

Authority functions by this new climate in ministry today. In a more traditional society the Church was a place where you put up with limits. Today, however, people have high expectations of their leaders. The parish is not a place to put up with things you would not tolerate in other circles. Neither is a religious community. In fact, many ministers and those with named authority in religious congregations experience a crisis of "inferiority." People are demanding, and the skill deficit between their training and their current job seems more apparent.

Some human activities, however, cannot be carried out with functional authority. They cannot be separated from the person carrying out the activity. Faith, for instance, grows only where there are persons to whom one can relate. One needs someone with whom one can identify, with whom one can build a personal relationship of trust. Here trust and character are more important than every type of competence.[11] By character we mean someone who proves himself or herself trustworthy.

Faith requires a personal authority whom you trust and to whom one gives decisive significance.[12] Faith also needs community. Community involves a relationship to people who share everyday life and interpret practical experience in the light of faith, an obedient community. Faith is fed by integration into a community or by support by a trustworthy person. Authority required for faith is mediated by a reliable individual, a stable group, or a combination of the two. Because of these realities, obedience includes the establishment of credibility.

Religious build the faith community through their vow of obedience as they foster credibility on several levels. First, the public nature of the vow of obedience calls religious to be trustworthy before others who see them as women and men of the Church. The Church struggles for the authoritative legitimacy to promote

11. We are not opposing the two. Both in a broad sense are part of competence in these settings.

12. Here we see human faith as the starting point of religious faith.

faith in modern culture. While the authority of the Church rests in mystery, its credibility has to be humanly established to be believed. When this credibility is weak, the community suffers.

Authority is attributed not by those who claim it, but by those who hold it trustworthy. Breakdown of trust feeds a loss of faith. Religious can help to establish the credibility of the Church by the integrity of their personal lives.

Second, credibility comes from standing for the truth. Religion should to be linked to the truth of people's needs through practical responses by congregations. The choices of religious congregations need to relate to the real issues of people's lives. Commitment to truth in response to real needs fosters credibility.

Third, religious can take an active role to promote the societal credibility of the Church as a whole. Today something is perceived as legitimate, not just because the Church says it, but because it also makes human sense.

Needed church reforms such as the rights of women cannot be ignored by religious orders. Promotion of the credibility of church in many societies depends on a response to this crisis. Economic and political reforms in third world and poverty situations, as well as over-consuming first world countries, are necessary for credible witness. A half-hearted response is not only weak ministry; it is scandalous.

Fourth, the institutions sponsored by religious congregations need to be credible as an expression of religious obedience. This is accomplished through good performance, signs of competence. Hospitals are not Christian if they are inefficient, schools not gospel-oriented if poor education is given. Poorly prepared homilies and disorganized religious education programs are failures in obedience. They undermine church credibility. When closeness to the Church and congregations breeds contact with the exercise of power and authority unrelated to people's lives and concerns, there is need for conversion in the area of obedience.

Finally, true authority is established through individual trustworthiness and witness to a life of satisfaction and other-centeredness. What is presented in the name of the Church has to be Good News to those who receive it. To use Christian symbols that are culturally alienating or insensitive to women, people of color, and marginated cultures is not good news. Immediate contact with those who have public roles in the Church is not credible when it is marked by fear, verbal or sexual abuse, abandonment, lack of concern, or failure to enable others for leadership.

Vowed obedience establishes the credibility of authority through its public witness. In a world without a center, finding a Center and listening with one's whole heart is a public testimony, a life work. It is a witness which transcends function. Obedience is deeply personal for it touches human integrity. It involves being more than a minimal self, uncommitted to social relationships, public life, and service. Obedience re-establishes trust through people who embody meanings and values upon which the whole community depends.

This is the stretch of obedience which serves society. The world still works only because people by and large trust one another and can take one another at their word and keep it. Religious, through their vow of obedience, have a special role in maintaining this "ecology" of social living.

Chapter Twenty

New Times for Obedience

Any understanding of vowed obedience must involve relationship to authority. Since there is a crisis of authority in our culture, these are "new times" for obedience. Changed perceptions of authority influence religious congregations as well as the wider culture. Religious have experimented with collegial forms of decision-making and government since Vatican II. At the local level there have been shared forms of leadership, with different members assuming coordinating functions in the group for short periods of time.

Some religious live alone, and maintain a link with a regional or local leader. Others connect to groups which meet periodically for prayer and discernment. While these new forms of bonding and authoritative relationships merit study and reflection, I do not wish to treat them here. Others have done so.[1] They stand as symbols of new times. We will focus instead on the problem with relationship to authority in general, and how this affects religious.

Many adults in the first world church seem trapped in negative postures toward authority. These authority issues never move toward any resolution. The sociologist Richard Sennett refers to this as the stance of negation.[2]

---

1. Patricia Wittberg, *Pathways to Re-Creating Religious Communities* (New York: Paulist Press, 1996).

2. Richard Sennett, *Authority* (New York: Knopf, 1980). I will be following Sennett's analysis, applying it to religious life.

A negative posture toward authority is not dependent upon situations of conflict or cooperation, perceptions of competence or its lack. Rather it is a consistent, repetitive, and energy-consuming phenomenon in which a negative response is given to authority regardless of how it functions. Negation is evoked because authority functions. A negative posture toward authority actually functions as an authority bond for some individuals. This stance of negation can occur in religious communities.

The cultural climate surrounding authority affects the practice of vowed obedience. Descriptions of cultural patterns cannot, however, render a conclusive analysis of the situation of obedience today. Many factors enter into the practice of obedience. The mystery of faith, the motivation of piety, and a common commitment to the gospel bring to the relationship of religious and those in authority forces which cannot be reduced sociologically.

Yet the spiritual bond of authority within a religious community is understood within the cultural patterns of its members. The insights of sociology help to describe these standards. This knowledge also highlights the countercultural challenge of the vow and its witness value.[3] In order not to overlook this information, let us investigate the bond of negation.

Authority is an interpretative process, not a thing. Some sociologists locate authority in the credibility of ideas, rules, and persons to whom we ascribe it. Sennett focuses on how the social exchange between the "strong" and "weak" results in an interpretation of authority.[4]

Authority is a search for solidity and security in the strength of others. It is an emotional bond whereby we interpret the conditions of power, give conditions of control, and influence a meaning by defining an image of strength.[5] Recent church documents reflect a similar notion of authority. Vatican II acknowledged that both the content and the process by which authoritative direc-

3. Sennett comments on first world culture, but similar insight can be gained from examining, for instance, the influence of tribal culture in Africa or traditional culture in Japan and Asia.

4. Sennett, *Authority,* 25.

5. *Ibid.,* 3.

tives are made have bearing on their capacity to be vehicles of the Holy Spirit.[6] How the bond of authority is formed is pertinent to church and religious life.

The formation of the authority bond in modern society gives rise to a paradoxical situation. What is peculiar to modern times is that formally legitimate powers in dominant institutions inspire a strong sense of illegitimacy among those subject to them.[7]

People distrust the government, politicians, "city hall," TV, and at times, the Church, priests, and religious. In religious communities, members complain that congregational government is unrelated to them, does not care, is elitist. This climate is different from the '50s. Then authority held a distinct place in society and the Church.

An authority bond is a unique human bond. It is between two people who are unequal in power. How is this bond forged by negation? Negation occurs when the authority bond is formed through rejection of the authority figure. Authority, however, remains the point of departure in the relationship.[8] The destructive element in the relationship is that an individual feels tied to the person he or she is rejecting.

Three ways of forming a bond with authority through negation are: 1) disobedient dependence; 2) idealized substitution; and 3) the fantasy of disappearance of authority. Disobedient dependence involves the compulsive focus of attention on the wishes of authority. Then one does the opposite. It is different from genuine independence or autonomy. The need to go against authority, rather than initiative, motivates it.[9]

Disobedient dependence is practiced as a person proposes something which he or she knows authority cannot accept. An authority figure becomes an "authority" through the capacity to say no. If someone is strong enough to say no, that person is strong enough to be an authority.[10]

6. *Lumen Gentium 12,* 12 and 25, *Dei Verbum* 10, *Gaudium et Spes,* 43.
7. Sennett, *Authority,* 26.
8. *Ibid.,* 28.
9. *Ibid.,* 34.
10. *Ibid.,* 35.

Setting up a situation in which authority has to say no creates a feeling of safety. Dependence on authority and transgression of it are inseparable in this stance. A bond is created through these opposite wishes. Even if authority "agrees" to the wish, people change the nature of the demand to maintain the bond they need. This dynamic actually tightens the bond between the authority figure and his or her subjects. This can occur in the life of a religious and in a community as a whole.

Idealized substitution is the process by which the authority figure is used as a negative model. Whatever she or he is and does, the opposite is what the subjects want. For instance, religious may focus on the perceived negative traits of a person in leadership. They may criticize a leader as too aloof. If the person becomes more friendly, however, the individual will be criticized for the change. The point is, members cannot imagine authority except as the opposite of what they have. The fear which operates in idealized substitution is a fear of being cut loose, having no moorings or point of reference. Members depend on the person in charge as a point of reference.[11]

The fantasy of disappearance is the belief that everything would be all right if only the people in charge would disappear. The subject again is caught. There is a need to fantasize that everything would be all right if only the authority figure did not make his or her presence felt. This is coupled with a fear that without that presence there would be nothing. There is both fear of the authority figure and fear he or she will go away.

The result of this negative authority bond is a situation of double-bind: everything wrong is the fault of authority, yet there is a need that the authority be present. In post-Vatican II religious life, we experience religious who seem "at sea" without conflictual relations with congregational, ecclesial, or other forms of authority.

These three forms of a negative bond with authority appear pathological. They are. However, they are also culturally reinforced. We are interested in them as cultural phenomena rather than as developmental problems. The situation of obedience

11. *Ibid.*, 38.

today is one in which these negative patterns find easy acceptance by others.

The cultural presence of these patterns calls for a different response than if they were only the problem of individuals. The cultural reinforcement of negation of authority replaces the natural and healthy process by which fear of authority is overcome and relationship to it matures. Healthy authority relationships are hampered in our culture. This forms the context in which obedience is lived. Let us examine the historical roots of this problem.

Historical roots of negation

According to Sennett, rejection of authority is not tied to a concrete betrayal. Rather, its origins are in the eighteenth-century belief that the legitimacy of rulers must be destroyed in order to change their power. The King had to be destroyed in order for the people to be the new authority. To disbelieve was to be free. To destroy the legitimacy of authority was to destroy its force.[12]

There is an analogous movement in religious life since Vatican II. Religious life moved from pre-enlightenment times into the twentieth century in a matter of thirty years. This movement involved constructive and destructive assumptions of modern thought. As a result, culture's negating spirit crept into religious community because it touched alienations experienced in religious life.

In the eighteenth century, the market system expanded a negative spirit toward authority. "The invisible hand" of the market was the measure of fairness or authority in an economic system. The system moved away from person-to-person relationships. Yet, "the invisible hand" of the market was an abstraction. It was tied to no single person. If the market was disturbed and people were out of work, no specific human being could be held accountable.

The invisible image gave the illusion of freedom from previous constraining authority relationships. Yet, it was not enough to fill human authority needs. There was an attempt to find someone

---

12. Sennett, *Authority,* 43.

responsible, to establish images of human strength and control and make them more concrete. It was fulfilled in the image of the nineteenth-century "boss" as a paternalistic figure. Modern authority was forged in this model.

Nineteenth-century bosses were drawn as ones who would promise protection and be figures of strength, but they did not come through.[13] They differed from earlier authority figures who were patrimonial rather than paternalistic. Earlier authority was patrimonial because through them the "patrimony" of the family, land, and power were passed on. Later paternalistic figures, the bosses, had no patrimony to pass on.

When the land-based economy broke up, so did the basis of patrimonial authority. With no property to pass on and no guarantee of position passing to the next generation, patrimonial authority became paternal authority. It was based on domination without a contract of inheritance. Symbols of authority continued, but the material realities upon which it was based stopped.

There is an analogous situation today in religious life. Religious authority has less material authority over a religious. For instance, religious authority often cannot mission a religious to a job. They do not create jobs. Many religious congregations no longer control hiring as they did. Unlike before, many cannot employ their own members.

When material bases of authority are weak, authority is more symbolic. When a father could no longer guarantee his child a known place in the world, he had to legitimate his authority on bases other than materiality alone. Authority was based on symbols and beliefs.

In the nineteenth century, power was legitimated outside the family by appeal to the roles within the family.[14] Bosses were drawn to be like fathers, and workers were expected to assume their role as "children." Bosses were to offer protection, like a father, and workers were to be loyal, appreciative, and passive.[15]

13. *Ibid.*, 45.
14. *Ibid.*, 57.
15. This child-parent relationship is also in much of the literature surrounding obedience in the nineteenth century.

When bosses could not offer protection because factors in the market were beyond their personal control, authority relations were transformed. The authority relationship still promised nurturance. Yet, its reality denied the essential quality of human nurturance, that one's care will make another grow stronger.

Authority structures in the marketplace were impersonal. Authority could demand obedience without promising nurturance. For instance, a subject with a grievance faced a system in which no specific human agent could be held accountable. The bureaucracy could be blamed ultimately, but it was untouchable. In this system, the leader rules but is absolved from taking responsibility for the engine of rule, the bureaucracy.[16] Authority transformed itself into power alone. The authority bond was removed from its nurturance and trust-building responsibilities.

Paternalistic authority patterns resulted. There were new sociological patterns by which authorities could portray strength and arouse feelings of fear and promise protection. While these emotions were elicited, the authorities would not come through. Power was non-dialogical. Society made it permissible for the leader to care for subjects only insofar as it served his or her interest.

Today, for instance, middle managers find themselves out of work after years of service to a corporation. A relationship that appears to incorporate one into the firm leaves one out without recourse. The modern climate of negation of authority is grounded in an authority image that elicits the emotion of submission but offers no concern.

Paternalistic authority patterns are far more powerful than power in the normal family. Paternalistic authority occurs when one person is authorized to control the boundaries of reality for other people. People cannot object to such control. If they do, the authority claims he or she is being betrayed and maligned.[17] Shame is introduced into obedience.

Normally in the family, control is neither all love nor all power. There is a mixture of both. The authority of a healthy parent can

16. Sennett, 77.
17. *Ibid.*, 66.

be challenged. Normal parents are not humiliated by such a challenge. They regard it as a sign that children are maturing. Shame is used in a healthy family to mark boundaries of behavior which are necessary to socialize the child.[18] This is healthy shame.

To maintain control in an authority bond of negation, unhealthy shame is introduced into obedience. Through playing on feelings of shame, authority tries to control when it no longer has the material means to control.

Modern society adds to the conditions in which people are vulnerable to shame. In traditional society, people inherited their place in the social order. In modern society people feel personally responsible for their place in the world. In modern society, there is a reversal of the "survival of the fittest."

People feel shame about dependence in a world which claims that all have equal opportunity. If one is not the "fittest," it is one's own fault or that of someone else.[19] If Mary has not "progressed" to the scale of Sue, Mary is to blame. I once heard a religious echo the dilemma of finding one's place in a confused system of authority vulnerable to shame. The religious remarked, "There are two kinds of people in my order, parents and children. I want to be a parent."

The malignancy in modern authority is its offer of a false love and no concern. It is built on illegitimate forms of social control. The subject is influenced but cannot in turn influence those who are "taking care" of him or her. Negation, in this system, makes sense. It is an effort to avoid this relationship. Negation occurs in public life more than in private life because a family offers alternatives to this dilemma.

In normal family life, the rhythm of growth and decay helps to resolve problems with authority. As individuals grow older, they assume authority themselves. By doing so they break the funda-

---

18. See Erikson, *Childhood and Society;* and James W. Fowler, *Faithful Change: The Personal and Public Challenges of Postmodern Life* (Nashville: Abingdon Press, 1996) part II.

19. Sennett, *Authority,* 47. See also Michael Lerner, *The Politics of Meaning: Restoring Hope and Possibility in an Age of Cynicism* (New York: Addison-Wesley, 1996) 6.

mental power of authority to inspire fear.[20] The waxing and waning of parenting disrupts the relations of authority. No such possibility exists in the public realm. Authority lacks this fluidity.

Negation allows the need for strong people in one's life. Yet by rejecting their legitimacy, dependence can occur without vulnerability.[21] Fear of dependence is overcome by attacks on the integrity of the authority figure.[22] If it is not legitimate for another to make demands, then we are protected against feeling weak or ashamed. The destructive element in this cycle is that the content of authority, what authority should be, is cast aside. Legitimate needs for authority for the individual or group are not met.[23]

By definition, the subject under paternalistic authority has no influence on the one in charge. The "weaker" can only resist by being the negation of whatever the powerful want them to be. Negation of authority, however, never transcends the terms of power used by authority. The vision of a better order, or a better authority, is not generated by this resistance.

A way out?

Is there a way out of this modern quagmire? Sennett claims that authority which is legible and visible creates the possibility that other authority relations beyond negation can emerge.

Authority is visible when those who are in positions of control are explicit about themselves. They are clear about what they can and cannot do and are specific about their promises. Authority is legible when the authority bond is formed through a healthy process. Through discussions and mutual decision-making, some people are given authority by others but are forbidden to lord it over them.[24]

Legible authority occurs when people participate in the nuancing of "commands." Rules are reinterpreted and abridged at

20. Sennett, *Authority,* 159.

21. *Ibid.,* 46.

22. Stephen Carter stresses this point in *Integrity, op. cit.,* chapter 12, commenting on attack of political leaders in our society.

23. Sennett, *Authority,* 74.

24. *Ibid.,* 168.

times through public discussion. At various levels of "command," freedom is created to redefine categories as problems arise.[25] Subsidiarity is practiced. Rather than the one in charge specifying what he or she wants and how it is to be done, decisions are made, when possible, by those involved. Authority becomes a process of making, breaking, and remaking of meanings that are visible and legible.[26]

The creation of legible and visible authority is a challenge to religious of modern times. The chaos of negation is fed by the illusion of uninhibited power and nonapproachable disinterestedness. The ultimate deception which entraps is the image of authority as a controller who also does not care.

Malignant use of authority is an escape from mutuality. It frees itself from dealing mutually with others by arousing feelings of shame and inadequacy in them. Authority like this offers two options to others: to continue the cycle of negating, or to break the cycle by walking away.

Ecclesial and congregational authority has a healing ministry to those who suffer from this cultural problem with authority. The scriptural warning, "it would be better for you if a millstone were hung around your neck and you were thrown into the sea than for you to cause one of these little ones to stumble" (Luke 17:2), makes explicit that gospel use of authority is not to be as in the culture. Religious institutions are called to provide alternative standards, not only for the good of members, but as a witness to better authority in church and society.

Obedience and ecclesial life

Authority in our lives is a deep human need. Religious continue to search for authorities in their lives even when "freedom from authority" is called for loudly. Authority is never a replacement for the inner authority of the person. We assume that

25. *Ibid.*, 183.
26. We see a model of this type of process by the American bishops in the proceedings from which the Economic Pastoral was produced in the United States.

healthy inner authority is augmented and supported by recognition of authority in one's life.

The resolution of the tensions surrounding authority cannot be done in a unilateral way. Adults need to assume authority in the Church in a meaningful manner. This is key to de-mythologizing authority and breaking the cycle of negativity. This is especially true for women as they search for significant means to share in the ministry of authority in the Church. In both first and third world cultures, woman's role has to be supported by its importance in cultural traditions. It also needs to be freed from the repressive aspects of those traditions. The Church needs the service of authority of women to lead it in the next millennium.

A major challenge to church authority today is how to maintain a visible and legible authoritative stance around controversial issues. This requires taking a stance without communicating a disinterestedness and withdrawal that leaves only exit or negation as options. Religious orders have a profound role to play in the Church in this regard. As they move from the sidelines of negation to assume a fuller responsibility for mission in the Church, vowed obedience calls them to create systems which support visible and legible authority in the Church.

Political-mystical signs

The root meaning of the term obedience is "to hear." Obedience connotes a readiness to listen and to attend to what is other than oneself. Obedience dwells in the deep recesses of conscience. It is the willingness to recognize a will and reality outside one's own as carrying a validity and identity fundamental to one's own good and sense of rightness. Religious obedience recognizes legitimate congregational authority as a mediation of this "otherness." It holds community as a medium for listening to the gospel.

At the center of Christian obedience is Jesus' own submission to the will of him whom he called Father. The deepest meaning of religious obedience is love. Obedient love shares in the life of Jesus as a disciple. Jesus asked his disciples to submit their wills to his. "For those who want to save their life will lose it and those who lose their life for my sake will save it" (Luke 9:23-24).

Obedience is not giving up one's will but using it for the Kingdom. In this sense the ongoing path of obedience is marked by three characteristics: a growing sense of providence, repentance, and vocation.[27]

Providence

What are signs that one is walking the path of obedience? An obedient person has a growing sense that the world is under God's guidance and is trustworthy. In interpersonal relationships, one can rely on the sameness and continuity of others in community and ministry. The person can depend on others, as well as being a trustworthy person upon whom others can depend.

Obedience develops a growing belief that God has a purpose for each person. The world is seen as ultimately benevolent, in spite of setbacks and disappointments. Reliance on divine guidance is a "must" in all details of life. The obedient person does not see this as a deficiency in personal competence but as a mode of proceeding which calls him or her forth as a person.

Faith gradually rules more areas of life as the road to spiritual dependence is walked with an obedient heart. A sense of providence has radical political overtones. Listening to God's Word provides a countercultural voice. It gives an inner affirmation that can stand against the injustices of our times.

Repentance

Obedience leads to an acceptance of an appropriate level of moral responsibility for a particular situation. One is not immobilized by guilt or caught in excessive self-righteousness. A person develops a healthy sense of how one is an agent in the problems of life. Such persons can take responsibility for what they have control over in life and let go of the rest.

These people are able to experience remorse, regret, and sorrow when appropriate, for they have a sense of the "other" that

---

27. Capps develops these themes through a discussion of the beatitudes. See *Deadly Sins and Saving Virtues,* chapter 9. I am indebted to his analysis which I adapt for religious.

both confirms and holds out to them a sense of accountability. This in turn bonds them with others. It creates an affective unity in the communities in which they share, even though there are problems. They can ultimately forgive themselves and others and avoid being trapped in unhealthy guilt and unrealistic expectations of others.

The life and ministry of a religious is marked by a spirit of repentance that is not maudlin but life-confirming. It witnesses to others the humility which can collaborate. It has the freedom of spirit to take initiative, make mistakes, and still bond and work in union with others. In a world torn by age-old animosities and endless cycles of violence, obedience witnesses to the higher order. In this Heart we can let go and keep on because we know we are loved.

Vocation

Obedience, over a lifetime, gives a religious a deep sense of personal vocation. With vocation comes its attendant qualities of purpose, dedication, personal competence, and effectiveness. This inner sense of vocation lives counter to a world that is stagnant, binding, and without much future. A religious is a cheerful participant in the scheme of creation and providence that grounds a sense of purpose and dedication.

In a world where nothing is important except number one, religious obedience is a capacity to participate in a productive situation for others and bring it to completion. Obedience links personal competency to its fruitfulness for others. It looks at the needs of the whole, rather than personal achievement alone. The Kingdom is the mirror to measure its worth.

A life of obedience is gradually filled with a spirit of expectancy that all good things will be given to an obedient heart. It lives in equity with others, open to the repentance that a life of conversion requires. A life of obedience ultimately fills one with a spirit of self-worth. One has grounded one's life on values, which take a lifetime to learn and share.

Chapter Twenty-One

Celibacy:
From Ambiguity to Integrity

Celibacy is thought to be the only vow of the religious, since it captures the radical commitment of a religious vocation.[1] A desire to love God with one's whole self is made explicit in the decision not to marry. It is hard to know whether celibacy is the only vow. We do know it joins with poverty and obedience to mark a life path grounded on the conviction that one is called by God. Other reasons for this promise do not sustain religious life.

The vow of celibacy is about love. Its practice leads to the chasms and peaks involved in any personal struggle to love. Celibacy crosses the muddy waters of the unconscious and delves into a private current of invitation and threat. No life center is more deeply personal. No other road of development is so unique, chaotic, and enlivening.

A religious chooses to love celibately. The love matured through celibacy is not an absolute love or a perfect love. It is simply one's own love, transformed and directed toward God and others.[2] The path of celibacy is concrete and individual. It flows from personal history. It aims at integrity in love, in spite of mistakes.

The face of celibacy will be different at various junctures in life. The middle-aged brother, watching the children of his college buddy, reflects on the children he did not father. He experiences

---

1. Sandra Schneiders, *New Wineskins: Re-Imagining Religious Life Today* (New York: Paulist Press, 1986) 114.
2. At a mystical level, human love and divine love become one.

the vow differently than the novice does. She may grapple with the injustice of leading on a former friend. The discipline of celibacy may mean letting go so another can search for a life companion.

Celibacy is about sexuality. We will leave many things unsaid about celibacy because much has been written by others. Instead, we will offer a paradigm which touches the broad range of life experiences that a promise of celibacy affects. Celibacy will be considered within the wide understandings of sexuality in the faith community and the society.

Pastorally, celibacy is often seen as a higher calling in the Church. However, religious are challenged before all else to live the common life of sexual integration held out to the whole Church. There is no celibacy which circumvents the daily challenges of sexual integrity drawn in the gospel and lived by church community.

History

For centuries in the Western world, sexuality was linked only to procreation. Since procreation is a powerful human capacity, the Church sought to protect it. It confined procreation and sexuality to the stable union of marriage. All sexual acts were judged by their role leading to or properly expressing intercourse.

Since procreation was for marriage, so was sex. Any sexual acts outside the proper expression of sex within marriage were considered gravely sinful. Human life itself was at stake in indiscriminate sexual expression. All homosexual acts were against this natural order and thus sinful. Autoerotic actions were a misuse of sexual power meant for procreation.

The vow of celibacy could not avoid being touched by this general understanding of sexuality within the Church. The mystical tradition always protected religiously motivated celibacy. It gave it a loving, affective dimension by centering it on love of God. However, general pedagogy regarding the vow took on the biological, legalistic, and mechanistic understanding of sexuality that pervaded the Church.

By Vatican II, genital sexuality was redefined. It was described less in reference to children and more in its potential to create a lifelong bond with another. Procreation and conjugality were recognized as equal dimensions of sexuality.

At the same time, religious explored their vow. They moved from a narrow understanding of celibacy which robbed them of close friendship or warm expressions of affection. They searched for a deeper relational life with others. Warnings against particular friendships and rules about modesty lessened. Sanctions against contact with members of the opposite sex were dropped. Strictures against physical contact with children in the classroom were no longer in the vocabulary of religious formation.

In the transition which followed Vatican II, celibacy retained its identity as the vow not to marry. "The rest" too often remained a matter of exploration. The sexual revolution in first world culture called into question all sexual mores. Even past attitudes formed by family and society in the lives of religious were challenged.

The practice of the vow of celibacy took on the ambiguities of this transition. Today there are many questions regarding the boundaries of celibacy. Yet, religious know cultural values alone are insufficient to define the practice of this vow.

Toward a definition

In common thinking, sexuality and genitality, or the genital experience of sex, are identical. Sexuality, in this view, is explicit genital activity or actions which lead to it. Sexuality, however, is a broader human experience than genitality alone.

Human sexuality is a power of encounter, a dynamism of openness, of communion, and of creativity.[3] Sexuality, in this view, is linked to a wide range of human experiences. Sexuality becomes a way of being in the world. Genitality, or an orientation to pleasure and procreation, is only one dimension of sexuality.

A broader definition of sexuality is not meant to be evasive. Daily, celibates are challenged to integrate the call of sexuality, to bond with others, into their lives.[4] Struggles with genitality are

3. William F. Kraft, *Whole and Holy Sexuality* (St. Meinrad, Ind.: Abbey Press, 1989). I will draw on Kraft's analysis throughout this chapter.

4. Vincent J. Genovesi, *In Pursuit of Love: Catholic Morality and Human Sexuality* (Wilmington: Michael Glazier, Inc. 1987) 141. Genovesi's thought also influences this chapter.

part of this summons. A wider view of sexuality, however, points to the lifegiving and love-making powers of sexuality in the relationships of every celibate, powers that are not explicitly genital.

The relational capacities of human sexuality are not just genital. They are also cognitive and affective. Since sexuality involves a range of human capacities, sexual maturation concerns the capacity for relationship, not just the capacity to have genital sex. Through our sexuality we enter into the mystery of human loving as family members, friends, ministers, and sisters and brothers in community.

Religious are aided in their understanding of celibacy today as the Church has moved beyond a solely biological framework for understanding sexuality. Procreative sex is not just a means for the continuation of the species. It marks the relationship between love and fruitfulness. While most express this gift through having and parenting children, religious also experience love and fruitfulness. Religious know love and fruitfulness through the mystery of Christian virginity. Virginity is more than being single. A single life can be lived by anyone in secular culture. Christian virginity is a stance of belief.

Christian virginity is the free choice of celibacy as an expression of love of God.[5] It is a commitment in faith to relationships, communion, creativity, and generation of new life, but with a different touch.[6] The vow of celibacy finds its roots in the spiritual tradition of virginity. This tradition overshadows sexual abstinence as defining the vow. Sexual abstinence is a necessary but minimal biological understanding of what celibacy involves.

The vow

Religious life is based on the belief that one has been touched by God. The vow of celibacy is a response to this touch. Fundamentally, the vow of celibate chastity entails the obligation of perfect continence in celibacy for the sake of the Kingdom (Canon 599). It is a promise to enter into friendship with Jesus. It is a

---

5. This is a spiritual choice.
6. Josef Fuchs, *Personal Responsibility and Christian Morality,* 6ff.

pledge to trust in the continuing power of the Holy Spirit and to live gratefully before God who gives all.

Scripture testifies to the religious experience that inspires the vow. In Mark, we see Jesus "looking steadily" at the disciple, and being filled with love, saying "come follow me" (Mark 10:20ff.). The reality of being loved by Jesus poses an ultimate question to the religious. Life cannot go on without attention to this call.

The response of a religious is to set aside the usual path to Christian marriage. Why this is so is a mystery. Through celibacy religious express the desire to give their whole life to God. We hear in Mark an echo of this experience, "What good is it for persons to gain the whole world, yet forfeit their soul?" (Mark 8:36). Celibacy is a call of love. As with all calls to a life of love, it is a soul-defining experience.

Why do some Christians experience this gospel call? We can only presume to know the reasons. Celibacy is a calling and a gift. The Christian community witnesses to this and points to where the gift has been given through the ages. They name it a grace of God.

There are reasons for celibacy which have been recorded in the history of this experience. Celibacy gives one a greater freedom for ministry; it allows one to focus on the concerns of God. Celibacy is a sacrifice. People differ as to how much these "reasons" concur with their experience. For instance, many married people do not feel their spouse is a distraction from God, but rather a window on God's love.

Vowed celibacy is distinct as an adult life-style in the Church in that it is a calling to love and know God in a singular rather than partnered way. Celibacy is a calling given for the individual and for the whole Church. Beyond that, celibacy shares in the mystery of all love. Why does Ann marry Tom instead of Jim? From the outside, all love is a mystery.

We do find in biblical poems and mystical allegories images of a life-defining relationship with God. For example, wisdom is personified in the Old Testament as a symbol of Godself.[7] In 1

7. Johnson, *She Who Is,* 86ff.

Corinthians: 1:24, St. Paul tells us Jesus is this wisdom of God. The religious experience at the heart of celibacy is mirrored in the pursuit of wisdom.

"I loved her more than health and beauty, and I chose to have her rather than light, because her radiance never ceases. All good things came to me along with her, and in her hands uncounted wealth. I rejoiced in them all, because wisdom leads them; but I did not know that she was their mother" (Wis 7:10-12).

The text speaks of an ongoing relationship of love, which develops over time, is life consuming and all encompassing. It also alludes to the hiddenness of love, elusive to the grasp, yet undeniable. Just as those who are married grow in love, a religious gradually grasps the love which God has for her and the place he holds in God's heart. In time, the religious finds God in all things. Celibacy, as the search for wisdom, is a promise to pursue relationship with God above all else.

Vowed celibacy is the consecration of our sexuality, our way of being a man or woman in the world. As a vow, it touches our embodiment, or how we manifest ourselves, experience, behave, and are seen by others as men or women. Celibacy is a symbol of our core commitment to God because it concerns the deepest recesses of our selves. It is a commitment of our total life and the transformation of our future love.

There is no divorce of spirit and flesh in the vow of celibacy. Love of God and others is not abstract. I love with my body, my senses, my perceptions, my attitudes, my behaviors. How I express myself with my body is an act of relationship to God.

God loved us, too, through flesh. Through the dedication of his flesh, even to the point of the cross, Jesus made his love concrete. It would have been impossible for us to grasp his love at the same depth without this manifestation of love. Our response of love is also this specific.

To see, hear, touch, yearn for, think about, speak to, or relate to another is an embodied and sexual act. Celibacy touches all aspects of our embodiment and relational capacities. Most religious see sexual intercourse in conflict with their vow of celibacy. However, it takes reflection to connect habitual demeaning of others as also inconsistent with the vow. Here celibacy challenges us to a better relational life.

 Celibacy is more than continence. Reduced to a biological interpretation alone, the transformative "work" of the vow is overlooked. Celibacy is to teach us to love, the real task of our adult lives. Cultural views of sexuality, however, are weak in providing a vision of sexual integration which supports this vow.

What is sexuality?

 People view sexuality in diverse and contradictory ways. Many judge the appropriateness of sexual actions on the basis of ideas about sexuality as a whole. What sexuality is in their minds dictates how it is used. Others do not reflect on its meaning at all. Religious draw on these cultural understandings of sexuality. In crisis situations, cultural views generally lack the value perspective which supports the promise of celibacy.

 First world culture is individualistic. Morally, this translates into relativism, the notion there are no general norms binding on everyone. While celibates understand intellectually the meaning of celibacy, they depend at times on the relativism of the culture, not Christian teaching, for its practice.

 Reliance on culture occurs for many reasons. The controversy over sexual teaching in the Church and the restrictive teachings in the past regarding sexuality in religious orders lead some to dismiss the Church as a reliable guide regarding sex. Others have never had the opportunity to think past poor pedagogy regarding sexuality. In its place they have adopted a cultural view.

 There are a range of views of sexuality in the culture. Some adopt a recreational approach to sex and a subsequent ethic. According to this thinking, the purpose of sex is to provide individuals with entertainment, pleasure, or escape from the humdrum of living. This view is depicted in the media. One can choose on a Saturday night to go to a movie, go bowling, or have sex. All are equal and legitimate. Inappropriate sex would be violent sex or actions that contradict cultural sensibilities, such as rape or incest.

 Others find this a little crass and adopt a relational ethic. Here, the human meaning of sexuality stems from the role sex plays in relating one person to another. Sex is to fulfill spiritual, emotional, intellectual, and physical needs. Sex is appropriate as long as there is some type of mutual relationship between the partners and neither is manipulated or exploited. The purpose of sex is to express and bond a relationship. Whatever is agreed to by two consenting adults is ethical.

Selfishness, manipulation, exploitation are sources of evil in this understanding. They are wrong, but not the sexual actions themselves. The meaning of sexual actions, beyond that of their service to enhance a relationship, is not important. The relational ethic is attractive and operative in our culture. Celibates easily drift toward this ethic, especially when their commitment is challenged.

The Church does not accept either of these ethics of the sexual revolution. The recreational view puts too much stress on the physical element of sex and ignores important relational considerations. Sex for human beings is more than the sex drive alone.

Sexual bonding is a limited guide to sustaining relationships. Relationships ultimately demand a commitment of the person in areas of living beyond sexual compatibility. Sex plus emotional intimacy is closer to the human meaning of sexuality. Intimacy involves the capacity to blend one's life with another through shared commitment on many levels, not just sexual ones. Recreational sex obviously is outside the promise of celibacy.

The relational view is also inadequate. It gives too much emphasis to the romance of sex, to the neglect of important social dimensions. Sexuality involves family and needs for stability and long-term relationships. The relational view does not link sex to the human need for stability and permanency. It also lacks a strong view of sexual integration. Sexual integration happens over the long term in sexually active relationships, in fidelity to the social stance of spousehood and its multiple commitments. The relational view underplays these realities. People carry the scars of the transitional relationships which the relational ethic upholds.

Religious who engage in sex out of this relational understanding are living outside the vow. It is not easy to work through these relationships. Yet, if religious find themselves in them, they can talk over questions such as these with another.

What is the capacity of this behavior to lead to true integration, regardless of how much short-term good is derived? Is there real commitment in a relationship when a sexually active relationship is "fit into" an otherwise "celibate" life-style?

Can the benefits of either life-style, marriage or celibacy, be derived in this situation? Is it just? Is it fair to engage another in a sexual relationship which ultimately reduces that person's freedom to seek a partner who is free to be committed to him or her?

Church and the cultural ethic

The Church takes a different stance toward sex than does the recreational and relational view. It proposes an ethic which the Church calls integral. An integral ethic encompasses all the dimensions believed present in human sexuality: the physical and pleasurable, the intimate and relational, and the relationship between sex and parenthood and the family.[8] Healthy sexuality encompasses each dimension and holds it in proper balance with the others. An integral view sees the role of sex in human fulfillment differently than the culture does.

Psychologists remind us that people commonly address needs for self-acceptance, belonging, and desire for sexual pleasure by seeking out genital relationships. The need for relationship and intimacy, however, is deeper in the human psyche than is the need for genital sex.

Experience proves that genital activity provides no guarantee of intimacy and that intimacy is possible without genital expression. For those who meet their needs for love and intimacy within a genital relationship, it is the deeper relationship of love which provides the meaning of their shared sexual life, not the other way around. The attitude of the Church toward sex shares this perspective.

Homosexuality

The vow of celibacy relates to all sexual activity, both heterosexual and homosexual. Homosexuality is understood by the Church in light of its beliefs about human sexuality in general.

---

8. See Lisa Sowle Cahill, "Can We Get Real About Sex," *Commonweal* 117:15 (Sept. 14, 1990).

There is much we do not understand about homosexuality today. More research is needed on its causes and meaning, especially its possible biological and genetic origins. However, the stance of the Church to date regarding homosexuality stems from certain fundamental convictions.

The Church upholds homosexual persons as persons. Homosexuals are those people who experience a predominant, persistent, and exclusive attraction to sexual activity with members of their own sex. This experience is often a given, and not something chosen.

Many people have, at some time, a sexual attraction to members of their own sex. In adolescence, homosexual experience is not unusual as a developmental experience. Some feel a sexual attraction to both sexes, yet are attracted predominantly to one sex.

The Church reserves the term homosexual for those for whom sexual attraction to members of one's own sex is an established and pervasive orientation in their adult years. A homosexual person has an attraction to members of the same sex, yet a person can be homosexual in orientation without having acted upon this psychosexual attraction.[9]

Homosexual activity, choosing to engage in explicit sexual activity with a member of one's own sex, is inappropriate.[10] In the Church's understanding, human sexuality is fundamentally the two-in-one flesh expression of two different sexes.[11] Sex is meant

9. This is a debated fact among psychologists. Some would hold a person must have had some genital experience in order to be aware of his or her orientation. Others claim that actual fulfillment of this desire is not necessary for awareness of one's orientation. The Church asserts the latter view lest the impression be given that sexual activity has to precede awareness of orientation. See Gerald D. Coleman, S.S., *Homosexuality: Catholic Teaching and Pastoral Practice* (New York: Paulist Press, 1995) 17–22.

10. The Church assumes that both homosexual and heterosexual people can, for various reasons, desire homosexual activity. It is judged inappropriate for both. In other words, one does not need to be homosexual to engage in homosexual activity. Individuals may seek to fulfill a range of needs through homosexual behavior, as through any sexual behavior. For celibates, both homosexual and heterosexual activity is inappropriate.

11. Lisa Sowle Cahill, *Between the Sexes. Foundations for a Christian Ethic of Sexuality* (New York: Paulist Press, 1985).

to bond a person to someone sexually different. When that difference is not present, a core complementarity inherent to sexual bonding is missing.

The Church understands sexuality as generative and bonding. This is a meaning found in sexuality, not one put onto it. Sex between same-sex partners cannot create this unity because the sexual difference is not there. Two people who are sexually the same cannot be brought into the sexual otherness inherent to the meaning of human sexuality.[12]

Homosexual persons are often discriminated against in our society. The Church sees this as an evil and opposes all forms of discrimination. The vow of celibacy calls religious to share in this stance of the Church.

Same-sex friendship

Religious often live in same-sex living situations. They have special opportunities to develop life-long friendships with members of their own sex and the opposite sex. A challenge of celibacy is to love these friends in a way that is integral. Later we will consider friendships with the opposite sex, while here we deal with same-sex friends.

The oneness and difference of same-sex friends call them to a unity in friendship, but not a sexually genital one. Differences between friends of the same sex are interpersonal, not explicitly sexual. Same-sex love as friendship and intimacy is to be developed, but not same-sex sex.[13] Here religious walk the common road of all in the Church toward sexual integration.

There can be a desire for physical intimacy among same-sex friends without the presence of a persistent homosexual orientation. Even if same-sex friends mutually strive for a shared sexual pleasure, they cannot achieve a unity in one flesh. This is a physical impossibility. The unity they can achieve, the unity of friendship, can actually be harmed by sexual activity.

---

12. Kraft, *Whole and Holy Sexuality,* 109ff.

13. James Hanigan, *Homosexuality: The Test Case for Christian Ethics* (New York: Paulist Press, 1988) 97ff.

Friendship has a value in itself. It does not need sex. In fact, a key life support for all, but especially for a homosexual person, is the development of a stable friendship with at least one person.[14]

Sex plunges same-sex friends into ritual actions which they can only simulate, but never actually achieve.[15] Physical love-making reflects an intimacy not upheld in the true public relationship which exists between the parties, especially for celibates who have made primary commitments elsewhere. A disparity exists between private behavior and one's public stance. This marks a lack of authenticity in sexual expression.

The real basis of intimacy in same-sex friendship flourishes without a genital dimension. Emotional warmth, compassion, and tenderness are human qualities rooted in sexuality and are true expressions of it; yet, they are not specifically genital in nature or focus.

Same-sex activity between friends is understandable as a human search for love. However, it lacks the capacity, as sexual activity, to draw one out of oneself into the "other," the transcendent dimension of sexuality. For this reason, it is inappropriate.

This stance is not meant to underplay the sexual tensions which can enter in a relationship between two people who truly love one another, same sex or not. Yet, the Church's view is clear on how sexual behavior leads or does not lead to sexual integration. Later we will look at the range of human wants that persons attempt to fulfill through sexual activity. It may point to the deeper needs friends seek to fulfill in attempting sexual activity.

Sexual expression is only appropriate in the context of a mutual commitment in the faith community. Committed love as marriage is the condition necessary for genital expression to truly lead to human integration as love.[16] For the relational ethic, love

14. Bishops' Committee on Pastoral Research and Practices, *Principles To Guide Confessors in Questions of Homosexuality* (Washington, D.C., National Conference of Catholic Bishops, 1973).

15. Hanigan, *Homosexuality,* chapter 4.

16. One may ask, why not then same-sex marriage? The Church does not sanction same-sex marriage because partners cannot accomplish the unity of marriage, understood as a unity which transcends sexual difference. Also,

is always a necessary condition for expression of genital sexuality. Love, for the Church, is not always a sufficient condition for these expressions.[17] Only a pledged love, or marriage, is sufficient.

There is no other human relationship in which we are more vulnerable to another than in a sexual one. Respect of the person is a key criterion of authentic sexuality. Thus, the Church holds that only when vulnerability is mixed with the unique love of a pledged commitment does genital sexuality reach its true human potential.

Chastity

Chastity is for all Christians, not just those who are single or celibate. Donald Goergen identifies chastity as a virtue that accepts a person's striving for pleasure and "attempts to put that striving in the service of other human and Christian values." Chastity moderates one's sexuality and enables a person to place genitality's intense physical pleasure at the service of love.[18]

Virginity and chastity are not the same. Spouses are not virgins, yet they are chaste when their physical relationship expresses the commitment and love they have for one another in daily life. For various reasons religious might not be virgins, but they can begin a life rooted in Christian virginity with a promise of chastity in a vowed commitment. Virgins can be unchaste when they retain their virginity but engage in sexual behaviors inconsistent with their life stance. This is true even if their behavior does not involve the "loss" of physical virginity. This understanding of vowed celibacy is more challenging than a biological one alone.

---

children cannot be generated from this union. Even when reproductive technologies are used, a child does not come from the specific union of persons. See Coleman, *Homosexuality,* 119ff.

17. Vincent Genovesi, S.J., "Sexuality" in *The New Dictionary of Theology,* 947–54.

18. Donald Goergen, *The Sexual Celibate* (New York: Seabury Press, 1974).

Celibate chastity calls for an integrity of behavior that is not easy, as one enters into the complications which arise in human intimacy. One is neither married nor a child. All relationships in a celibate's life have to be judged as to their place in the primary relationship promised to God and the commitment to grow in love implied in the vow. Let us go on now to explore this promise in more detail.

Chapter Twenty-Two

Faces of Sexual Integration

Comparisons between marriage and celibacy are dubious. Examination of one in light of the other often clouds the integrity of each one. Yet, the affinities they share lure us into an attempt. Marriage and celibacy uniquely express the relationship between love and fruitfulness. Yet, they enrich their participants and the community in different ways. An analogy between them clarifies that celibacy is not just an internal state. Like marriage, it is a way of living and being in the world. In this sense, a life of celibacy is sexually single rather than partnered.

Celibacy is more than an internal aspiration or desire. It is a sexual reality lived in a well-defined social context. Celibacy is lived in a style of human relationships different from that of couples. In this sense, marriage is the institution of sexual partnering whereas celibacy is an institution of sexual singularity.[1]

Celibacy is not oriented toward partnering. Because of this, the sexual expressions appropriate to celibacy are those of affection. These are the social conventions of warmth and tenderness, rather than signs and gestures which involve genitality.

The sexual language of the celibate is to be consistent with the life-style in which he or she has chosen to experience intimacy

---

1. M. Rondet, *Le célibat évangelique dans un mode mixte* (Paris: Desclee de Brouwer, 1978) 15, as quoted in Andre Guidon, *The Sexual Creators* (Lanham, Md.: University Press of America, 1986) 206. See also Donald Goergen, *The Sexual Celibate,* 108.

and interpersonal relatedness.[2] Sexual expressions of the celibate are those of intentional friendship, rather than coupling. It is inappropriate, therefore, for a celibate to engage in intercourse or the physical intimacy which leads towards it.

Coupling and intentional friendship

Society often considers intimacy and sex as the same. In the culture, a life without sex is a life without intimacy. The faith community has a different view. Sex alone is not necessary for happiness. Human intimacy, however, is a far deeper and non-negotiable need. Celibacy and intimacy are not only compatible, but necessary.

Intimacy is the willingness to give and receive expressions of deep personal warmth, affection, and tenderness. Celibate life offers many opportunities for intimacy. Prayer, community, ministry, and family provide means for intimacy, yet friendship is often the most important door to this experience. What makes relationships of a celibate intimate, yet different from marriage? Celibate relationships are characterized by intentional friendship, whereas married relationships are distinguished by coupling.

Intimacy for the celibate is discovered in the mutual interest of friendship, not in the "us" of coupling. What is the distinction? Virginia Finn puts it this way: in friendship "your focus is on me, not us, and mine on you, not us."[3]

Intentional friendship is inclusive. The sexual relationship of coupling is exclusive. Inclusivity translates into open bonding and relinquishing possession. Friends can "feel" the inclusivity of friendship in its capacity to welcome and relate to others. There is a marked fluidity of relationship in intentional friendships.

2. Andrew Guidon uses the notion of sexuality as a language. Sexual behavior must be consistent with the reality of the partners to have integrity. The intimacy of physical behavior is to be consistent with the public social commitment. Genital activity on the part of committed celibates, therefore, is a language inconsistent with the social reality of the partners. See *The Sexual Language* (The University of Ottawa Press, 1976) 83.

3. Virginia Finn, "Two Ways of Loving" in Mary Ann Huddleston, *Celibate Loving* (New York: Paulist Press, 1981) 29–45.

At a congregational gathering, a casual comment alluded to the subtle inclusivity of intentional friendship. One member came to sit at a lunch table with another and remarked, "I'll sit with you, since you are not attached." Did the person have no friends? This was not the case. All people are "attached" to their friends in some way. However, the person commenting sensed that the energies of the member were not preoccupied with those friendships. The person was open to many relationships and actively sought them.

In intentional friendship, there is no one dimension friends share together that may not be shared with another. There are confidences exchanged between friends that will not be made public. However, any dimension of self that is shared could be shared with others if chosen.

In marriage, the sexual sharing of the couple is necessarily exclusive. Married partners are intentional friends, yet their relationship is distinct because they are also a couple. They are a couple, not just sexually, but in many other dimensions of their lives. Even legal recognition is given to the privacy of their communication.

Coupling creates difficulties in open relationships among members of a religious community. If extreme, members feel they have no relational place in the community. People are "taken."[4] Friendship is not guaranteed in religious life nor do religious develop all friendships within community, but the style of celibate life is one which should promote opportunities for friendship.

The sexual expressions appropriate for intentional friendship are the expressions of affection common to a culture. They are the same gestures married partners would extend to those other than their spouse. It is understandable that, at times, celibates desire the intimacies of genital sex with close friends. Married people also could be attracted to the same with a friend or a colleague. However, primary commitments lead both to choose otherwise.

Because the life-style of the celibate is single rather than partnered, genital expressions of sexuality are always inappropriate. Intercourse or foreplay contributes to the merger and creation of

---

4. This can extend to patterns of friendship beyond coupling when new members cannot find a place because patterns of relationship are set.

the affective center of coupling. Celibate friends do not have this bond with each other.

The social commitment of celibate friends is different than marriage. Friendship may be lifelong but not lived in the social stance of spousehood. Celibate friends may need to move away from one another. Their responsibilities require them to follow the calls they choose as primary in their lives. Integrity in friendship grows in the light of these commitments.

Placement of emotional energy and focus are distinct in intentional friendship and coupling. On occasion, celibates do engage in "coupling" relationships, which resemble a marriage in energy and focus, yet may lack genital relations. These relationships occur with a member of the opposite sex, or same sex. Yet, the vow calls celibates beyond them.

If celibacy is only biological then the lack of sexual activity would qualify these relationships as proper for celibate life. However, a fuller view of celibacy questions their energy and focus. Many drift in and out of such relationships as they grow in love. The call of celibacy invites us beyond nesting in these relationships. Celibacy challenges us to ask and discern who and what is the center of our emotional energy?

Central to celibate loving is freedom of the heart. Vowed celibates do not create and maintain an "us" or a shared center through which to live, as does a couple. Celibates do share their lives with those they love, yet they are sexually and emotionally single. They merge with no one person as a life partner, even though they have deep and lifelong friendships. Celibates love their friends, but they love *them*, not the them in an "us."

The presence of "coupling" in community today has many roots. It is an indication of transitions and tensions in community life. Coupling can be an effort to heal from a time in religious life when emotional intimacy was not allowed. It can be an attempt at emotional survival in some community situations. Ministry commitments also move religious to live in numerical "twos."[5] These "twos" may be a couple or may be friends, or may

5. Some communities have a tradition of missioning members in twos. Obviously this has nothing to do with coupling.

not be either. The difference between intentional friendship, "coupling," and companionship is deeper than geography.

Intentional friends know, "We have posited 'oneness' elsewhere, in our primary commitments, and are free . . . to be an unencumbered 'me and you' together."[6] This commitment creates a style of relating which comes from the depth of who a celibate is. Celibates' friends love them in their difference, and do not demand of them a merger.

Dimensions of sexuality

The path of sexual integration in celibacy involves many dimensions of sexuality. People think superficially that celibate relationships are asexual and that celibates live without a sexual life. Human sexuality is far more complex.

Sexuality is far more deeply rooted in our psyche than its genital expression. Living without genital sex is not living without sexuality. Sexuality is both the physiological and psychological ground of our capacity to love. Innate, dynamic, and integral to being human, it is God's way of calling us into communion with others through our need to reach out and touch—emotionally, intellectually, and physically.[7]

Sexuality includes the capacity to relate to others with emotional warmth, compassion, and tenderness. These affective qualities are rooted in sexuality and are true expressions of it. Yet they are not specifically genital in nature or focus.[8]

When we act as loving individuals, we are acting as sexual beings, even though we are not involved in genital relations. Many loving relationships between parents and children, friends, and colleagues involve no suggestion of genital involvement.

There can be pressure to engage in inappropriate genital relations in any relationship. The genital expressions of love can be more or less important or imperative depending on how well developed the human affectivity of the partner is. In other words, it

---

6. Finn, "Two Ways of Loving," 38.
7. Genovesi, *In Pursuit of Love*, 141.
8. *Ibid.*, 142ff.

is not unusual to find that to the extent one's affective qualities are underdeveloped and unappreciated, there is a preoccupation with the genital or physical aspects of sexuality. This can lead to behavior that is destructive and/or futile because although physical sexual needs are real, they are not our highest needs.

Jane has been professed for three years and is a pastoral associate in a small parish. She lives in community with three others, the next in age is twenty years older than herself. Jane's community is an average mix of care, concern, misunderstanding, and forgiveness.

Jane met Jim, an associate pastor in the next parish. Jim has a network of friends in the parish, yet struggles to live in the parish rectory with a pastor who seldom speaks to him. Jim's description of parish life is, "I eat pasta and he eats out." The pastor is kind but distant.

Jane and Jim met at a deanery meeting. Socially they began to go out about a year ago. They found mutuality in a relationship where both could relax, blow off steam, and find companionship. Jane and Jim are friends. There is a pressure from time to time to allow the potential physical dimension of their friendship to take over. They have to work at developing their relationship at the level of affective sexuality. They count on each other for friendship but avoid moving into a partnered life-style.

Experienced religious have seen relationships like Jane's and Jim's go many ways. Many remain friends and develop a good relationship. Some allow the physical side of the relationship to take over. Others leave and marry.

In friendship, it is difficult to separate the person from the patterns of relating that develop in a relationship. Religious can find themselves in a relationship which is going in a different direction than they intended. It begins as a social relationship, yet involves increasing brushes with potential sexual situations.

Questions which help to discern the direction of a relationship are the following: What do we generally do together? If there is physical affection expressed and the physical dimension of the relationship stopped, would we still be interested in each other? Do I feel comfortable in this relationship? Does it distract me from other things I value: prayer, community, other friendships? How do others see this relationship?

Because issues of intimacy, sex, and relational needs can be confusing, exciting, and challenging, all at the same time, a good spiritual director can help one be honest, acquire self-knowledge, and gain confidence and freedom in relationships. There is an apprenticeship to love that must be faced. Many goods can come from not being afraid of relationships. Yet, the illusions which also arise must be sought out. This is true for both heterosexual and homosexual relationships.

The common learning is that if our highest human needs go unrecognized and remain unmet, no satisfaction of our physical sexual needs is likely to result in a sense of human fulfillment. Rollo May puts it this way, "For human beings the more powerful need is not for sex, *per se*, but for relationships, intimacy, acceptance, and affirmation."[9] We long for intimacy. Human experience testifies that a genital relationship is no guarantee of intimacy, and intimacy is possible without genital expression.

Sexual integration is the capacity to move beyond oneself in loving and warm relationships in a manner that respects the truth of oneself and the other. For a celibate this happens in a major way through the development of sexual affectivity. This growth occurs in our spiritual life, relationships, community, and ministry. Let us explore what this means.

Affective sexuality

Affective sexuality refers to feelings, emotions, or moods that move toward or incorporate some form of intimacy. Through affective sexuality we are motivated to get close to another, to "touch" another affectively in some way. We not only seek relationships, but those which involve closeness. Even the desire for such relationships is evidence of affective sexuality acting in our lives.

Affective sexuality has varied expressions. It can be expressed through physical signs, a kiss or hug, a caring gesture meant to communicate a closeness which is distinctive of a relationship.

---

9. Rollo May, *Love and Will* (New York: W. W. Norton and Co., 1969) 311.

Friends know what certain looks mean, looks of caring, of delight, of acceptance, of a shared sense of humor. Community members recognize when they are being reassured, comforted, and supported. They know when others are "on their side" personally. When care is expressed, affectivity is involved.

The spiritual dimension of affective sexuality is a faithfulness and presence that sustains all love. Consideration, warmth, hospitality, kindness all are ways our affectivity is shared. While some celibates fantasize that genital relations cure all ills, married people know that these affective signs are the glue of a happy relationship.

In close relationships, affective sexual behavior can be an end in itself or it can be in the service of and part of genital behavior. Affective sexuality does not need to lead to genital behavior. Intention is the determining factor whether affective sexuality is an end in itself or is a means to genital behavior.[10]

We know our intention by asking, just where do I want this gesture to lead? Do I want a sexual relationship with this person which is different from the commitment we have? Am I interested in this person, or in the physical relationship which we share, or might share? People are different. Friends learn from experience to make choices to keep their expressions of affection at the appropriate level. They choose to avoid situations in which problems will likely occur.

Celibates need to be aware of what their gestures communicate in ministry situations. Does Mary walk up to George, Ann's husband, at a parish dance, and put her arm around him? A married woman might do this with a man other than her spouse, and maybe not.

Does Tom hug his parishioners indiscriminately when they leave Mass? Sometimes this is appropriate, sometimes not. Many feel welcomed by it. Some people find it invasive, others offensive. For instance, people who have been physically or sexually abused may find any uninvited touch alienating rather than pastoral. When religious are conscious of their affective needs, they can meet them in ways that respect the reality of the other person.

10. Kraft, *Whole and Holy Sexuality*, 37ff.

The initial years of a celibate commitment involve learning that one can live a life of celibacy, abstaining from genital behavior and the affective behavior which leads to it, and still be fulfilled. The commitment of celibacy, however, takes a different shape in later life. Middle-age celibates accept in a new way that they have not passed life on through children of their own. They acknowledge there is no life partner with whom they will share their remaining years. Older religious are challenged to a new kind of love in relinquishing possessions and willingness to affirm others.

Sometimes religious "drift" into situations in which poor choices in close relationships are made. Keith Clark comments that religious often set up roadblocks on the road to genital intimacy rather than put on the brakes. This approach comes across in terms such as, "at least we did not do. . . ."[11]

Religious who have not confronted the intention behind their affective behavior are called by their vow to ask themselves honestly, just what do I want? Looking into the mirror of the vow rather than the illusionary mist of societal practices is a step toward integrity.

Beginning religious who are testing their capacity to live a vow of celibacy do so by living it now. They strive to make better choices if they make mistakes. The desire to live the vow and the capacity to make concrete progress is a sign of a sincere vocation. Celibacy is not a denial of genital sexuality, but an integration of it.

Genital sexuality

Genital sexuality refers to the behavior, thoughts, fantasies, desires, and feelings that involve or encourage genital behavior.[12] Genital behavior and genitality are different. Sexual intercourse and masturbation are explicit forms of genital behavior. Feelings and fantasies that do or can activate genital processes are modes of genitality.

---

11. Keith Clark, *An Experience of Celibacy* (Notre Dame, Ind.: Ave Marie Press, 1982) 168ff.

12. Kraft, *Whole and Holy Sexuality,* 59ff.

Genitality incorporates thoughts and feelings that can, but need not, be expressed in genital behavior. Signs such as genital erection and lubrication and the presence of sexual desires and fantasies indicate activation of genital sex that may or may not be promoted or realized in genital behavior.

Genital sexuality in itself or as only a biological process does not exist. Rather, genital sexuality is an expression of the whole person. As we misuse, celebrate, or realize our genitality, we are doing the same to ourselves.

Our genitality also has a quasi-sacramental function in our lives. The processes of genitality, that of being excited by another, point to the basic direction of human growth, that of going out of ourselves. Our genital sexuality in this sense is a sign of our transcendence. We are meant to go beyond ourselves, bond with others, and create new life.

Genital sex takes time, place, and commitment. When discussing this reality with college students, some usually protest that their apartments offer enough "time and place" for good enough sex. But "time and place" in the above statement refer to the relational time and continuity for true relationship to exist over the long haul. This is the description of marriage.

Marriage does not guarantee authentic genitality, but it does offer the conditions in which it can occur. When love has no time or social place, tension and frustration eventually emerge explicitly or implicitly. Healthy genitality is the capacity to give and receive genital expressions of love as part of a broader love commitment that is emotional, functional, and spiritual. This is a description of the pledged love of marriage. Celibates are called to follow the common road of all Christians in sexual behavior. The faith community holds that sex is for marriage.

The celibate life-style does not afford the kind of time, place, and commitment that can foster loving genital relations. Time is integral to the meaning of married love because married love is the desire to love someone for a lifetime. Genital sex is part of a love which involves not only a physical presence but a spiritual and functional experience of spousehood. Shared commitment integrates the persons of the partners through the project of marriage. Celibates, however, who engage in genital relations are try-ing to integrate their lives around two all-inclusive commitments. Celibacy is a way of loving, not a ministerial commitment alone.

Vowed celibates who engage in genital behaviors behave in a way that may be understandable and normal, meaning not pathological, but this is not healthy or moral.[13] It may reduce ten-sion and afford pleasurable satisfaction. It will not, however, per-manently achieve health or wholistic sexual growth. In fact, such behavior violates personal wholeness and holiness.

Celibates on the road to sexual integration learn to sublimate their genital desires into their broader life goals. Some will fall in love and struggle with these choices. Others may never fall in love and yet be relational people. Both will develop their capacity to deal with life's moments of intimacy and loneliness realistically and constructively according to the first choice in their lives.[14]

Primary sexuality

Elements of the varied aspects of sexuality can be found in the sexual ethics of the Church. Recently, the Church has discussed whether sexism is a sin. This is a very interesting question in light of the history of moral reflection on sexuality in the Church.[15]

Some find an exaggerated emphasis on sexuality in the moral life of the Church. The faithful over the years have become pre-occupied with avoiding sins of a sexual nature. As a result, less at-tention is given to other sinful behavior, not sexual in nature, but nonetheless damaging to others. Some go to the other extreme, leaving their sexual lives relatively unexamined. Balance in sexual practice tips different ways on the scales of history.

Today gender relations occupy a focal place in church con-sciousness, to the point that we discuss the sinful nature of sex-

13. "Pathological" here is used loosely to mean not repressed.

14. See Clark, *An Experience of Celibacy,* chapters 13 and 14.

15. John Mahoney, *The Making of Moral Theology* (Oxford: Claredon Press, 1987) 27–36.

ism. On what basis is sexism a sin?[16] Sexism is not directed toward genital behavior. As a human behavior, it involves more pervasive interpersonal relations. Is it a sexual sin? If it is, how is it? To reflect on these questions we need to consider a third mode of sexuality, primary sexuality.[17]

Primary sexuality refers to how men and women are present to reality. All persons, including hermits, have primary sexual relations. Primary sexuality accounts for the fact that we experience life differently as a man or as a woman.

Development of primary sexuality includes integration of male and female elements in each personality. Jung claims we integrate the masculine and feminine dimensions of life as *animus* and *anima*. This is done in part through interaction with members of the opposite sex.

Primary sexuality is involved in core issues in our lives. How do I view my body? How do I care for it? How do I see myself as a man or a woman? How do I view men? What are my spontaneous reactions to women?

Gender and learned behavior account for differences between men and women. People debate the nature of these differences, beyond physiology. Some claim there are specific characteristics ascribed to men and women, such as, men are aggressive and women passive. Others find this overstated. They claim there is no one system of characteristics based on gender alone.[18] All human beings share the same personality potentials, yet culture supports development of certain characteristics according to gender. Regardless of where one stands in these debates, the development of primary sexuality is an adult task. It is also part of the vow of celibacy.

We develop our primary sexual self through interaction with persons of the opposite sex, nature, the fine and performing arts, literature, dreams, prayer, and the formation of values. These ac-

16. This is not a formal analysis of sexism as a sin. It is a pastoral reflection.

17. Kraft, *Whole and Holy Sexuality,* 25ff.

18. For a discussion of appropriate and inappropriate theological uses of the distinction between the sexes, see Carr, *Transforming Grace,* 49ff.

tivities assist in healthy sexual integration. They form part of the vow of celibate chastity, even without explicit "sexual" overtones.

Primary sexuality engages our perceptions of appropriate work roles. How does gender influence our attitudes towards the competencies of men and women? How often does this "sexual" issue enter into a life of ministry?

Primary sexuality influences theological perceptions of men's and women's roles in the Church. It touches the capacity to recognize, for instance, male and female conceptions of God in the tradition. Primary sexuality forges a link between sexuality and spiritual growth. Women can welcome feminine images of God, going beyond traditional male depictions if they so choose. Men will move past restrictions to spiritual development in their culture, such as, "only women go to church."

Primary sexuality involves learned behavior about what it means to be male or female. Personal history as a man or woman can have a negative impact on spiritual growth.[19] Replacing old tapes and behaviors by new ones is a task of adult life. To answer these calls of sexual integration is an expression of the vow of celibate chastity.

Healthy primary sexuality creates a harmony between a person's inner self and one's embodied self. It influences how women and men regard each other, how the arts and nature foster spiritual growth, how prayer is fed by good music, and how well we execute liturgy. All ways in which our senses are brought into the development of our spiritual self engage our primary sexuality. The vow calls us to grow in these areas of human living.

Sexism, by men or women, is a failure of primary sexuality. We can ponder whether there is more pain due to deficits in primary sexuality or from inappropriate sexual activity in today's Church. The need for better relationships between sexes in the Church challenges all vowed religious. Viewing sexuality as primary, affective and genital awakens a religious to the depth of development which the vow of celibate chastity inspires.

---

19. Lucia Capacchione, *Recovery of Your Inner Child* (New York: Simon and Schuster, 1991) 267ff.

Celibacy and personal goals

Vowed celibacy is a framework of love meant to lead to sexual integration. Integration for a celibate occurs through primary and affective dimensions of sexuality and the non-expression of genital behavior.

Celibates, as all adults, can seek to meet non-sexual needs through sexual behavior. Often it is not sex itself which is the internal pressure. It is other personal goals sought through genital behavior. All humans desire a core of human experiences for love and acceptance. Celibates need to be alert to these desires within them and find non-genital means to realize them.

The culture suggests that worthwhile human goals can be reached through genital sex alone. The faith community sees this as illusion. Celibates learn that human needs sought through sex alone have their true source of satisfaction in deeper human activities of love, commitment, intimacy, and meaning.

Celibates struggle with all adults who seek sexual integration. They try to become respectful and loving people who avoid exploitative, manipulative, and deceptive sexual behavior. Married, single, and vowed religious share this challenge of chastity. Chastity, lived in different frameworks of life, is the common road of all Christians.

Some argue that celibate and married Christians do not have a common road of chastity. Those who are married have a sexual partner. They do not feel the loneliness which enters the non-partnered life of the celibate.

Yet, loneliness is part of the life of any adult. It enters all life-styles differently. Marriage partners have celibate relationships. They have them with all others except their spouse. Their fidelity is to one alone, in good times and bad. Central to any adult life-style is a surrender. Chastity is a dedication and self-control prompted by love in all life-styles. A celibate learns to deal with the inevitable loneliness of his or her life-style creatively. A religious meets needs usually supported by genital activity in adulthood in a different way.

Sexuality and human needs

The central motivating force in healthy genitality is love.[20] Genital love makes love immediate and concrete. The need of a celibate to give and receive love is no less real. In marriage the need for love, however, is not met through genital sex alone. Instead, the context of a loving relationship gives meaning to genital sex. For the vowed celibate the need for love is met through a deepening spiritual life, family, community, ministry, and friends.

Sex can be motivated by the need to reduce sexual tension and experience pleasure. For vowed celibates sexual needs do not go away with the profession of vows. It is normal to want to fulfill those needs. Celibates learn to integrate them through suppression rather than repression, through mortification, discipline, humor, prayer, and redirection of energies.

Over time, celibates learn their vulnerabilities, when their sexual needs are likely to be more of a challenge. In these situations they discover ways to make choices in the direction of celibacy. As do partners in marriage, celibates foster their pledged love, even when painful.

Escape and search for ecstasy are drives that seek outlets in genital activity. Sex can be an attempt to lessen painful feelings of anxiety or depression. Yet, loveless sex is only a temporary remedy for these feelings. Sex "at any cost" is a symptom of deep hurt within.

It is human to want to escape, to leave the humdrum of everyday life and "get lost" in another. However, ecstasy can be a consequence of loving genital relations but not a good motivation for them. Escape through sex is short-lived, and the return to reality is filled with disappointment.

The need for connective and transpersonal experience in celibate life is real. Prayer, communion with nature, love of the arts, and the non-genital intimacy of friendship are all possible avenues of fulfillment. When celibates search for ecstasy through sex, there can be lack of connective experience in these other areas of life.

20. Kraft, *Whole and Holy Sexuality*, 91ff.

Sex is a way to feel special. However, feeling special is a consequence, not a goal, of loving sex. People who love one another find joy in pleasuring their partner. To seek to be special through sex alone is a fleeting satisfaction. When genital sex is sought simply to satisfy the need to feel special, exploitation is involved. Exploited persons may momentarily feel special but later feel alienated and abused.

Can a celibate fill a need to be special without a sexual partner? This is a spiritual question. Yet, married people ask similarly. Would life have been different if I married Joan instead of Sarah, Paul instead of Rick? Would my "needs" have been better filled?

These ponderings do not have answers. They indicate the limits of any life choice, rather than imply celibacy is the wrong one. Basic to all commitments is a decision to keep wanting what and to whom one is committed.

Celibates find they are special through warm and tender relationships with a wide variety of people. They form intentional friendships with some and contribute to the community in a satisfying and meaningful manner. A sense of one's unique way of loving is mirrored back as friendship, family, community, and ministerial relationships grow.

People search for self-completion through sex. Yet those who find wholeness do so because of a committed love. Celibates seek self-completion through their varied relationships, development of talents, and progress in their spiritual life.

Relationship to Jesus opens one to knowledge of self. Self-knowledge grows as one knows Jesus. Jesus does not replace other people in celibate life. Celibates need friends, just as Jesus needed friends. Yet, without an active and growing spiritual relationship, celibacy lacks its grounding in love.[21]

Power, hostility, and past experiences motivate genital sex. Surrender and mutuality in pleasure are significant experiences of people in love. Sexual energy, however, can be expressed in power plays that create, in a non-genital way, the experience of con-

---

21. A whole area which will be left untreated is the deeper relationship of genitality to spiritual dynamics. It is beyond the scope of this text.

quering or withholding. Exploitative use of power in the life of a celibate can express a weak sexual identity.

Hostility also motivates sexual behavior. Hostility is expressed through the need to punish, humiliate, reject, and control. A celibate can adopt an abusive relational style. Verbal, emotional, and sexual abuse can enter into relationships. Vowed celibacy calls for a commitment to deal with these issues and their perpetrators as part of a wholistic life-style.

Some engage in genital sex as a search for a substitute mother or father. When there is a significant age difference in the partners this unconscious need can be operative. Members within a same-sex community are vulnerable to exploitation by these drives. Their presence magnifies the responsibility of a community to create sexually safe formation programs for its new members.

When there has been sexual abuse in childhood, genital desires can be repressed or compulsively acted out. In such cases, clinical healing is needed so that a celibate life can be embraced. Hurts from the past need not become prescriptions for the future. Celibacy is lived through each person's unique history, never a perfect one. Acting out sexually, however, can postpone healing of these issues rather than help them.

People can seek sex simply as a search for intimacy. Some have never had much intimacy with anyone, including parents and friends. It is understandable to transfer fundamental needs and desire to be loved into a desire to be genitally intimate.

Genital satisfaction, however, is not an adequate replacement for the intimacy of love. Celibates who experience the intimacy of love will have genital desires, but they are more likely to make sense of them, to control them creatively, and to integrate their genitality into the total project of their lives.

The sexual integration called forth through the vow of celibacy has many faces, seasons, and moods. Our needs drive us at various times toward others in ways with which we may not be familiar. We explore relationships, we make mistakes, we learn about ourselves and our God.

Celibacy's hidden integration goes on like the field planted in the gospel, which grows up overnight, unknown to the planter.

On one level, a celibate commitment takes energy and alertness to grow in necessary honesty and skills to live it integrally. On another level, its flowering is hard to measure. Along the journey of human search and desire, the capacity to love appears as a gift. The celibate finds that through fidelity, one day he or she has become like the tree in the gospel, a place of love where many can gather and a few find a home.

When and where does one become a loving woman, a loving man? Celibacy has deep roots, engaging our life energies. It comes to life within the adult tasks of our development. We look now at the life passages it navigates.

Chapter Twenty-Three

From Cost to Consolation

Vowed celibacy is more than the practice of continence. It is the journey by which one becomes a loving person through commitment to the person of Jesus Christ. The religious integrates and negotiates the life tasks of the adult years, identity, intimacy, and generativity, through a celibate life which is religiously motivated. Love of Jesus and his people is expressed through a vowed celibacy, rather than marriage or the single state. Religious develop in love through the vows and the charism of their community.

Vowed celibacy engages the major life crisis of adolescence and adult years: identity versus identity confusion, intimacy versus isolation, and generativity versus stagnation. These challenges provide the context in which the love of a celibate person takes flesh. God summons each to growth by these invitations of life.

Each religious follows a singular path to God. A religious vocation is given according to a particular charism, at a specific time in the Church and the world, with a personal mission. There is no such thing as a uniform vocation in this sense. Each religious has special issues in his or her life history. The vows embrace the challenges, gifts, and difficulties of one's particular life course. By all these means, Jesus grows in intimacy with the religious and reveals himself.

Vowed celibacy, in this sense, is not a once and for all decision. It shapes the path of sexual integration and adult maturation long after a religious makes an initial promise. Yet the path of celibacy involves questions asked by other Christians.

Adults ask who they are and what their relationship is with the next generation. They seek loving relationships and strive to overcome the tendency to exploit, resent, and manipulate. They search for the meaning of life and their place in it. Religious share the developmental struggles of all adults, but through the sexual stance of a celibate choice. Erikson points to some practical issues of this growth.

Identity versus identity confusion

Individuals usually come to a sense of personal identity in late adolescence and early adult life. Identity is a self-recognition, an experience of oneself as a center of continuity and sameness. Identity involves the capacity to make an occupational commitment or take on a productive social role. Since people know who they are, others can count on them.[1] Identity confusion is simply the opposite: the person cannot "take hold." There is lacking a sufficient sense of self. A person is one way one day and another way the next.

A sense of identity is involved in recognition of a call to vowed celibacy. Celibacy is not an exterior choice alone. The choice of celibacy is part of "settling one's vocation." It involves a recognition that "this is me," and a feeling that "my deepest self is at home."[2] Identity is formed through these life choices.

A sense of identity before entering religious life is essential. One needs a basic sense of self, distinct from others.[3] Yet, identity is deepened and solidified through the formative processes of religious life. Incorporation into a community, adoption of the social stance of a religious, and ongoing formation add new dimensions to personal identity. Social sexual identity is part of this stable sense of self. Celibacy is not only an internal choice but a socially recognizable stance.[4]

1. Capps, *Deadly Sins and Saving Virtues*, 46ff., 95ff.
2. We say this realizing that some experience a call to vowed celibacy after living another adult vocation.
3. Merkle, *Committed by Choice*, chapter 3.
4. Here we are not speaking of sexual identity in a more basic sense of heterosexual or homosexual identity. While this is a formation issue, its treatment is beyond the scope of this writing.

New religious and seminarians must live celibacy practically, as they "try it on" as a life stance. This is necessary for celibacy to become part of their identity. Good modelling from those who have integrated celibacy into their lives is beneficial. New members and seminarians can be disillusioned and violated by exploitative relationships within and outside formation circles. When vowed members tolerate inappropriate behavior by peers or new members, they teach that celibacy is not part of the social identity of the group.

Ambiguity in sexual practice complicates formation of celibate identity in religious institutions today. To allow these situations is a failure in celibacy of the whole community. Those with integrity who are willing to walk with new members, sharing their struggles, give them a gift which cannot be bestowed by others. They support their discernment through clarity of living. They witness that fidelity and happiness in the life-style are within reach.

Virtue-vice struggle

The virtue-vice struggle surrounding identity is fidelity and pride.[5] Fidelity is the ability to sustain loyalties. In late adolescence, fidelity overcomes the drive toward pride or a sense of false identity. Religious struggle with fidelity over pride throughout their lives. The search to be faithful goes beyond a developmental stage; it is a life challenge.

Pride is an overly high opinion of oneself, an exaggerated sense of self-esteem shown in haughty and arrogant behavior. Healthy pride is a good self-concept and sense of personal worth. It is integral to sexual integration. False pride is a conceit and hypocrisy that finds joy in doing harm. Pride causes isolation. It is a denial of the need for others and for community. Pride makes one inaccessible and unreachable in community and ministry. It undermines others and makes pompous demands for attention.

Pride is self-deceptive. It hides anything that could taint a high self-opinion. Even "self-improvement" can flow from the self-

---

5. Here again I am indebted to Capps and Erikson as previously cited.

centeredness and self-absorption of pride. Here "growth" is never linked to its significance for others.

Ultimately, pride has religious overtones. Pride falsely places the individual at the center of the universe. Focus on God and the ego-inflation of pride are incompatible. Pride prevents a deeper identity which only relationship to God can give. It offers a false self of personal illusion.

Fidelity, on the other hand, is the capacity for duty, truthfulness, genuineness, loyalty, fairness, and devotion. Fidelity recognizes that self-worth is not based on qualities possessed independently of relationships with others. Fidelity builds community because it acknowledges the support, love, and nurturance of friends and community.

Fidelity is a mark of identity in religious life. Healthy religious know themselves. They found their identity in commitments to significant others and their spiritual commitment to God. Fidelity can face the inevitable contradictions of life. It demonstrates its power before reasons for infidelity: disillusionment, disappointment, and frustration. Fidelity survives personal crisis because it is rooted in a deep sense of self.

Many adults develop fidelity through sexual partnering. Celibates develop fidelity through surrender to God, friendship, ministry, family relationship, and communal bonding. The celibate witnesses particularly to the faithful love possible in these relationships.

Fidelity grounds the identity of a religious by offering a different basis of self-worth than pride. Pride suggests one is the center of self worth. Fidelity fosters self-worth through its capacity to mutually bestow and receive it.

Religious life offers opportunities to call and be called. Vowed celibacy challenges religious to recognize the value of others, not just themselves. Affirmation of the worth of others is key to community living and a sign of healthy personal identity.

Religious find their identity in Jesus through the same process of being chosen, called, and converted to recognition of his love for them. Through the experience of mutual love, the religious is de-centered on self. The deception of pride is overcome. In faithful love, the religious receives a self-worth that cannot be taken away because it is given by Jesus himself.[6]

Intimacy versus isolation

The next stage of life embraces a new form of adulthood. The giant leap is taken from receiving to giving love. Intimacy is the capacity to share a mutual trust and to regulate cycles of work, recreation, needs, and desires to blend our lives with another. We commit ourselves to concrete affiliations and partnerships despite the hardships and compromises involved in them.[7]

Incorporation into a religious community is an experience of intimacy for religious. Incorporation invites us to blend our lives with the community. By becoming minister, friend, family member, and disciple, the tension between bonding and isolation surfaces. Close friendships, relationships with mentors, and spiritual growth are other invitations to intimacy. Being "sister" or "brother" requires the blending of intimacy. When the capacity for intimacy is not present, isolation manifests in a mechanical and distant style of relationship, once characteristic of religious life. Community life becomes impossible.

Isolation, the negative pole of this crisis, is the inability to risk involvement with others. Members stand aloof or engage in competitive and combative behavior. Lack of investment in relationship weakens community life. Suspicion, backbiting, outbursts of rancor are all faces of the competitive and negative spirit of isolation.

---

6. Here a quote from Rahner illustrates the concreteness of this love as he answers the question, what happens when we love Jesus? "We may begin with the unhesitating assertion that in loving Jesus we love an actual human being, a real person. We seek him, we think about him, we speak with him, we feel his nearness, we have the perception, the sensation, that our own life is very substantially co-formed through him, through this other, through his own thinking and feeling and perception, through his life and love, and so on." *The Love of Jesus and the Love of Neighbor* (New York: Crossroad, 1983) 39.

7. Erik H. Erikson, *Childhood and Society*, 263. Experientially, intimacy involves the desire to know and be known.

Relationships of intimacy move outward to connect to the wider community. The "protective partnerships" of isolation seek to create a "world apart." Different from the privacy needed for friendship, "protective partnerships" promote withdrawal from others for personal survival. Because they are dependencies where people try to find their identity in another, they preclude real intimacy.

The virtue-vice polarity of intimacy versus isolation is lust and love. Lust, in its traditional form, manifests itself as a drive for unrestrained sexual gratification. However, lust has a more subtle side to it, as the lust for power. The central dynamic of lust is the desire for momentary gratification.

Lust is not selective of a partner. Whoever is available fulfills its needs. While intimacy desires a future with another, lust lives for the moment. Lust "burns its bridges" as it moves from person to person to satisfy its needs. Lust uses people and then drops them. A lustful style of relationship is opposed to love, even without a sexual component.

Disloyalty, cruelty, and unwillingness to assume responsibility for the consequences of one's actions are forms of lust. There is no real giving of self or receiving of another. Love, on the other hand, is the antithesis of lust. Love involves selectivity.

Healthy relationships are selective. A religious chooses friends and decides to invest in some relationships and not in others. A religious is selective in choosing a community. Love chooses this congregation, not that one. Lust makes no real choices. It drifts from person to person, situation to situation, trying to fill its needs. When reciprocity is expected, lust will move on.

Love softens the antagonisms of close relationships. In relationships between opposite sexes, love downgrades and overcomes gender tensions. It supports the other through mutual devotion.

Love finds intimacy satisfying and draws on its energy for activities outside the relationship. Love endures, lust fades. Love's energy never ends. It defeats lust by outlasting it.

Lust undermines community life, even if explicit sexual behavior is not present. Lust drains a community of energy by expecting the "other" to meet its every need. It knows no end to its criticism and blame of others when expectations cannot be met. It encourages dyadic withdrawal which weakens links with the wider group.

Lust only plays at intimacy. It refuses to engage the other in terms of mutual giving and receiving. It exploits individuals and the community. It takes but does not give back. Unfortunately, lust is not always easy to identify because in intimate relations there is always a blend of "love and hate." Lust can masquerade as intimacy. However, lust is discerned by the footprints of disloyalty and cruelty it leaves in its wake.

A celibate experiences the tension between love and lust when lust solicits inappropriate sexual behavior. Celibates can excuse lustful behavior by the claim that they are meant to "love everyone" and be bound by no one. A "love them" and "leave them" style of relationship can develop under the guise of celibacy. This is blantantly lustful and adolescent, not celibate. Loving celibate relationships, on the contrary, are characterized by mutual respect, equity, reconciliation, compassion, and integrity in sexual language.

Society counsels that love is learned in the academy of lust. The gospel offers the school of love. Since lust has forms other than explicitly sexual ones, continence alone does not overcome it. One can be sexually continent, yet a lustful celibate.

Moving from lust to love involves continual transformation. The call of vowed celibacy is to learn love, in a different style than a partnered relationship. Hospitality, forbearance, mutuality, other-centered interest in another, listening, and compassion are fruits of this search.

Conversion to love embraces a life of reflection. Do I use people? Am I loyal? Do I give back to the group? Do I keep confidences? Can I blend my life with others? Is it possible to change my plans? Can I risk sharing myself? Do I hide behind some protective image: my work, my race, my gender, my status, as a shield from real sharing?

Religious ask these questions in dialogue with trusted others and with Jesus. In prayer, Jesus reveals our greatest needs for love along with our potential to be friends, ministers, loving family members, and intimates. Spiritually, we appreciate Jesus for who he is rather than just for what we expect from him. We seek a fleshy heart of love rather than the stoney heart of lust. Because we have received love, we can give it away.

Generativity versus isolation

Middle adulthood invites the crisis of generativity or concern for establishing and guiding the next generation. Most adults raise children and live out their call to be generative. The religious, too, has a path of generativity.

Erikson reminds us that monastic communities live their generative call in a unique way. They renounce the right to procreate in order to center attention on ultimate concerns. In place of caring for their own children, they make central to their life discerning the Care that grounds all existence.[8]

Care marks the outcome of this crisis. Generativity is more than productivity. Generativity is emotional investment in the next generation or in whatever has been produced or created. The sentiment of generativity is captured when we are urged "to plant trees under which we will not sit."

Stagnation, the negative pole of this crisis, is the inability to sustain interest in what we have produced. Stagnation invests in the self as one's own prized progeny. Self-absorption, inability to care for others, loss of interest, respect, or sympathy for those for whom one has responsibility are signs of stagnation. The interpersonal impoverishment of stagnation fosters boredom and self-indulgence.

Stagnation distorts thinking. Self-preoccupation deforms perceptions of the world and others. In a religious community, the rumblings of stagnation are devastating and contagious. When large numbers of members struggle unsuccessfully with the same life crisis, the drift toward stagnation can be strong. Stagnation is more than the death of a ministry or project. It is the death of the spirit.

8. Donald Capps, *Deadly Sins and Saving Virtues*, 52ff., 101ff.

The virtue-vice tension of generativity versus stagnation is care and acedia. Acedia is the deadly sin of apathy. Acedia is often translated as sloth, suggesting the unwillingness to work or invest energy. But acedia is more subtle.

Acedia is a listlessness for the spiritual goods which the religious entered to pursue.[9] Acedia directs withdrawal of investment in anything that really matters. Lethargy, listlessness, and paralysis of the will are insidiously present and active. One withdraws from everything except the most trivial and surface interests.

A religious could be a workaholic but suffer from the pull of apathy. Apathy suppresses more profound desires and longings. These persons find they no longer care, hope, or believe in the values they once pursued. There is no restlessness and longing for the deeper things of life.

The religious caught in apathy can be very busy, going from one thing to another filling time. Boredom and restlessness are present not because of lack of activity. These individuals are not engaged in their vocation, hence they are detached from a true center of energy.

Apathy can drive religious to meddle in the affairs of others. Ceasing to do their own "personal work," they escape by becoming authorities on "what's wrong with others." Apathy destroys community life and harms individuals.

Apathy is more than lack of interest in the next generation. One author likens apathy to the activity of the Olympian gods. Lacking any genuine interest in humankind, the gods amused themselves by devising conflicts, conspiracies, and deceits. Their purpose was to obstruct the gratification of the desires of other gods and relieve themselves of boredom. They "toyed" with others instead of investing in them.[10]

Blocking, holding back, refusal to undertake good works which are "too much effort" are obvious forms of apathy. Jesus captured the spirit of apathy when he referred to children who asked par-

---

9. In the tradition, acedia is spiritual sloth. See S.T. II-II, Q. 35.1.

10. Stanford M. Lyman, *The Seven Deadly Sins: Society and Evil* (New York: St. Martin's Press, 1978).

ents for bread and were given a stone. In the intergenerational life of a religious congregation, the inability to invest, affirm, and take interest in the next generation is apathy.

A particularly destructive form of apathy is very subtle. It actively undermines and inhibits the growth of the younger generation in an arbitrary, capricious, and malicious way. Instead of care, it does people in and takes pleasure in it. This behavior reflects a lack of sexual integration and is challenged by the vow of celibacy.

In the tradition, apathy is the most serious deadly sin for religious because interest in the spiritual life is anesthetized. Religious living is propelled by spiritual desire. When desire is dead, there are no means to revive it.

The life of the Spirit is given, not created. The cure for apathy is spiritual regeneration, not a self-improvement program. A desire for God is enough for God to work and love a religious to new growth. Twelve-step programs acknowledge need of a higher power as key toward healing. The spiritual emptiness of apathy is at its core a refusal to desire. It is a spiritual crisis, a crisis of care.

Generativity requires a spiritual self possible only after identity and intimacy are reasonably navigated. No one can give another this self. Generative adults are invested because they want to be. Acedic adults do not care, and no one can make them care. Even if younger members of the community try to inspire an indifferent older member, it is unlikely they will be effective.

The indifference of apathy is offset from within. No one can do another's inner work. In the multi-age relationships of community, the young cannot rescue middle-age and older adults from apathy. There is great risk that the young person will be drawn into the older member's pathology and take on the cynical and despairing attitude. The young must attend to their own developmental tasks. Destructive and addictive relationships in a community can result from a cycle of enmeshment based on such a "rescue" of others.[11]

---

11. Capps, *Deadly Sins and Saving Virtues*, 108.

Care is an interest in the younger generation. It desires to leave behind a legacy. This care extends to life itself. Care takes steps to reduce or eliminate destructive effects of past choices as well as attempts to bring earlier projects to greater fulfillment. It does so, not out of egotistic needs to continue its own contributions, but out of a sense of responsibility to those who follow.

Vowed celibacy involves the extension of care to one's congregation, church, and society, despite the disappointments and disillusionments of life. In contrast to earlier struggles with appropriate limits in relationships, the vow challenges the middle-age and older adult to care at all and to develop a new kind of care. This care is only possible through a deepening of the spiritual life.

Care is not a self-initiated battle of the will. Care is sustained by knowing God's care for the world. Opened to a fresh sense of God's love, and grounded in God as all Care, one offers to the world a new kind of love.

Personal responsibility is transformed to a share in God's caring love. Care matures relationship with self, others, and the world by acknowledging one's need to be needed. Care flows from a healthy dependence on God and desire for mutuality with others.

Care is fully possible for a religious only on the difficult road of spiritual dependence. This road is easily avoided at mid-life when society recognizes the religious as competent and higher in status than when they first began. It is a time when religious are susceptible to the temptation to ride the tide of externals and avoid deeper questions.

If we have turned off the road to spiritual dependence, we can still find the Care we seek. We find it as did the disciples on the road to Emmaus. Through desire, we encounter Jesus leading us back, telling us of his dying and rising in our lives, and breaking bread with us. Unlike us, God never forsakes what God has generated. As we depend on God through awareness of the forgiveness and reconciliation needed by our middle years, we know the meaning of long-term love and its seasons of growth and hope. This love ultimately defeats death in all its forms.

Chapter Twenty-Four

New Times for Celibacy

The roots of vowed celibacy are in the mystery of love. Celibate love is a readiness to move out of oneself, trusting in God's love at the core of life. God's love for the celibate is an experienced love. It is known directly and mediated through the love encountered through others. It is a love which transforms, calls, surprises, and heals.

Jesus desires life for those who follow him. "I come that they may have life, and have it to the full" (John 10:10). Through celibacy a religious shares in that life. Jesus told his disciples to come to him for life. "Let anyone who is thirsty come to me" (John 7:37). Celibacy in this sense is a radical turn to Jesus, taking him at his word. Through celibacy, the religious lives in Jesus.

One does not give up sexuality in celibate love but integrates it. Yet in modern culture, religious live celibacy in a society that struggles with the meaning of sex, commitment, and personal identity. They live in a time of violence and confusion over boundaries in relationships. The Church dwells in this culture also and shares its struggle. This situation creates new times for celibacy.

Since celibates are touched by the ambiguities in sexual practice today, they seek healing for themselves and for others when necessary. They live celibacy in these new times with an ability to be countercultural, peaceful, and compassionate.

Countercultural

The fidelity of vowed celibacy grounds a maturity which resists the cultural tendency to just go with the flow. A sense of identity marks a person with the ability to stand independently. Celibates express their love and care by the way they handle problems in an indifferent society.

The capacity to do what is right is needed today. In a crisis, religious witness by facing issues rather than avoiding them. In cases in which sexual exploitation and social exclusivism create violence and havoc, the challenge is even greater. Today religious institutions suffer from the injustices caused by the inappropriate sexual conduct of some of its members. Yet they cannot hide from these problems as do many in the culture.

Perpetrators and victims need to be treated with justice and care. Financial and legal justice has to be coupled with spiritual and moral fortitude to carry the cross which each situation involves. Yet, vowed members of these institutions are called to go on with their lives and to define themselves and their celibate stance with integrity.

The different touch of the celibate gives rise to a special type of fruitfulness in society today. As a celibate seeks fidelity over pride, love over lust, and care beyond acedic pulls, love is shared in the midst of a fragmented world. Beyond service alone, this love is marked by presence, creativity, and insight. It is a love offered to many and to a special few over a lifetime.

The deepening identity of a religious is a support for others. People who search for meaning can find a rootedness in a celibate's sense of self. This is not because they are celibate but because they have allowed their celibate promise to call them to a maturity.

Their different touch reaches the marginated and excluded and can provide an anchor for those "at sea" in life's journey. Celibacy is countercultural as it witnesses that life's questions are deeper than the superficial answers of society. Vowed celibates are willing to bet their lives on their vision. In spite of the sexual tensions which plague church and society today, celibates continue to live their call.

Peaceful

Fruits of a celibate life are happiness and contentment. A loving person overcomes inner contentiousness in order to create peace in relationships. A celibate heart avoids the violence and destructiveness of lust. It creates trust instead of mistrust, harmony over acrimony, and builds bridges rather than barriers.

At a recent profession Mass of a black religious, I watched a white religious lead the entrance procession with the cross, walking the rhythmic step of the black community. This was not her natural step. She had spent years living and working among the poor and in multi-cultural communities. She had learned this step in this process. Ministry called her to a culture not her own. It expanded her personal identity to be bicultural in some way.

The black sister, willing to make vows in a predominantly white community, had a love that was bicultural. Contrary to the racism in the society, she was willing to be sister with those who were too often racist. Both religious experienced intimacy and care through faithful presence in a poor parish situation. They sought peace daily in the midst of the violence that surrounded them.

The commitments of these two religious witness to a racial peace neither may have anticipated earlier in life. Born into a society where racism is a force to overcome, both chose to live differently. Community living invited them beyond these deep cultural impasses. It called them to a love across racial lines.

Love develops where peace is sought. This is not a peace without conflict. It is a love where peace is the ultimate goal of any conflict. Religious community is meant to testify to a unity that seeks peace and embraces difference.

Compassionate

Celibate love fosters a care that is compassionate. Religious are often in positions in which they can make life better or more difficult for others. Compassion is the capacity to feel with others. It operates, not from a position of superiority and distance, but from a stance of immersion in human struggles.

Compassion involves the willingness to give help which is within one's power. It is an active love which continually cares. Compassion overcomes the inner voices that say "we have cared enough." It avoids the acedic pulls of resentment, "we've earned our stripes." Compassion remembers the struggles of life and does not withdraw; it does not excuse itself and hold others accountable.

Compassion is needed in the midst of the great pluralism in society today. It withholds harsh judgments of others and avoids comparison of one's life situation with those not lived. It lives joined to Jesus, whose Care knows no end. It sees life from his perspective and thus can recognize the vunerable in its midst.

Love which defeats death

Awareness of the poor marks the experience of celibate love. The marginalization of the poor taps the fidelity of religious. Today masses, named non-persons by the economic yardsticks of our culture, wander the world. They are throw-away people, at home and abroad, suffering from the mechanisms of oppression.

The heart of a religious is drawn to the poor. One religious put it this way, "I do not understand all the mechanisms of the economic market, but I surely see the results of it in the lives of the poor." Through direct service, social analysis, or both, religious look upon the faces of the poor. They seek to defeat the death which haunts them economically, socially, and spiritually.

Religious who allow the poor to impact their lives live more evangelically radical and actively ethical than they may have intended when they began their journey. The call to act justly, love tenderly, and walk humbly with their God impacts them as relationship with God grows and deepens. Fidelity, care, and generativity spill over into the world.

Love transforms the diocesan office as well as the hospital corridor. It enters the political race for school board and buys a hospice for AIDS patients. It does social analysis and celebrates liturgies. It teaches piano and it mentors spiritual directors.

Care leaves the tried and true and trusts the Spirit to meet new pastoral needs. It walks on new ground so the next generation can follow. Care is angered that people make clothing in sweatshops in Taiwan, and migrant children lack proper education. It makes room for battered women in its home, and sends its senior men and women to tutor those who cannot read.

Care does the accounts for a high school budget and teaches altar servers love for the liturgy. It corrects spelling and transports children in costumes to rest homes to cheer the elderly. It practices with the choir and prays with the Scripture group. It builds homes for the homeless and translates the gospel into a tribal language. It reads to the lonely and visits the sick. It cooks supper for the community, does the laundry, and cuts the grass. It consoles the dying and baptizes the newborn. It counsels the troubled and prays without ceasing for others.

Religious know the intimacy of friendship, community, and relationship to Jesus. Yet intimacy is also the reach of insertion into parishes, towns, countries, and cultures into which a religious ventures because of a congregational call. The sexual integration of vowed celibacy is seen in the gentle eyes of the aged religious who still welcomes the awkward visitor, providing hospitality and making the stranger feel at home.

Those who have found God in all things can point to the Care which holds the world together. Religious share in the fruitfulness of all creation. They live in harmony with creation in a way which invites peoples to claim the earth as their home. They bid all to turn from the ways of death and embrace life in its many forms.

Fruitfulness is nature's response to death's active pull. The fruitfulness of celibate love shares this energy. It testifies to the action of Spirit who brings all creation to completion, calling us beyond our present imagination.

At the cusp of a new millennium, the Church joins with others of good will to offer society a new style of life. The world hungers for fresh forms of living in which people are judged not only on a scale of wealth or power that divides them, but on the basis of the humanity that unites them. Religious communities are to be "communities of the way" who model concretely the possibility of this vision.

New community of baptism

Religious life makes a statement about human life as a whole. Celibates contribute to the future of human communities through the style of living they embrace.

Celibates form real communities in various cultures. They witness to a community based on neither friendship, blood, nor natural ties. Through vows, religious place their lives and what belongs to them in the keeping of others in the community. The community receives their word and holds it for them. It makes claims on them for faithfulness and constancy.

The relationship of community is a new relationship. It is one of binding and being bound, of giving and being claimed. It is a relationship that points to the future.[1] By making promises in the presence of others, religious influence their future. They determine themselves to do the actions they intend and promise. They seek by commitment to find their freedom, not destroy it.

The new community created by religious vows is a visible form of the new community of baptism. It is more than a mystical community; it is a concrete and practical one. Community forms part of the identity of religious. Through community, religious distinguish between all the things they could do and the ones they will do.

Is community really that important in modern times? Religious say it is. When people act, their willingness to change, to move forward, to continue, is linked to the sense of being bound to whomever or whatever calls them forth. They identify with the object of their promises. In conflict, many will put energies there, which they are unwilling to invest elsewhere.

For this reason adults make commitments: to free them to do something in the face of the impossible task of feeling called to everything. On such basis, all community functions and the future of community rests. Community is the limit that grounds all openness to the universal. For this reason, all human beings need community.

Religious seek to build community in all ministries. People today suffer many times from one of two things. One group stands before an ever-widening range of options and a confusing rate of change. Another group is crushed by the lack of opportunities and stare blankly into a future which has no place for them.

---

1. Farley, *Personal Commitments*, 18ff.

Both conditions of modern times break down the will and moral resources for community. People need support to trust and enter into the mutual obligation to build the community they so desperately seek.

Today's society is filled with desires but resists making any commitments to fulfill them. Religious community stands in counter-witness to this situation. Religious promise to do all that is possible to keep love alive and to be faithful to what they have promised. In face of feelings that come and go, religious sustain commitment to community, acknowledging the human limits both they and it share.

Community is a major means by which religious express the relationship between love and fruitfulness. They support the human search for community in every way they can. Religious have learned that their yearning to belong to others and to God can be satisfied only through some form of mutual commitment. They share their learning with the world, as a special gift of their fidelity, love, and care.

Becoming what we love

The three vows involve more than ethical practice. They are invitations to union with God in the life of each religious. The vows are a way of loving in time. Religious not only love in a faithful, caring, and compassionate way. These qualities become part of their person, as a reflection of the life of Jesus in them. In time, religious become what they love.

Living the gospel through the vows unites the life of the religious with Jesus. Christ becomes alive in their lives, giving their love a different touch. To describe this process, we have used many images in this book.

There are seasons to love, so we speak of growth in religious life in a developmental way.[2] The vows engage the religious in the life challenges of the adult years. They also reframe and restructure the unfinished business from childhood. Fidelity to them leads toward a wholeness that reflects the unique history of each religious.

2. *Ibid.*, 41ff.

The vows also have a linear quality. They are a road with detours and fast lanes and boundary lines for steady traffic. They involve choices and turns, crossroads and maps. Goodness or malice collect as baggage on this journey. Religious travel light so as to get to their destination. Yet, they bog down with the weight of negative potentials. They spin their wheels and fail to move toward their goal.

Choices made by religious not only affect the present, but also the future. Because the vows are one road and not another, choices are not neutral. New choices are qualified as fidelity or betrayal, furthering the journey or referring the religious back to the map for direction and purpose. Religious and their congregations choose to ratify their commitment many times along the journey. This requires trust that God continues to call them anew.

Finally, the life of the vows has a spiraling quality to it. We end where we began. In this sense, there is nothing new under the sun. Even today, the eldest can watch the new entrant and know there is something intangible and universal in every beginning vocation. This is true in ragtime, war time, or at the cusp of a new millennium.

Nothing changes, yet all is new, but not as it was before. This level of the vows is the hardest to describe, yet it is the ground upon which the rest is built. It involves the life of contemplation and political-mystical presence to God's own self. Moments of recognition at this depth penetrate the mystery of God in which the vows are lived.

The mystery of Jesus' life stands ever present to the religious, to live in and from which to learn. We grow in knowledge of Jesus, not as an idea or belief, but as a person loving us and creating love within us. Nothing is the same because of the touch of Jesus, yet all is the same. Our lives stand in the ever present mystery of his life, death, and resurrection.

Whether a beginner or one who has journeyed many years, we stand equal in these moments, for they are gifts to be received. As those invited to a banquet, the oldest and the youngest can have their fill, and each finds the abundance of the mystery they both share. We become what we love through the vows, and learn this is truly the best part of our journey.

Gathering the fragments

This book has examined religious life in terms of key cultural, social, and faith questions of our times. It has not said everything. It is offered as a contribution to the wider conversation around these issues today. Religious life lives on, not in books, but in the committed love of its members. Those willing to face the moral hazards of this time will be those who will give shape to religious life in a new millennium.

The capacity for religious life to grow and flourish is in keeping with its nature as an expression of the life of the Spirit. Response to the call of the Spirit is not inevitable, yet the Spirit acts against many odds. Through graced human freedom the pull of entropy is overcome, and forward movement occurs. May these considerations spark new energy for those who seek this movement in religious life. May they trust in the goodness of God's faithful love in its continuing renewal.

Index

accountability, 21, 26
alienation, 4
American bishops, 230, 245
analogy, 39, 40
Aquinas, Thomas, 96, 274
Aschenbrenner, George, 169
associates, 91, 155–157
Aubert, J. M., 99
Augustine, St., 204

Bainton, Roland, 153
baptism, 88, 94
    see community of baptism
        under each vow
Basch, Michael, 170
Bateson, Gregory, 39
Becker, Ernest, 182
Bellah, Robert, 16, 18, 72, 144, 176,
    177
Berger, Peter, 216
Berry, Thomas, 30, 41
bourgeois, 17
Browning, Don, 174, 175

Cada, Lawrence et al, 31, 144
Cahill, Lisa Sowle, 242, 243
canon law, 104, 114, 116, 118, 129,
    158, 171, 172, 204, 237
Capacchione, Lucia, 260
Capps, Donald, 139, 170, 176, 177,

182, 187, 193, 206, 207, 209, 211,
    232, 267, 268, 273
Carr, Anne, 68, 259
Carroll, Denis, 31
Carter, Stephen, 153, 229
celibacy (celibate chastity),
    234–247, 248–265, 277–285
    abstinence, 237, 240, 266, 272
    abuse, 264, 268, 278
    canon law, 237
    charism, 266
    chastity, 246
    community, 249–252, 268–274,
        279, 281–282
    consecration, 239
    embodiment, 239
    freedom, 251
    friendship, 242, 250
        coupling, 249–252, 272
        heterosexual, 253–255
        intentional, 249–252, 272
        same-sex, 244–246, 255
    homosexuality, 242–244
    identity, 267–269, 277
    incorporation, 267, 270
    insertion, 281
    integrity, 256, 272, 278
    intimacy, 242, 247, 249, 254, 264,
        270–272

Jesus, 238, 263, 266, 269, 272–
    274, 276–277, 280–281
lifestyle
    single and partnered,
        238, 248ff.
loneliness, 261
love, 234, 237–239, 255, 262–263,
    265, 269, 271–272, 277–278
    way of loving, 258, 272, 278
marriage, 245–246, 248–251, 257,
    261
ministry, 255, 262–263, 268, 278,
    280–282
mystical/contemplative, 234, 235,
    239, 262, 277
    compassionate, 279–280
    countercultural, 277–278
    peaceful, 278–280
sexism, 258–259
sexuality, 236–237, 243, 252, 277
    church history, 235–236, 258
    church views, 242–246, 249,
        258, 277
    cultural views, 240–242
    dimensions of
        affective, 248, 252, 254–256
        genital, 256–258, 262
        primary, 258–261
    integration/maturation, 237,
        254, 258, 262, 264, 268, 278
    language, 248–249
    ministry, 255, 262–263, 269,
        272–273, 280–282
    practice as
        defeat of death, 280–281
    new community of baptism,
        281–283
    ecclesial, *see* church
spiritual regeneration, 275
surrender, 261, 263
transformative way, 256, 266–281
    identity–identity confusion,

267–270
    fidelity–pride, 268–270
    intimacy-isolation, 270–273
        love-lust, 271–273
    generativity-stagnation, 273–
        276
        care-acedia, 274–276,
            280–281
    virginity, 237, 246
certitude, 29
chance, 29, 31, 36, 47
change, 47, 53–55, 57
    as circuit, 48
    as difference, 59
    as gift, 61
Chardin, Teilhard de, 31, 33, 40, 45,
    55
charism, 22, 42, 49, 62, 91, 104, 107,
    117, 134, 157, 189, 216
choice, 96, 100, 135
    categorical, 71, 80, 101
    transcendental, 77, 101
Christian life, 86–91, 97, 99;
    see vows
church, 70–71, 77, 85, 90–91, 103,
    105, 113, 115, 121, 126, 128, 138,
    141, 149, 157, 192, 193
Ciccarelli, M., 119
Clark, Keith, 256, 258
Coleman, Gerald, 243
communication crisis, 6
community, 144–159, 281–283
    baptism, 142
        see community of baptism
    characteristics/modern
        community, 145–151
    as circuit, 59
    communitarian/associational
        ties, 155–157
    core/selective participation,
        155–157
    cultural religion, 18–19

cultural theories, 16, 18, 60–61
diversification/unification, 60,
    156–157, 279
energy, 135, 156
equilibrium, 59
experimentation, 154
faith, (religious), 69, 72
frameworks, 109, 155–157
life style enclaves, 144
manifold engagement, 145, 155
ministry, 138, 148, 150–151, 153
    see individual vows
moral calls, 92–94
moral hazards, 26, 158
practices, 139–140, 149, 158, 220
regulators/bonding, 61
nineteenth century, 120–121,
    138, 141–142, 150–151
society, 150, 154, 157, 279, 281
traditional/modern, 142–145,
    155
vows, 22
    see individual vows
witness/value formation, 68, 90,
    106, 155, 167, 218, 220
complexity, 33
Conn, Walter, 105
conscience, 79–82, 87–88
    communal conscience, 90
contemplative religious, 107, 152
continuity, 46, 48, 55
conversion, 105
    see transformative way/vows
cosmology, 30–31
counsels, 96–100
countercultural, 22, 26, 152, 154, 184,
    214, 232–233
creation, 44, 281
    see evolution
criteria of discernment, 16–17, 29,
    37, 60, 90–91, 135, 158, 282
critical discernments, viii, 17, 23, 26,

29, 60, 134–135, 141, 172, 230
cultural transition, 138, 155–158, 221

Darwin, Charles, 30
"defeat of death," 151–156
    models for ministry, 154–155
    see individual vows
Dei Verbum, 223
different touch, vii, 71, 85, 101, 103,
    110, 237, 278, 283–284
discernment, 54, 58, 90, 93, 95
discipleship, 85, 98, 100
    see Jesus under each vow
Dodd, C. H., 96
dogma, 90
    see individual topics
Donovan, Vincent, 30
Dorr, Donal, 126
Dulles, Avery, 140

Eberle, Gary, 7
Ecclesia Catholica, 118
ecclesial identity, 157–159
ecological movement, 7, 45, 281
Economic Pastoral (USA), 230
egotism, 100
energy, 34–37, 47–48, 54–55, 57, 60,
    64, 132, 134, 285
    ecclesial, 157–159,
        see individual vows
    ministerial, 132–135,
        see individual vows
entropy, 33–36, 39, 43, 47, 110
epigenetic principle, 174
equilibrium, 45–46, 55, 57, 61
Erikson, Erik, 173–174, 208, 228,
    268, 270
Eucharist, 89, *see* sacraments
Evans, Mary, 127
evil, 42–43
evolution, 31, 41, 61
    evolutionary perspective, 30, 33,
        38, 41, 46, 54, 56

human beings, 61–62
path, 46–47
theories and religious, 30–33,37,
　　44, 46, 49, 53, 58, 60–61, 63,
　　113, 150

Fagan, Sean, 79
faith, 20, 65–73
　　Christian morality, 72, 81, 93
　　eschatological, 10–11
　　human faith, 66–69, 87
　　outlook, 66, 71, 77
　　religious faith, 69–70, 82, 85, 87,
　　　　99, 101
　　transcendental data, 67–68, 82,
　　　　89, 137, 189
Farley, Margaret, 42, 59, 98, 103,
　　109, 168, 172, 282, 283
Finn, Virginia, 249–252
finitude, 19, 20, 71
Fischer, Kathleen, 87, 138
Flannery, Austin, 22
flexibility, 54, 55, 58
Fowler, James, 43, 199, 228
fragmentation, 11, 19, 26, 38, 135,
　　216, 278
framework, 86, 101, 103
Francis of Assisi, 179
Fransen, Piet, 216
freedom, 44, 53–62, 64, 97, 104,
　　137, 145, 179, 189, 216, 278
Frost, Robert, 67
Fuchs, Josef, 78, 88, 166, 237
future, 42, 108, 131

Gaudium et Spes, 44, 72, 79, 153, 223
Gemelli, Agostino, 119
genetic structure, 55
Genovesi, Vincent, 236, 246, 252
Goergen, Donald, 180
Gonzalez, Paula, 30
Gottemoeller, Doris, 103
grace, 43, 45, 63, 64–66, 70, 86, 96

101, 102, 164
Grosh, Gerald, 180
Guidon, Andre, 248, 249
Gumpel, Peter, 166
Gutierrez, Gustavo, 17

Haight, Roger, 68, 102, 110
Hannigan, James, 244, 245
Hargrove, Barbara, 18
Hart, Thomas, 87, 138
Hassel, David, 199
Haught, John 29, 32, 38
Hehir, Brian, 154
hereditary structures, 58
hermeneutics, 29
Hines, Mary, 28
Hodgson, Peter, 192
Hofstadter, Richard, 30
Holland, Sharon, 118, 119, 120,
　　123, 124, 126, 127, 131
hope, 20–23, 43, 65, 88, 89, 110,
　　187, 195, 207–208, 214
Hostie, Raymond, 31, 114
human condition, 64–65

identity, 6, 21
　　congregational, 129, 131, 158
　　see vow of celibate chastity
imagination, 21
innocence, 22
integrity, 20, 63, 94, 182–185
　　see vow of poverty

Jesus Christ, 70, 80, 89, 93, 96–97,
　　101–102, 104
　　see individual vows
John Paul II, 82
Johnson, Elizabeth, 39, 80, 203, 238

Kairos, 99
Kaufmann, Franz-Xavier, 217
Keane, Philip, 32
Keenan, James, 168, 175

Kerkhop, Jan, 20
King, Martin Luther, 146
Kingdom, 75, 89, 90, 96, 99, 101,
    196, 214, 232
Kraft, William, 236, 244, 255, 256
    259, 262

Lasch, Christopher, 13, 21, 33
law, 55
legalism, 117
Lerner, Michael, 228
life crisis, 173–174
linear thinking, 32, 48, 53
Love, 20, 23, 44–45, 61–62, 64, 71,
    86, 88–91, 101, 103, 105, 107,
    138, 163, 166–167, 176, 198,
    214, 231
    see individual vows
Lozano, John, 96, 100, 201
Lumen Gentium, 11, 70, 223
Lyman, Stanford, 274

MacIntyre, Alasdair, 140
MacNamara, Vincent, 42
Mahoney, John, 258
marriage, 100, 106
mass and minority, 57–58
    styles of commitment, 133–135
Matera, Frank, 96, 98
May, Gerald, 71, 102, 163, 164, 165
May, Rollo, 254
May, William, 178
McCool, Gerald, 137
McCormick, Patrick, 64, 165
McCormick, Richard, 91
McKenna, Thomas, 11
McNamara, Jo Ann Kay, 136
memory, 22–23
Merici, Angela, 118
Merkle, Judith, 17, 49, 55, 66, 75,
    77, 97, 131, 136, 144, 146, 165,
    175, 183, 197, 204, 267
Metz, Johannes, 17, 18, 19, 179,

191, 193
Miller, Alice, 170
mind, 39–43
minority and majority, 35, 56, 61
Misner, Paul, 126
mission, 90, 107, 110, 132, 134–135,
    137, 138, 151–154, *see* individual
    vows
models for ministry, 154–155
Mojzes, Paul, 186
Molinari, Paul, 166, 214
Monad, Jacques, 31
moral call, 86, 91, 98
    Christian essential, 92–93, 99
    Christian existential, 95–102
    essential 92, 95, 99
    existential, 92
moral choice, 80–81, 284
moral hazards, 23–27
moral tastes, 166–169, 208
multi-cultural, 147, 220, 279
mutuality, 45, 61, 100, 108, 148,
    159, 211, 230, 276
mystery, 19, 28, 70–71, 81
mystical, 32, 106, 110
    see individual vows

nature, 63–64
    see evolutionary perspective
negentropy, 34–36, 43, 47, 61
new science, 32, 37
nineteenth century, 23, 114ff.
    religious life, 124–135, 136, 159
        canonical processes, 115–118,
            128–130
        characteristic elements, 137–
            141, 159
        incorporation, 120–121, 123
        institutes of simple vows,
            114–115, 118, 120, 126, 127
    new needs, 125–126
    practices, 139

secular institutes, 116, 118–124,
    127, 130
    consecration, 120, 123, 128, 131
societies of common life, 116, 124
styles of commitment, 122, 124,
    127, 131, 132–135
styles of ministry, 132–136
vows, 123–124, 129
nonfulfillment, 42
North American church, 19
nostalgia, 20–23, 141
Nygren and Ukeritis, 5, 26, 132

Oates, Mary, 127
obedience, 197–204, 205–220,
    221–233
    affective bonding, 197, 204–205,
        209, 211, 217, 218, 220, 233
    authority, 204, 216, 217–221
        legible, 229–230
        negation, 221–230
        paternalistic, 226–227, 229
        patrimonial, 226
        shame, 227–228, 230
        visible, 229–230
    canon law, 204
    charism, 216
    church, 204–205, 213, 215–216,
        218, 223, 225, 230–231
    community, *see* affective bonding
    congregational, 208, 210–211,
        213–215, 218, 230–231
    credibility, 218–220
    disaffection, 198–201, 206, 219
    historical forms, 201–202, 221,
        225, 230
    human faith, 197–198
    Jesus, 198, 200, 202–203, 206,
        213, 214, 231
    mystical/contemplative, 231
        providence, 232
        repentance, 232–233

vocation, 233
practice, as
    community of baptism, 217–
        220
    defeat of death, 214–217
    ecclesial, *see* church
religious faith, 197–198,
    201–202
society, 214–217, 219–220
transformative way
    trust-mistrust, 205–208
        hope-gluttony, 207–208
    initiative-guilt, 209–211
        purpose/dedication-greed,
            209–211, 215
    industry-inferiority, 211–214,
        216
        competence-envy, 212–213,
            218, 219, 232
    vow, 203–204
O'Connell, Timothy, 81
O'Donnell, John 19
order, (universe), 36

Palmer, Helen, 177
paradigm, 8, 29, 45, 48, 70
paradox, vii, 3, 6–12, 48, 70, 89,
    116, 143
paralysis, 21
participation
    core and selective, 156–157
paschal mystery, 15, 19, 20, 77, 88,
    89, 93 102, 154
Paul VI, 171
personhood, 64, 86, 88
Pieris, Aloysius, 98, 191
poor, 53, 154, 280–281
    see ministry, individual vows
Populorum Progressio, 10, 171
postmodern, 7–9, 214
poverty, 163–172, 173–185,
    186–196

addiction, 163–165, 189
canon law, 171, 172
church, 192–193
commitment, 172, 185
community, 179–181, 183, 187–
189, 193–194
desires: transformation, 163–
172, 183, 184, 187
Jesus, 168, 180–182, 185, 187–
189, 191–194
inculturation, 190–191
Kohut, 169
love, 181, 189, 195
material possessions
family living standards, 171
historical forms/practice,
170–172
practice today, 179–181, 185
mystical/contemplative
gratitude/awareness of the holy,
194–196
longing, 187
self-mastery, 187
practice, as
community of baptism,
188–189
defeat of death, 186–188
ecclesial, *see* church
social teaching, 170, 171
society, 187, 191, 196, 214
transformative way
autonomy-shame, 177, 179,
180, 187, 191
will-anger, 178–179
integrity-despair, 181–185, 187
wisdom-melancholy,
183–185
vision, 183, 185, 188
practices, 66, 134, 139–141
predictability, 33
pre-Vatican, 15, 32, 86
Primo feliciter, 130, 132

Provida Mater Ecclesia, 130
purposefulness, 36, 42, 48, 54, 61

qualitative/quantitative, 35, 64, 77
quantum theory, 33
Quesnell, Quentin, 45

racism, 147, 279
Rahner, Karl, 88, 96, 108, 270
randomness, 29, 46, 47
Rasmussen, Larry, 4, 135, 139,
142–145, 147, 153, 155, 157, 215
redemption, 76
redundancy, 40
relationships
radial-tangential, 56–57
styles of commitment, 132–133
relativism, 39
religion, 17, 20
cultural religion, 18–20
religious life
constitutions, 131
developmental perspective,
174–175, 283
foundations, 45, 76–77, 85,
88–91, 106 109, 113, 157, 214
historical/cultural forms,
107–108, 113, 123–124,
125–135, 136, 145, 157, 225
institution, 121, 158
repetition, 55
renunciation, 98, 136
resentment, 20
responsibility, 37, 87
revelation, 28, 88, 89
and evolution, 29, 37
risk, 67–69
Rondet, M., 248
Roof, Wade Clark, 166

sacraments, 89, 158
salvation, 65, 71, 74–77, 137
cultural theory of, 15, 17, 19, 20

Sastre Santos, Eutimio, 6, 115, 116, 117, 118, 121, 124, 129, 158
Schillebeeckx, Edward, 4, 65, 69, 188, 189
Schneiders, Sandra, 234
scripture, 72, 89
secular culture, vii, 14, 15, 18, 53, 60
segmentation, 23
Segundo, Juan Luis, 33–34, 36, 39, 40, 43, 47–48, 57–59, 61–62, 64, 67–69, 74, 88, 115
self creation, 17, 18, 20
Selznick, Philip, 147
Senior, Donald, 96, 104
Sennett, Richard, 59, 221–230
sexism, 258
sin, 43, 64, 88, 90, 110, 178
Sobrino, Jon, 40
Spirit, 11, 35, 36, 98, 103, 121
stagnation, 23
Stahel, Thomas, 26
Stefano, Frances, 40
struggle, 4
success
　cultural view, 16, 53
suffering, 20, 164, 189
survival of the fittest, 30, 61
synthesis, 35

telos, 29
Tetlow, Joseph, 3
Tillich, Paul, 77
time, 46, 48, 62
Toynbee, Arnold, 3
transcendence, 102, 110, 215
Troeltsch, Ernst, 157
truth, 8, 38–39, 80

Ulanov, Ann and Barry, 212

values, 66–67, 167, 182
Vatican II, 4, 11, 88, 117, 130, 131, 143, 223, 235
vocation, 87–88, 91
vows
　adulthood, 86–87, 105, 175
　baptism, 94, 107, 109
　choice, 71, 77–82
　　categorical, 71, 78, 101, 104
　　transcendental, 77–78, 101, 104
　consecration, 102, 104, 105, 151
　core of religious/mystical life, 175, 283–285
　existential Christian call, 100, 109
　framework, 103–110, 159, 175
　human faith, 68, 71, 82
　keys of understanding, 159
　lifestyle, 107, 282
　public profession, 123, 129, 134, 191, 214, 218, 220, 231
　public responsibility, 91, 106, 134, 153, 154, 157, 176, 186–188, 191, 214
　reach of salvation, 74, 76, 81–82
　religious conversion, 105–106
　religious faith, 70–71, 74, 82, 100–102, 105, 106, 158
　secular context, 131, 138
　separation from the world, 151–152
　way, 72, 78, 107, 113, 134, 136, 141, 154, 157, 176, 194–195
　virtue-vice, 174–176, 183–185
　see celibate chastity, poverty, obedience

way, vii, 88–89, 121
Wilber, Charles, 24
will of group, 23
Wittberg, Patricia, 31, 132, 221
Wogaman, Philip, 158
Wolff, Edward, 171
women, 89, 180, 219, 231